SIMONS SAYS

*The Simons bookplate, showing
the City of Detroit flag, the
birthdates of both Detroit and
Leonard N. Simons.*

Leonard N. Simons

SIMONS SAYS

Faith, Fun, and Foible
Leonard N. Simons

Selections from his writings and talks

Leo M. Franklin Archives of Temple Beth El
Birmingham, Michigan   1984

Produced by Wayne State University Press,
Detroit, Michigan, 48202.

Published on the occasion of the eightieth birthday of Leonard N. Simons by
the Leo M. Franklin Archives of Temple Beth El, Birmingham, Michigan, July
24, 1984.

Library of Congress Cataloging in Publication Data

Simons, Leonard N., 1904–
  Simons says.

  1. Simons, Leonard N., 1904–   —Addresses, essays,
lectures.   2. Jews—Michigan—Detroit—Biography—
Addresses, essays, lectures.   3. Detroit (Mich.)—
Biography—Addresses, essays, lectures.   1. Title.
F574.D49J572 1984   977.4′34043′0924   84-7316
ISBN 0-8143-1779-0

Manufactured in the United States of America.
Designed by Richard Kinney.

This book is dedicated, as my life has been, to
Harriette
my dear wife of more than fifty-four years

My thanks to the
Wayne State University Press
for editing, designing and
producing *Simons Says*
Leonard Norman Simons

Table of Contents

Foreword

This is a feast of writing. In the scholarly world there is the tradition of dedicating such a "Feast of Writing"—a *Festschrift*—to a distinguished colleague when he retires or reaches a significant birthday anniversary. Such books are usually composed of writings by the man's friends, writings on topics close to the heart of each of the contributors. Looking forward to Leonard Simons' eightieth birthday on July 24, 1984, some friends of his thought it appropriate to have him speak for himself, rather than to have others speak for him.

Leonard is a businessman who, as the following pages testify, has dedicated a large portion of his life speaking for and of others. If there is a worthy cause, he is in its vanguard, leading the way with his good sense and sensible wit. His first rule in speaking and writing surely must be "Never bore your audience." Hence, the most delectable feast to be given in honor of Leonard's attaining the age of octogenarian is a collection of some of his choicest morsels composed in honor of his friends, his city, his beliefs, and his religion.

It is the rare charitable organization, social service agency, human action committee, church roll, or public commission in his home town, in Detroit, that does not have the name of Leonard Simons embedded in its records as benefactor. As you will read in the following pages, his interests are ecumenical, ubiquitous, and omnifarious, but his concern is single-minded: human welfare. A man of faith, he has spent much of his effort and time in the service of Judaism. But as a part of the greater brotherhood of man, he put his talents to work for all, black man and white, Christian and Jew. Hence, the pages that follow have something to say for all of us.

And what Leonard Simons has to say cannot be separated from how he says it. For this reason, the informal presentation that has his vigor and personal touch has been kept. He combines wit and humor with those serious matters that are close to his heart in order to bring the message home. He is deadly serious without being deadly.

Many of the talks, like the accompanying photographs, prominently display Leonard Simons. That is as reasonable as it is necessary. When he undertakes a charitable task—raising funds for a senior citizens home, for a church program, for a college scholarship, for a health care center—he throws himself into the project with all the force and enthusiasm at his command. He is no shrinking violet; he refuses to stay in the background, which is one of the reasons he is so successful and so sought after in fund raising. Modesty is a virtue, but it does not build a new hospital, or fund cancer research, or sustain a newborn state, or offer a youngster a college education.

An omnivorous reader, as well as a collector of books, Leonard composes his scripts from a thousand sources, but the way in which he weaves together the thoughts and insights are his alone. This is not simply a Jewish feast; it can be enjoyed by all.

BERNARD GOLDMAN
WAYNE STATE UNIVERSITY

Acknowledgments and Disclaimer

*N*ever *in my* wildest dreams did I think that many of my talks and writings would one day become a book. Now that they have, I regret that I did not keep meticulous records of the sources from which I drew my wisdom, my enlightenment, and my wit. If I had, I could now give the proper by-lines. But I can give here, happily, recognition to some of the brilliant and clever people whose words and thoughts have helped determine and influence my thinking, my beliefs, and my life. Thank God some are still with us; some of blessed memory are not. Their teachings, advice, and thoughts I have borrowed and made my own. Some I know only through their writings, others from personal contact; their words have made this book possible.

Among the rabbis are Jacob R. Marcus, Samuel Sandmel, Nelson Glueck, Maurice Eisendrath, Leo M. Franklin, B. Benedict Glazer, Morris Adler, Samuel Silver, Abraham Joshua Heschel, Robert Gordis, Richard C. Hertz, Irving I. Katz, and Minard Klein.

The nonclergy are Philip Slomovitz, Trudie Weiss-Rosmarin, Cecil Roth, Lion Feuchtwanger, Lin Yutang, Sydney J. Harris and those master funny-bone ticklers Leo Rosten, Sam Levenson, Joey Adams, and Robert Orben, who gave me written permission to quote him. And there are many other friends and acquaintances too numerous to mention. To all I extend my profound thanks.

Reader, feel free to quote verbally anything you like in these pages. Some of the thoughts and humor are original, but which, I honestly do not know. As my dear grandmother used to say, "Enjoy, enjoy!"

Leonard Norman Rashall Simons
July 24, 1984

13

Postscript

One last very special thanks I extend to my dearest friend and partner of over sixty years, Lawrence J. Michelson. His confidence in me, his sympathetic support at all times, his patience, understanding, and encouragement in all I have tried to accomplish both inside and outside the business world, have earned my everlasting gratitude.

This I Believe

Edward R. Murrow, Columbia Broadcasting System radio and television news analyst, war correspondent and author, sponsored the "This I Believe" series. The series invited prominent people to express their beliefs on the CBS national radio network.

I believe with all my heart that man was put on this earth to serve mankind. The satisfaction I get whenever I have the opportunity to accomplish something worthwhile for someone or some group is proof to me that life's biggest thrills are secured from deeds of kindness and goodwill. For me to earn warm thanks, expressed in a sincere handshake, for something which I have done is reward beyond measure.

When I was a boy, I lived with my grandparents. Here

This article was one of a series of newspaper articles and radio broadcasts which appeared throughout the United States in 1951. Locally it was published in the Detroit Free Press with the following editor's note: Leonard N. Simons, a partner in Simons-Michelson Company, who is also active in welfare, business, and interfaith circles, reveals here his personal creed.

were two people who had very few of the material things, yet I never heard them complain. The affection and respect they had for each other and for those with whom they came in contact made an indelible impression upon me. In the tradition of my religion, when a boy reaches thirteen, he comes of age, becomes a man. At the time, my grandfather gave me these words of wisdom:

> Love, respect and generosity are the three most important words in the dictionary. If you have certain talents that permit you some day to make a lot of money, then remember this, my boy, "A shroud has no pockets."

My grandparents' philosophy of life has been the inspiration for my own.

Twenty-three years ago I became a partner in an advertising agency. I determined then that I would set aside a part of my time to the job of helping, without payment or fee, organizations and people who had need for the type of assistance which I was particularly qualified to give.

Since that time I have lived by that plan, and while our list of business clients is far from the most impressive one in our profession, the list of charitable, civic and national organizations which we have assisted represents an effort on my part really to place service to my fellow man on as high and universal a plane as I can attain. That list gives me the most satisfaction when I take inventory of my assets.

I am indeed fortunate because I lead a full and happy life. I believe that by trying to live usefully I have become a better man myself and in so doing have earned the respect of my neighbors and the love of my family. What more could anyone ask?

I believe that death is not final, if, by virtue of what I have been able to contribute to the happiness of others, I continue to live in the memory of many of the people with whom I have been associated.

It is my belief that the money I earn is only as good as the good it can do during my lifetime. Beyond what I need for my family's security, the rest belongs to the service of my fellow men.

I believe that I should try to help, in my own small way,

to create a better world in which to live and in which to raise a family by continuing to extend a friendly hand to those who need my help. I try to judge men by the goodness in their hearts. I have found peace of mind in trying to do the things that I hope will find favor in the eyes of God.

Years ago I read a statement of Charles Schwab, former president of the United States Steel Corporation, and it strengthened my own philosophy of life. He said: "Most of my troubles have been due to my being good to people. If young folks want to avoid trouble, they should be hard-boiled and say no to everybody. They will walk through life unmolested. But they will do without friends and won't have much fun."

I believe he is right and that my own true worth, my real wealth, is the large number of friends I have. If I reach a ripe old age, I believe I shall be able to draw on a rich storehouse of memories.

Confessions of a *Schnorrer*

D*r. Simons thanks* you, Dr. Hertz, for that introduction. I like to remember what happened to me when I was given the title of Dr. Simons for the first time back in 1957. Wayne State University gave me an honorary doctorate at their June commencement before thousands of people. I was thrilled, of course, at the honor. When the program was over and everyone was leaving, I walked out of the auditorium in my cap and gown.

I was excited and was on cloud nine going to my car in

Talk given at Temple Beth El, April 1980. All talks in this volume were given in or around Detroit.

The caricature of the author is by Detroit Free Press artist Dick Mayer, a gift of the Detroit Historical Society on its 50th anniversary, November 1978.

the parking lot. I wasn't paying attention, and I nearly walked into a moving car. It almost hit me. The driver stuck his head out his window and yelled, "What the devil is the matter with you? Why don't you look where you're going, you jerk?" I looked sheepishly at him, held up my diploma, and answered, "Doctor Jerk to you!"

When Temple invited me to speak tonight I was told to pick any subject I thought you might like to hear discussed. So I chose the title, "The Confessions of a *Schnorrer*." A *schnorrer* is someone who is always petitioning people to give money, to make donations to worthy causes, to support their fellow man. I have always been quite proficient at fund raising. For many years I had the dubious distinction of being the *town schnorrer*. At one of the annual Jewish Welfare Federation campaign dinners, the late Justice Henry Butzel got up and said, "In the early days of this century, I was known as Detroit's *town schnorrer*, but now Leonard Simons has succeeded me in that unofficial capacity."

And I'll show you how the Essence of Judaism affected my life. Now do not be afraid. I am not going to sermonize. That's the rabbis' job. But, I must say that the Essence of Judaism is the most important ingredient of our religion. It is the intrinsic quality that gives our religion its identity. Together with belief in God and prayer, it is the major reason for our survival as a people.

What is the Essence of Judaism? It can be explained in one word, *zedakah*. In ancient days, *zedakah* was considered an act of duty. It is a deed of righteousness, of compassion and loving-kindness, a prerequisite of social justice. It is a divine commandment. Our ancestors shared their wealth with those less fortunate, both Jew and non-Jew, because our Jewish Bible teaches that all wealth belongs to God.

In today's world, we oversimplify *zedakah* by defining it as charity or philanthropy. Incidentally, in the Hebrew language there is no word for charity or beggar.

I'm proud to say the Essence of Judaism brought me inner satisfaction and gave me many new and stimulating interests; it expanded my knowledge, permitted me to become a world traveler, helped me become acquainted with a long list of outstanding men and women who helped countless thousands of men, women, and children with the kinds of assistance that met their particular personal problems. It has helped me fulfill my life.

Yes, as I reflect back, it has been a great life. I think how true the statement is: You only go around in this world once, but if you do it right, once is enough.

Larry Michelson, who has been my boyhood friend and my business partner for over sixty years, encouraged me in all my extracurricular activities. He worked with me on many of them. Sixty years is a very long time. Would you believe that in all those years, Larry and I have never had an argument of any kind? Well, it's true. I like to think of Larry and me as a modern day, Jewish version of Damon and Pythias.

From our earliest days, just about every worthy cause in which we were involved—sooner, or later, but usually sooner—became a fund-raising project. We start by just giving money, but soon we are asked to help raise funds. This proves that *zedakah* and fund raising go together; they're partners; they go hand in hand; one follows the other. Fund raising augments the classic eight degrees of *zedakah* and helps fulfill the Essence of Judaism.

It seems no organization ever has enough money. So you not only go to meetings and give money, but then you go out and ask others to give money. I remember a little rabbi from out of town who called on me to solicit my annual contribution for his *yeshiva*, his religious school. He happened to catch me on a day when I wasn't in a good mood. I didn't feel like giving him anything. So I gave all kinds of reasons why I wouldn't give that year. There were too many campaigns, business wasn't so good, and all such alibis. All the time I was talking to him he was making notes in a little black book. Finally my curiosity got the best of me and I said to him, "I'll tell you what I'll do rabbi. Show me what you've written in the book, and I'll give you a check. He handed the book over to me and I read: "Ehr ist mashoogeh—but git gelt" ("He's crazy, but he gives money").

One of my favorites in town is the Jewish Home for the Aged. I have been on its board about forty-five years. Detroit has some of the finest facilities, accommodations, and programs anywhere to bring happiness and prolonged life to a great many of our needy Jewish old folks.

There are many cute stories that can be told about the

Home. I remember one Sunday morning board meeting. When it was over, I talked to a resident whom I knew. We exchanged pleasantries, and when he asked me how I was feeling, I said I was a little tired of going to so many meetings. "I've been working on various committees for over forty years." He looked at me and said with a grin, "That's not so long. I've got ties that are older."

The Home had a party at which I was the master of ceremonies. After it was over, I was stopped by an old-timer who expressed his appreciation for my efforts by saying that he hoped and prayed he would live to be as old as my jokes.

The Home's doctors watch the health of the residents very carefully. They are constantly examined and checked. One man was telling his tale of woe, about his aches and pains, to the M.D. The doctor said, "You know my friend, we can't make you any younger." And Mr. "Friend" replied, "I don't want you should make me any younger. I just want you to make me get older."

I've told the Home to save me a corner room with a good view. If you want to feel young, always hang around older people.

Another one of my favorite organizations is the Jewish Welfare Federation. I think it does a fantastic job of planning and budgeting for its various agencies with full regard for their relative needs. This money is given to help all of our local Jewish charities as well as the State of Israel and Jews throughout the world who need financial assistance. Through the Allied Jewish Campaign, over $18 million will be raised again this year. That is amazing *zedakah* from around seventy-five thousand local Jews.

I have been identified with Federation since before World War II. I was a vice-president for a few years, and I was co-chairman of the 1959 Allied Jewish Campaign. I still work on the campaigns.

Because of my activities with Federation, I've been invited to the UJA (United Jewish Appeal) Study Missions in Israel. The last time I was in Israel was a year ago, and I'm frank to admit it was, as always, a tremendous thrill. I keep thinking about the fact that I am actually standing on this holy land where our ancestors lived so many generations ago. I imagine I'm a part of that history. My wife and I also get a big thrill when we visit the Leonard and Harriette Simons Forest in Jerusalem, given to the Jewish National Fund by our friends and acquaintances.

I have actively supported the JNF for many years. It is the largest employer of labor in Israel. They have done, and are doing, an unbelievable job of reclaiming the barren land. They plant millions of trees, pave the roads, and make the deserts bloom, and they have been doing it for many years, even before the State of Israel was established. They *knew* it was going to happen some day. They had faith.

In spite of wars and troubles of all kinds, the Israelis have a fabulous sense of humor. One of my friends went into an Israeli delicatessen and asked the waiter what was good to eat. The waiter said, "You name it, we got it." So he began calling off a lot of dishes that were his favorites back home, but the waiter kept shaking his head no to all of them. Finally my friend said, I thought you said if I named it—you've got it?" And the waiter answered, "That's right, but you didn't name it yet."

Two of my gentile friends who were with me on one of my visits saw a sign on the window that advertised kosher foods in Hebrew letters. One man said to the other, "What does that sign mean?" And the second one, a little more knowledgeable than the first one, said, "Well, to you it means nothing. To me it means nothing. But to the Jewish people that's Duncan Hines."

We were always told how helpful Israel's train conductors are. We asked one of them, "What time does the train get to Beersheba?" His answer was 11:02. "But," we said, "the timetable says it gets there at 10:15." The conductor replied, "So take the timetable."

Then they tell me about the Israeli tobacconist who made a fortune. He invented a *gefelt*-tipped cigarette (a play on Yiddish "filled").

We saw signs in some delicatessen windows that they sold "pickled *pupiks*" (navels, but affectionately applied to chicken gizzards).

My interest in extracurricular activities and in travel has taken my wife and me overseas over two dozen times. We were among the first to go to Red China. A year ago, after peace was declared, we went to Egypt. We also made two trips

22

to Iran before the king fell and the present troubles began.

We wanted to see the former Persia which is full of Jewish historical and biblical attractions. We were not disappointed. We saw, bought, and brought home many Jewish artifacts, most of which we gave to Beth El's Judaica Museum.

On our last visit to Iran in 1973, we wanted to see the twenty-five-hundred-year-old tombs of Queen Esther and her cousin Mordecai of Purim fame. After a full day's motor trip we arrived in Hamadan. Our guide took us to a handsome new building which is one of Iran's national treasures. It encloses the ancient tombs. We had to find the custodian of the key. Traditionally, he is the eldest Jew among the residents.

Within the tomb were two sarcophagi made of dark wood, side by side, each carved with intricate patterns plus a Hebrew inscription. Here was the tomb of the biblical heroine who had been King Ahasuerus' queen. The Persians called Ahasuerus, Xerxes I, of the family of Cyrus the Great and son of Darius the Great, the two kings who permitted the reconstruction of the Temple and allowed the exiles in Babylonia to return to Judah with the Temple vessels that had been stolen by King Nebuchadnezzar. Thus was created the period of the Second Temple in Jewish history.

These tombs have been guarded with loving care for twenty-five centuries. They make you realize how important Jewish history is in keeping our religion in spite of every conceivable form of intentional human cruelty for so many thousands of years. For me, that was an exciting and emotional experience.

We also visited the town of Isfahan. You may be surprised to learn that in ancient days its name was Al-Yahudiyyah—City of the Jews.

Harriette and I love to see new and different places and cultures. We love to meet people and study contrasts. We take at least one trip abroad each year. In fact, I've made out a new will which reads, "Being of sound mind, I spent all my money while I was alive."

Not too long ago, I was honored to be one of the few Jews ever elected an officer of the Greater Detroit Board of Commerce. They made me treasurer and asked me to help increase their annual income. So I raised everybody's dues.

At one of their dinner receptions for visiting dignitaries,

I was introduced to Frol Kozlov, one of Russia's top men in the Communist party. He spoke through an interpreter. He said, "How do you do?" And I said, "I'm pleased to meet you." Then silence. Neither one of us said anything. So I tried to make conversation by saying, "My mother was born in Russia." He said, "Is that so, where?" I answered, "Kiev." Then he said, "Then you've got Ukranian blood in you." And I responded, "Yes, I suppose so." He then asked, "Does that stamp you as a Red over here?" I replied, "To be truthful, I don't think I've ever told anybody about it." He leaned over toward me, patted me on the back and said, "Okay, I will keep your secret." A little later, when I went to the International Cancer Congress in Moscow, I tried to contact Kozlov but had no luck.

I have been fighting cancer for many years—by serving on the boards of the American Cancer Society Southeastern Michigan Chapter and of the Michigan Cancer Foundation. How did I get involved with them? Back in 1945, they came to me and asked me to head a fund-raising campaign to buy the property on John R. and Hancock, to build a cancer clinic and research institute. We did it; we raised $250,000. From that small beginning grew an $8 million building that carries the name of a famous Beth El member, The Meyer L. Prentis Cancer Center, which houses the Michigan Cancer Foundation and the United States government's Comprehensive Cancer Center. The Prentis family had asked me to find a fitting memorial for this fine gentleman. And I was able to arrange this tribute to Meyer.

In 1966, I went to the International Cancer Congress in Tokyo. The Japanese are most unusual people, so industrious and so clean. Their streets are immaculate. I say their birds fly upside down.

We had dinner with a Japanese couple. The man had been ordained a rabbi at Hebrew Union College the same year I received an honorary doctorate from HUC. I had met him in Cincinnati, and I wanted to look him up to see how he was getting along. This man had decided that Judaism was the answer to his quest for spiritual satisfaction. But the Jews who live in Japan, about one thousand, would not accept him as their rabbi. I guess the name Rabbi Hiroshi Okamoto did not sound kosher to them.

We took the rabbi and his family to dinner. They were

very poor. They had not tasted meat since they had left the United States. After listening to his problem, a group of us got together with Rabbi Hertz and raised some money which was sent to him each month for a year. This helped him get a Ph.D. at Oxford University in England. Now, thank goodness, he's a university professor and makes his living teaching.

Among my interests are the three Detroit Historical Museums. How did this come about? Well, about thirty-five years ago my friend George W. Stark, whom many of you remember was a *Detroit News* columnist, came to me. He had been offered $50,000 by the daughter of one of our former governors toward the building of a Detroit Historical Museum, provided others would contribute $200,000 within the next twelve months. Would I help raise the money? I became chairman, and we were successful. The next thing I knew, I was on the new, charter-created Detroit Historical Commission. I served for over thirty years under seven mayors. I am now retired, but Mayor Young made me president emeritus.

About five years ago we were traveling in France. We went to the little town of St. Nicolas de la Grave, near Toulouse, where Cadillac, the founder of Detroit, was born. The house was still standing but very dilapidated. The mayor offered to sell it to the Detroit Historical Society for 100,000 francs. I told him I'd raise the money for their town, if they would agree to repair the house and fix it up to look something like it did in the late 1600s and maintain it as a historical museum.

We kept our end of the bargain, and so did they. When everything was ready, a group from the Detroit Historical Society went over for the formal dedication. I was supposed to make a speech in French. In preparation, I studied for several weeks with a French teacher, but I didn't learn too much. I memorized my short talk. At the big banquet, I wanted to say "The last time I was here." In French that would begin, "Le dernier fois." But I came out with "Le derriere fois!"

To finish the story: in 1976, during the American Bicentennial, the president of France sent a telegram advising that he was making me a Chevalier (a knight) of the National Order of Merit, his country's second highest civilian award, for my services in connection with saving the Cadillac House and for helping to further good relations between France and the

U.S.A. The French ambassador in Washington came to Detroit on July 4th. At a luncheon, before the mayor and a large crowd, he pinned the medal on me and kissed me on both cheeks. But you know, he was not my type at all.

Old Central High School is now Old Main of Wayne State University, for whom I've raised a lot of money. On their campus you'll find the Nate Shapero Hall of Pharmacy, the Meyer and Anna Prentis School of Business Administration Building, the Charles Grosberg Religious Center, two buildings carrying the name of Helen DeRoy, the Vera Shiffman Medical Library, the Gertrude Levin Pain Clinic in the medical school, and the Helen Vera Prentis Lande Medical Research Building, and the Faculty Club Building financed by the Prentis Foundation. There also happens to be a Leonard N. Simons Building for the WSU Press, but I didn't raise money for that.

To continue my saga of fund raising. I'm on the board of Sinai Hospital. Of course it all began in 1941 with a campaign to raise enough money to build a local hospital under Jewish auspices. I was chairman of the Sinai money-raising Designations Committee for over twenty-five years. I'm still on the Executive Committee.

Today we have one of the finest general hospitals in America. It was created to give our Jewish physicians a place to practice. Most of our doctors could not get on the staffs of other hospitals in town because of discrimination. Today the picture has changed. There is a great shortage of doctors and nurses. Sinai Hospital is more important than ever because of its six hundred beds and most modern equipment and facilities.

Personally, I'm not so sure medicine has made much progress. If it has, then why do I feel worse than I did twenty years ago?

I have asthma or emphysema, and not too long ago I finally had a chance to use Sinai's facilities as a patient. I noticed that they put the initials "S.O.B." on my medical report. They're still trying to convince me that it means "short of breath."

As I think back, the one association that has given me the greatest satisfaction in my lifetime of trying to be helpful is my service to Temple Beth El over many years. The story starts again with fund raising. Temple was planning a cam-

26

paign to pay off the mortgage on the Woodward and Gladstone building. Larry Michelson and I were asked to handle the publicity and to work on fund raising. We did all the advertising, free of course, and Larry and I raised a lot of money. After the mortgage was burned, Rabbi Glazer came to my office and said he wanted me on the temple board.

Before his tragic death, Dr. Glazer was making plans to relocate our temple out north of Detroit, where many of the congregation were moving. He also wanted to reinstate the bar mitzvah which Beth El hadn't had for about fifty years. On his death both projects came to a halt. I agreed with him. I stubbornly pursued his plans and I take full responsibility for both of these changes. I fought for them, and I carried the ball for Dr. Glazer. I think you'll agree with me that both of these moves were excellent decisions by our congregation.

I must admit that serving Beth El has given me a tremendous amount of personal satisfaction and comfort. I learned a lot about my religion. I was proud to be called, if you'll excuse the expression, "a pillar of the church." That is, until I found out that the dictionary defines pillar as something thick, immovable, and holds everything up.

The time allotted me is just about up. If I had more time I could tell you many amusing stories about my experiences *schnorring,* fund raising, for the Union of American Hebrew Congregations, Brandeis University, Hebrew Union College—Jewish Institute of Religion, American Jewish Historical Society, Hadassah, Israel Bonds, Jewish Publication Society, Hillel, B'nai B'rith, American Jewish Committee, Hebrew University of Jerusalem, and others as well as all the nonsectarian organizations that I've worked for, giving and raising money.

I've spent the majority of my seventy-five years trying to follow the precepts of the Essence of Judaism, and, I confess, it has been the pathway to happiness for me. I thank God that I was able to do it.

I also thank my dear wife, Harriette, for letting me do it. We recently celebrated our 50th wedding anniversary. We believe the reason we were able to do it was not by just living *with* each other, but by living *for* each other.

You might also like to know that Harriette has already picked out the epitaph for my tombstone. It's going to read: "Here lies Leonard N. Simons—gone to another meeting.

Machers and Mavericks I've Met

*W*hen *Temple Beth El* asked me to
speak again this year, I thought I would continue to reminisce.
In other words: "Part II of Confessions of a *Schnorrer*." But,
then I decided it would be more fun to relate a few anecdotes
about some friends and acquaintances. And I've had many of
them, some greats, some near greats, and some ingrates.

I describe them as *machers* (doers) and mavericks. There
is hardly any difference between them. In most cases, mavericks are people with ideas and strong minds of their own.
They carry nobody's brand. And unlike cattle, they do not always do what they should do or are expected to do. Usually,
they are exceptionally smart, determined people. Because they
also are usually successful, the mavericks end up as *machers.*

Machers are people who are doers. They are not all
wealthy, but they are people of influence in organizations,
politics, business, civic affairs, religion, charities, etc; they are
the people who make things happen, who get things done.

American Jewry has a superabundance of men and
women who have earned the right to be called *machers.* These
Jews have been able to develop their capabilities to their fullest
potential because they live in this great free land of ours.

I once asked Dr. Jacob Marcus, the eminent Jewish historian of the Hebrew Union College's American Jewish Archives, what contributions Jews have made to American culture. He answered with a twinkle in his eye that if it were not
for a Jew, Emile Berliner, we would have no radio or television
because Berliner perfected the microphone.

Rabbi Marcus mentioned another Jew, Akiba Horowitz,
who loved America so much that he gave up his Jewish name
and took a good American name. He called himself Conrad
Hubert. Then he proceeded to discover the flashlight. It netted

Talk given at Temple Beth El, May 1981.

L. to R.: author, Nate Shapero, Sidney Allen

him $10 million. On his death it was found that his estate was divided equally among Jews, Catholics, and Protestants.

Then Marcus said, "but more important is the fact that Gregory Pincus is the man who perfected 'the pill.' " And, he continued, "What a remarkable contribution these three Jews have made to civilization. Before they perfected their discoveries, we wasted our time playing poker, and when we got up at night, without the courtesy of a flashlight, we stumbled over a dozen children in our house."

For tonight I have chosen some *machers* and mavericks whose names, I am sure, are familiar to you. They were my friends. Some of them were your friends, too. And, while they are no longer with us, when they were, they really helped make this old world of ours a little better and a more interesting place.

I have made some slides of pictures that I found among my old photographs. Without further ado, let's turn down the lights.

I will start with this picture of Nate Shapero, Sidney Allen, and me. We were at a New Year's Eve party at a ranch in Arizona back in 1953. The three of us came in costume, dressed up to look like what we called Abraham Lincoln's undertakers. At that time, I was president of Beth El and was taking my responsibilities seriously. Irving Katz was our secretary, and it was his job to keep me informed nearly every day with what was going on at Beth El.

Imagine my shock when about a week after this party, Irving mailed me a copy of the latest *Temple Bulletin*. Here's what a page looked like. There was my very undignified picture from the party, with the wording "Our president vacationing in Arizona." I was angry! I ran to the phone and called Irving. I started yelling, "How could you do this? Where is your good judgment?" plus much more in much stronger language. Irving was laughing, which made me angrier. Finally, he said, "Don't get excited; it was only a joke played on you by your good friend, Nate Shapero. He sent me the photo and story. The members did *not* get this *Bulletin*. We printed only *one* copy—*just for you*."

Now, you have seen the most unique copy of the *Temple Bulletin* ever printed. It was typical of Nate Shapero's great sense of humor. He loved a gag or a good joke. And he had a keen mind plus a million good ideas. He was an outstanding citizen who was honored by thousands of Jews and non-Jews for his good deeds. Suffice to say, nearly every worthwhile activity in town had some assistance from his person or his pocketbook. In the development of Sinai Hospital, for example, Nate was the biggest *macher* of all.

Nate was president of Beth El during its 100th Anniversary in 1950. It was his idea to produce a 100-year history book on our Temple. He got the board to approve $2,500 to pay for the book and then gave me the assignment to get the book out. The sum of $2,500 could not pay for much of a book even then, and so, we only had an idea but not enough money.

In 1954, when I had my 50th birthday, my wife, Harriette, told all my friends who asked her not to buy me gifts but to give the money they intended to spend to a Leonard Simons Fund at Beth El. Almost $20,000 was raised. We took most of the fund and gave it to the Wayne State University Press to produce *The Beth El Story*. I designed the format, but Irving Katz and our good friend, Dr. Jacob Marcus, contributed the contents.

At the Jewish Home For Aged. *L. to R.:* Myron Keyes, the author, Sidney Allen, and residents

The Press editors thought our book was a "smorgasbord of literature" and did not want to put their colophon, their trademark, on it and publish it. I insisted the Press owed me a favor; I originated its financially successful Board of Advisers. Also, the Leonard N. Simons Fund was paying the cost of the book. So they reluctantly agreed but weren't too happy about it.

The Beth El Story won an award that year as one of the fourteen best books of the year from the standpoint of design by the Chicago Book Publishers Association, the first time the Press had ever won an award of any kind. Nate Shapero said to me, "It's a good thing you had a 50th birthday, Leonard."

Nate's buddy and mine was Sidney Allen, father of former Temple president Jay Allen. We three worked together on dozens of worthy projects, and they were always successful. Sid was a *macher* at the Jewish Home for Aged. That was his pet.

This picture shows Sid with Myron Keys, who was president at that time. We were at a board meeting. We always

B. Benedict Glazer

Morris Adler

spoke with some of the residents. Many were a lot of fun to talk to. One cute old-timer told us his life's story in a few words. He said, "I set out in life to find the pot of gold at the end of the rainbow. Now, I'm eighty-seven, and all I've got is the pot."

I remember one old resident coming up to me after a board meeting. He said, "You're Mr. Sidney Allen, aren't you? Can I have your autograph please?" I replied, "But I'm not Sidney Allen." And the man said, "What's the difference. My young grandson can't read yet anyway."

Sid was very close to Beth El. He was a vice-president and would have been president except for his health. He was generous to a fault. He tried to help any friend whom he knew

L. *to* R.: Alfred Taubman, Charles Gershenson, Rabbi Adler, the author, Max Shaye, Isidore Sobeloff, William Avrunin

needed assistance. And because everyone had confidence in him, Sidney Allen could get nearly everybody to work with him on any kind of a project, even on something nonexistent, such as fund raising for the "Unmarried Widows of Korea." Everyone loved him. He was a good guy, a man's man.

Another great twosome in town was our own Rabbi B. Benedict Glazer and Rabbi Morris Adler of Congregation Shaarey Zedek. How they both loved a good, clean, funny story. When they told a joke, they'd explode with laughter, and you had to join them because their laughs were so infectious. They were both famous as pulpiteers and were inspirational leaders. Here indeed were a couple of great *machers* as well as great, truly great, rabbis. What a pity God took both of them from us so early.

I had been bar mitzvah at conservative Shaarey Zedek on Willis and Brush streets. Later, I joined reform Beth El. Rabbi Adler knew this. Whenever he introduced me to someone, he'd say, "I want you to meet my friend Leonard Simons. His roots are great but his branches are withered." Then he'd roar with laughter. He liked to say that most people wish to serve God, but in an advisory capacity only.

A member of his large congregation once came up to

him and said "Hi, Rabbi, remember me?" Adler wasn't sure; after all, who can remember every congregant? Adler said, "Close your eyes." The member did so. Then Adler exclaimed, "Now I know you! You always fall asleep as soon as the sermon starts." And the member replied, "Rabbi, you should feel complimented. If I did not trust you, I could not sleep."

I remember presenting Rabbi Adler as our speaker at an Allied Jewish Campaign meeting. This picture was taken that day; that's the rabbi next to me. Also at the front table are Al Taubman, Charles Gershenson, Max Shaye; and there are Isidore Sobeloff and William Avrunin. I had worked hard on a project of which I was proud. After the meeting Rabbi Adler thanked me for his introduction.

A year later, the new Jewish Home for Aged on Seven Mile Road—Borman Hall—was being dedicated on a Sunday morning. I had just returned from Europe that Friday, when I was asked to please handle the introduction of Rabbi Adler, our speaker. I said, "No way; I just got back. I cannot prepare anything on such short notice, and I will not talk extemporaneously when introducing a man like Adler." But the caller insisted, so I reluctantly gave in.

After panicking for a few moments, I thought of my last year's Adler introduction. It was Saturday. I drove downtown to my closed office and prayed I could locate a copy. Thank God, I found it. I changed the opening sentences and used the old introduction, word for word. When the affair was over, Rabbi Adler came to me with tears in his eyes and said, "Leonard, that was the finest introduction I've ever received in my life. I'll treasure it forever." I did not have the heart to tell him it was the identical introduction I had given him a year ago.

Dr. B. Benedict Glazer, "Babe" to his close friends, encouraged many of us to take an active part in Beth El affairs. I liked his many-faceted, interesting personality. He was warm and outgoing, an extrovert. He was immensely popular, beloved by Jews and non-Jews.

He was a scholar with an exceptional mind. He fought injustice at all levels His was the vision to plan our Temple's move to where our membership would relocate their homes. Dr. Glazer gets full credit for what we see here tonight. He planned our congregation's future. Unfortunately, he did not

Fred Butzel   Henry Butzel

have the pleasure—*nachus* (the proud pleasure)—of seeing how beautifully his dream was realized.

Dr. Glazer had a great sense of humor. He said he had a nightmare once: he heard God sneeze and didn't know what to say to Him. I liked his definition of a rabbi: a rabbi is someone who walks around all day with a worried look—on his president's face.

During the time Temple Beth El was campaigning to burn the Woodward and Gladstone mortgage, Rabbi Glazer made a pertinent sermon one Sabbath. A member of the congregation came up after services and said "Rabbi, that was a damn good sermon you gave, damn good!" Dr. Glazer replied, "Thank you, but couldn't you have expressed your compliment in a little more restrained way?" To which our member answered, "I can't help it, rabbi. You gave such a damn good sermon, I'm giving $5,000 to the Mortgage Burning Campaign." And, Glazer exclaimed, "The hell you say!"

This is a photo of Fred Butzel. But first let me tell you about the two famous Butzels I have known: Fred and brother Henry. If there ever were *machers* and mavericks, this duo of brilliant lawyers was unequalled. They spent many hours of their time, and many thousands of their dollars, to help Jewish refugees get a fresh start in America.

No one in Detroit had a more famous name than the Butzels. Fred and Henry, together with cousin Leo, served on just about every important local civic committee, sat on the boards of our most important corporations, and handled the legal problems of our wealthiest Jewish and non-Jewish citizens. They had the respect for their integrity and intelligence that all honorable men and women hope to achieve.

I count Fred Butzel as one of the ten all-time greatest citizens in Michigan history. A bachelor, he spent his life serving others. I am amazed that among the countless projects he headed, he found time in six different years to serve as chairman of the Detroit Allied Jewish Campaign! This picture shows Fred at one of the campaign meetings. Do you recognize Celia Broder and Henry Wineman sitting next to Fred? Three great citizens.

Fred told me that he was always available to serve Detroit's Federation in any way it needed him. When I was in my thirties, Fred came up to my office to ask my advice and help on some civic matter. I was so proud that he had considered me a Jewish *macher*. It was an impetus for me to try to do better. I liked his famous remark: "The trouble with being a leader is that you can't be sure whether people are following you or chasing you."

Then there was Henry Butzel, who became chief justice of the Michigan Supreme Court. He had been a president of Beth El as had his father before him. In the early days of the century, Henry had the dubious distinction of being Detroit's Jewish *town schnorrer*. But he turned his title over to me about twenty years ago at the United Jewish Charities 60th Anniversary dinner.

When I became president of Beth El, Henry told me about his experience as its president after serving one year. At the annual meeting he announced, "I guess I just am not cut out to be a Temple president, and I am *not* running for reelection." He added, "And they all applauded."

I used to pick up Henry and drive him to Allied Jewish Campaign meetings. At the age of ninety, he no longer drove. But he still wouldn't let me take his arm to help him, even in icy weather. When we got to the meetings, I usually gave him a cigar. He loved to smoke. He'd take out a little gadget from his pocket, insert the end of the cigar in the opening, squeeze it together, and chop off the tip of the cigar. He'd smile at me and say, "Now the cigar's kosher. I just circumcized it."

He once asked me what he could do—his smoking was

Meyer L. Prentis

discoloring his teeth brown. I suggested he wear brown suits and ties. He didn't like my idea.

These Butzel men were outstanding lawyers with tremendous practices. One of them, in his early days, had a library in his office with fifteen-foot bookcases from floor to ceiling to hold all his law books. It was said that if a new client came in with a lawsuit involving a book on the top shelves, he would *not* take the case.

Meyer Prentis, a good friend, was another of our great Detroit Jews. Meyer was a genius with figures, and his talent carried him up to one of the very biggest corporation jobs in the world as treasurer of General Motors. He had a brilliant mind. The last four or five G.M. board chairmen were trained by Meyer Prentis.

You really could not call Meyer a maverick, but what an outstanding *macher* he was! And how he loved Beth El. He served on its board for years. Meyer was cochairman of the successful campaign to burn the mortgage on our Woodward and Gladstone temple. When Dr. Glazer died and we searched for a new rabbi, Meyer Prentis served as cochairman of that very important committee.

This picture shows Meyer leading the procession at the temple when Dr. Hertz was inducted as our rabbi. And here's a group picture of the presidents of Franklin Hills Country Club taken a few years ago with Meyer in the front row on the right end.

Past presidents of Franklin Hills Country Club

How many of you know that Franklin Hills Country Club went broke during the depression years? The banks foreclosed on our mortgage. We were about to lose the club until Meyer stepped in. He paid up the mortgage and bought the club. He saved Franklin Hills for the Jewish community. When new financing was found, Meyer sold the club back to us for exactly what he paid for it. He could have made a big profit by keeping the property, but that was not his way. Money was not that important to him.

Meyer once told me about an accident Mrs. Prentis had when she lost control of her car. She smashed into five cars before she pulled herself together. Still, she was mighty lucky. It happened in her own garage.

Meyer was a great family man who took life and responsibilities seriously. He worried about other people. "ML," as he was fondly called, created a charitable foundation. He then taught his daughters and sons-in-law how to give his fortune to deserving causes and projects. And they have done just that. The tremendous good they continue to do reflects great honor on the family as well as on the vision and memory of Meyer Prentis.

Just for a change of pace, here's a picture of me with

L. to R.: Larry Michelson, Kim Novak, the author, Carl Shalit

L. to R.: Rabbi Hertz, Eleanor Roosevelt, Albert Colman, the author

the lovely movie star Kim Novak. She isn't a *macher*, but she is considered a maverick and very much alive. Notice where my right arm is?

I met Kim at a local party, and we seemed to hit it off nicely. I was trying to be as charming as I could. I told her it was a good thing she was a woman because a figure like hers would be wasted on a man.

While we were having our pictures taken together, she said something that sounded like "It's not jurisprudent of the parallel for military embrosures." I turned to her and said, "What did you say? I don't get you." And Kim replied, "That's what I'm trying to tell you."

Then there was that wonderful *macher* whom I greatly admired: Eleanor Roosevelt. She was no stranger to Beth El. She spoke here in 1947 at a Sabbath service under the auspices of our Jewish Welfare Foundation. Later, in 1954, sponsored by our newly formed Young Married Group, she spoke to a full house in our main sanctuary.

In this picture we see Dr. Hertz as he looked twenty-seven years ago, and that handsome man between Mrs. Roosevelt and me is temple member and attorney Albert Colman, who is still a temple stalwart.

I met the great lady in 1952 at the first commencement of Brandeis University. Eleanor Roosevelt was the speaker. She spoke for almost an hour without referring to a single note. We never heard a smoother, more brilliant, more inspirational message than that she gave the young graduates.

I was in the commencement ceremony because I had been a Fellow of Brandeis since the year it opened. The Fellows are a special group of people: as I understand this honor it gives us the privilege of giving and raising money for Brandeis. Most of the original Fellows had not graduated from a college or a university, but they were successful business men.

Nate Shapero, Dr. Glazer, Sidney Allen, and I once brought Dr. Abram Sacher, president of Brandeis, to Detroit to assist us in some fund raising for his university. That was twenty-nine years ago. In June of that year I went to Brandeis to march as a Fellow of the university in Brandeis' first commencement exercises. Dr. Sacher gave us cowls or hoods to wear over our gowns. The colorful hoods were supposed to indicate that were graduate doctors, engineers, etc. My degree

David Ben Gurion and the author

L. to R.: Ben Silberstein, the author, Larry Michelson, Maurice Aronsson

was L. H. D.—Doctor of Humane Letters. I told them that many of my clients and friends would never agree that I wrote "humane letters."

Recognize this famous *macher*? Former Israel Prime Minister David Ben Gurion. He is giving me a memento of my visit to Israel back in 1956 when I was part of the United Jewish Appeal Study Mission. At the closing dinner, we had our pictures taken. As we were about to get our gift, the photographer told us to say, *"g'vee nah."* Note my lips. I asked Ben Gurion what that word meant. He said, "Cheese, in Hebrew."

Ben Gurion was the backbone and the mastermind of Israel in those early days. He was a little giant. I heard him say that Israel was the only country in the world, where, if you call someone a Jew, you are not being an anti-Semite.

It was said that if Ben Gurion did not like you, he would have a tree in Israel uprooted in your honor.

To get back to our town—here's a picture of two great mavericks who became *machers,* Ben Silberstein and Maury Aronsson. They threw a party for Larry Michelson and me on the 20th anniversary of our advertising agency back in 1949. It was at the old Standard Club, *Alav ha sholem* (May it rest in peace).

Ben and Maury were my friends since childhood, and we remained good friends up to the day each of them passed away. Both were Beth El members.

Ben, on the left hand side of the picture, was a Detroit lawyer, a success in local real estate, who bought the First National Bank Building in Detroit. Later, he went out to California and became internationally famous as the owner of the fabulous Beverly Hills Hotel.

Ben had his own ideas about giving away his money, and he gave a tremendous amount. For instance, he bought a $200,000 statue by the great sculptor Maillol for the Detroit Institute of Arts. It was a larger than life-size nude. He named it "Crisco" because, as he put it, "Crisco is fat in the can."

Ben gave $100,000 at one time to the United Negro College Fund. He gave me $250,000 for Wayne State University's Medical School to establish a Pain Clinic in memory of his first wife, who had lived for many years in constant pain.

In the early days of that marriage Ben gave his wife, Gertrude, a one thousand dollar U.S. Bond every Hanukah or

Maurice Aronsson

Christmas. Then he'd tell her he'd put it in their bank safe deposit box. Every year she got a thousand dollar bond. Several years later, she noticed the date on the bond. Ben had been giving her the same bond each year!

Here's a picture of Maurice Aronsson at the 60th birthday party given in his honor by 350 friends. The giant birthday card congratulating Maury was signed by all the guests. I was the master of ceremonies that evening, and it was great fun.

Maury was nicknamed "Santa Claus" by his friends. Why? Because he was the softest touch in town. The list of people who borrowed money from him was a yard long. And he never charged interest on a personal loan to a friend.

Maury was a *macher* in the Jewish Home for Aged. He was chairman of the Detroit Allied Jewish Campaign which raised $6 million in one year, an all-time high for Detroit at that time. Others had the idea to build a Jewish-sponsored hospital in town, but it took Maury's leadership, influence, and generosity to convince Federation to go along with us. We first met at his home in 1941. Larry Michelson and I were there. The project was held up for a few years by World War II, but then we were able to start up again. Maury was a *macher* who could take a great deal of credit for the six-hundred-bed, outstanding medical facility that Sinai Hospital is today.

"Santa Claus" Aronsson was a terrific personality. He ran his very successful printing company in his own unique fashion. He used to tell his crew, "When I want your advice, I'll give it to you," and they all loved him. He would also often say, "I never lose my temper. I misplace or mislay it some-time, but I never lose it."

Incidentally, Aronsson Printing Company is still a success under his son Herby Aronsson. But Maury was a one-of-a-kind guy. He would sit at your desk and figure out his price on your print job in a couple of minutes. Of course, sometimes he forgot to figure in the cost of the paper, or the ink, but, as he explained, "I figure my cost at, let's say, one dollar, and I sell it to you for two. I make my 1 percent, and I'm satisfied."

Obviously, I cannot talk about all the important mavericks and *machers* I knew who helped make Jewish history in Detroit, for there were so many notables. I selected just nine men who were my close friends. They ranked extremely high in my esteem and in my heart. God bless their memories.

I'd like to tell you a little story about the new Bible translation by the Jewish Publication Society of America. About ten years ago I was on the Jewish Publication Society board. The Society needed money to finance the new translation. I was asked to prepare a campaign to raise Detroit's fair share. My plan worked and was duplicated around the country. The chairman of the Translation Committee of seven biblical scholars was my friend, Dr. Harry Orlinsky of the Hebrew Union College, one of the greatest Bible scholars alive.

Orlinsky and I kept in contact with each other because we both knew there was going to be more fund raising after the Torah portion was completed. Harry sent me galley proofs of the new translation as it went along. The first page he sent me showed that the scholars had *changed* the very first line of the Bible—universally known as "In the beginning God created the heaven and the earth."

I was shocked. To change this best known sentence in our Bible was sacrilegious to me. I immediately wrote Orlinsky and pleaded with them not to change it. We corresponded all year. I coaxed—I argued—I tried my best powers of persuasion . . . all to no avail. I was very unhappy.

Imagine my surprise when I received the finished copy of the new Torah book. They did change the first line. It now reads, "In the beginning *when God began to create* the heaven and the earth." But they put a small notation after the word "create." And at the bottom of the page they put, "or, In the beginning God created the heaven and the earth."

Harry Orlinsky

I'm sure Dr. Orlinsky would never admit that they re-tained the postscript wording because of my year-long plead-ing with them to save the time immemorial translation of the first line of the Bible. But, I like to think that I personally did help influence this little change of heart by the scholars and that I helped save this first line in the Bible for posterity. So sue me; I'm proud of the time and effort I spent working on these ten little words.

I remember one of my out-of-town trips for our office. Before I went to sleep I opened the Bible in the hotel bedroom. On the front page someone wrote, "If you are sick, read Psalm 18. If worried about your family, read Psalm 45. If you are lonely, read Psalm 92. So I read Psalm 92. When I finished, I glanced to the bottom of the page and I read, "If you are still lonely call 888-3468 and ask for Mary."

As President Reagan would say "Well"—that's about it for tonight. I hope you enjoyed my little stories. And it is fun to look at old nostalgic photos, isn't it? I love to look at my own fifty-one-year-old wedding pictures. They are great—with me in my tuxedo and Harriette on her pony.

I'll be seventy-seven years old in a couple months and I have emphysema. I won't say I'm completely out of condi-tion now—but I even puff when I go downstairs.

I love to play golf, but my doctor has warned me to stay away from the golf course. He said, "the way you look, Leonard, you would take a chance getting so close to those holes in the ground."

In retrospect, I've had a grand life, but if I had my life to live over again, I'd need more money.

This may very well be my swan song so far as speeches are concerned. I happen to be a person who is happy and proud to see young Jewish leaders—new *machers* and new mavericks—take over and the sooner the better.

Sydney Harris, the popular author and newspaper columnist wrote, "Growing older imposes a duty upon us to get more like a peach on the inside as we get more like a prune on the outside." He is so right.

I'm also getting used to my form of retirement—the time when a man goes from "Who's Who" to "Who's he?" from super to superannuated, when your passion turns to compassion.

I admit that when I hit seventy-five I felt a little despondent. I complained to Doctor Becker, and he said "*Cheer up*, Leonard. Look at it this way. If you were a horse, you'd have been dead fifty years ago."

Good night, and God bless you.

Detroit Historical Museum—
Kresge Hall

L. to R.: Edgar "Bud" Guest, the author, Stanley Kresge

G*ood evening ladies* and gentlemen. That was a very nice introduction you gave me, Bud Guest. Thank you. I'd like to tell you about the introduction I received recently at another affair. The chairman of the evening said, "For people who are *well known*, you do *not* need *lengthy* introductions. So I give you Leonard Simons; the less said about him the better."

Tonight it is my pleasant duty as president of the Detroit Historical Commission officially to thank two individuals who were primarily responsible for making possible our mil-

Talk given at the Detroit Historical Museum honoring the Kresge Foundation, June 1968.

lion-dollar museum addition. I'm talking about Gordon Rice for his inspiration to suggest to Stanley Kresge the idea of a Kresge Exhibit Hall. And to Stanley Kresge for his encouragement and assistance in helping us secure the munificent grant from the trustees of the Kresge Foundation.

In planning tonight's affair we thought we should try to make it a fun evening. So I hope you won't mind me reminiscing a bit. As I sat up here tonight looking at Stanley Kresge and Gordon Rice I could not help but think back to the days of old Central High School when all three of us were students in the building that is now called Old Main by Wayne State University. Those were the good old days when we were young and knew everything.

I don't remember what kind of a student Stanley was, but I do remember that Gordon and I were in the top 10 percent of the bottom 25 percent of the class. I think I was the only kid at Central High School ever thrown out of the Glee Club—for singing.

History was my favorite subject in school, but I never got good marks. My mother, after checking my report card, once said to me, "Well, there's one thing in your favor Leonard, with these grades, you could not possibly be cheating."

Stanley Kresge was one of my football heroes. He was a star end on the varsity football team. Gordon was a star basketball player. Me? I was a Star of David.

However, athletically, I was not a total loss. I played intramural baseball with Gordon. I remember how we'd put on our uniforms in the gymnasium locker room. Then we would walk from school to the baseball field which was about a mile away. On the way over we always had to stop at Gordon Rice's home which was on Cass Avenue near the school. We'd go into the house, and I'd help him make his bed and straighten up his bedroom. I think at that time his father was president of the Cadillac Motor Car Company, yet both Gordon and his brother Martin were taught by their mother to keep their room clean. We were the only three baseball players on the team with dishpan hands and housemaid's knee.

When Stanley, Gordon, and I went to old Central, Detroit had a population of less than a million people. James Couzens was our mayor. Later on he became famous as the father-in-law of Commissioner Mrs. Slattery. A new Ford cost

$400. The fire department used horses. Radio had just come into popular use. You rode the street cars for three cents, and there was no charge for transfers. Victor Herbert and also Mark Twain's son-in-law, Ossip Gabrilowitz, conducted the Detroit Symphony Orchestra. The new Main Library had just been built on Woodward and we kids used to play ball across the street on the site of the present Institute of Arts. We had a depression in 1921 also. Yes, those were the days that people talk about as being "the good old days": may they never come back again.

Time does go fast, doesn't it? It is hard for me to believe that I have been on the Detroit Historical Commission for twenty-three years. And it all started because my friend George Washington Stark asked me to help him raise the money we had to have if our city was to have an historical museum. We were successful and raised the money required to build our first unit. You know that our Master Plan calls for three more units down Kirby to Cass. I mention this in the hope that there is another "angel" in our audience tonight who will take the hint and emulate the example of the Kresge Foundation.

Don't everyone stand up at once, please.

I wish George Stark could have been with us tonight. The museum was his whole life. It was his dream. George, with his unrivaled memories of early Detroit, put his memories and articulation at the service of his fellow townsmen. His brilliance, his charm and wit as a speaker and writer, drew large audiences and spread knowledge of and interest in Detroit history. If any building ever was a monument to one man's efforts, this one is. Yes, Detroit can remember George Stark with thanks for the great historical museum in which we are enjoying our dedication dinner tonight. The dreamer is no longer with us, but his dreams continue to come true.

From the beginning we Detroit Historical Commissioners have tried to demonstrate that our major interest has not been the dry bones of history but its living spirit. And, like every other human institution, the Detroit Historical Museum cannot live merely by the exaltation of a worthy past. George Stark stressed that it must justify itself continually by linking our past with the present in a lively and interesting fashion. This I believe we are doing.

It was Gordon's idea to approach Stanley and the Kresge

Foundation to see if they would be interested in helping our museum expand by financing an addition to be called the Kresge Exhibit Hall. Stanley gave a sympathetic ear to Gordon, George, and me. The Kresge Foundation liked what we submitted. What Gordon's idea accomplished you can see all around you this evening.

And now it is our great pleasure to express our feelings and thanks to Stanley Kresge and the Kresge Foundation.

The Kresge name is one of the truly great ones in our community. Kresge's has been making history since the day just before the turn of the century when they opened their first store in Detroit on Woodward near State Street. Stanley's father, Sebastian S. Kresge, was a good citizen. He was a dedicated man, and he raised his children to be God-fearing people. He taught them that the true joy of living was in the pleasure of giving, and he taught them to have the healthy earthiness and warmth of plain people. He knew that we are all plain people and that a rich man is only a poor man with money.

They tell the story about a young man who applied for work at Sebastian S. Kresge's first store. Mr. Kresge said, "All right son, I'll give you a job. Start by sweeping up the store." The young man protested—"But I'm a college graduate." And Mr. Kresge replied, "Well OK—then watch me, and I'll show you how to do it."

Seriously, if any family has regarded its accumulated wealth as a public trust it is certainly the Kresge family. By establishing the Kresge Foundation they have created one of the greatest sources for good that America has ever seen. The Kresge Foundation name is repeated with impressive regularity in beneficent enterprises and endeavors in Detroit and throughout the United States, not forgetting Canada and a few faraway places such as Korea. To recount the Foundation's many benefactions in detail would be a worrisome task. But I don't think it would be out of order if I were to tell you that since the Kresge Foundation was established forty-four years ago last month, it has given away close to $100 million, give or take a few million. What's a few million dollars among friends?

Yes, the Kresge family has learned well that they can best pursue happiness by thinking of others, by being exposed to common problems, by being aware of the need for service and consideration especially to those less fortunate. That is why they have endowed the Kresge Foundation so generously. The Kresge Foundation knows that man does not live by bread alone. So, their contributions are also very generous to cultural projects, among which, happily, our museum is included.

Stanley and his wife, Dorothy, are very religious people. They live by the Golden Rule, and they do everything in their power to try to make this world of ours a better place for all of us. They know that there is a big difference between sticking your nose into other people's business and putting your heart into other people's problems. They know that there are vast areas of an economic, social, moral, and ethical nature where people of all religions can and should work together.

Talking about religion reminds me of something I read the other day. It was the definition of a dead atheist. He was all dressed up, with no place to go.

Well, so much for my bit of reminiscing. Stanley, I have thanked you in person several times for the gift of the Kresge Exhibit Hall. By now you must be convinced that we are truly excited and grateful for the much needed additional space which the Kresge Foundation made possible. On behalf of the four Detroit Historical Commissioners we publicly say, "Thank you, Stanley, for everything you personally have done for our community. May you and the other trustees, as well as the Kresge Foundation, continue to flourish as the Cedars of Lebanon."

Stanley, one more thing. There was an old American custom of leaving the latchstring out so that friends might come in to see you. While that old custom has vanished with the pressures of urban living, we want you to know that we preserve and cherish that old-fashioned spirit of the latchstring out. We have found a way to make it just as significant and real in 1968.

To remind the members of the Kresge Foundation of our continuing invitation, and welcome, we want each of the six members of the Foundation Board to have his own personal gold key to the entrance of the Kresge Exhibit Hall. So, if you will please come up here, Stanley, I will present you with the set of keys. And we hope all of you will visit us often.

Egypt: Museums, Mummies, Mosques, and Moses

Immediately upon hearing the excit-
ing news that at long last Egypt and Israel had signed a peace
treaty, a group of us from Wayne State University who were
to attend the Ninth Annual Jerusalem International Book Fair
arranged a stopover in Egypt. We spent about a week sightseeing in Cairo and in southern Egypt. We took a ship up the
Nile in order to go south!

As a lover of history, and especially Jewish history, I
could now fulfill my long dreamed about visit to Pharaohland.
Egypt is the birthplace, the matrix, of our Bible history. Our
Jewish patriarchs, Abraham, Isaac, Jacob, Joseph, and Moses—
all these and more—lived in this land.

The Egyptians call Abraham the first prophet of God.
After him, they substitute Ismael for Isaac. They consider sacred and revere such places as the Chapel of the Burning Bush,
the site where God first revealed Himself to Moses; the Springs
of Moses, where Moses drew water when he struck the rock
with his rod; Mount Moses (or Mt. Sinai or Mt. Horeb), where
God gave Moses the Ten Commandments.

Some say the Egyptian name Moses is derived from the
last half of the name Thutmosis. There were four kings with
this name in their famous XVIII Dynasty (1575–1308 B.C.E.).
Moses was born about this time. This also was when King
Akhenaton introduced monotheism to Egypt.

The Exodus, under Moses' leadership, took place in this
period. The importance of the Exodus in Jewish theology is
well known, and Egyptian sources have numerous details of
the Bible story. But no direct Egyptian references to the Exodus have been found.

In the great Egyptian Museum of Antiquities there are

Written for the Jewish Telegraphic Agency, April 1979.

countless statues, monuments, fragments of ancient relics and artifacts, mummies, jewelry, etc. About one-quarter of the exhibits are devoted to King Tut. There is one stela, an upright sculptured slab of stone, called the Victory Stela of King Merneptah II (considered the pharaoh at the time of the Exodus). It has the only known mention of Israel on any Egyptian monument. Carved into the stone is the wording that he had wiped out the Hebrews. "Israel is laid waste . . . completely destroyed. Their nation exists no more. . . ." That was about three thousand years ago. How wrong King Merneptah was!

Before World War II, as many as 100,000 Jews lived peacefully in Egypt as citizens. There are now 150 left, someone recently wrote. I was told by an Egyptian-Jewish merchant that he believed the number to be about 1,500.

In Old Cairo, the walled city of antiquity, we visited the oldest synagogue in Egypt, formerly called the Synagogue of the Prophet Jeremiah. It is now the Ben Ezra Synagogue, named after Rabbi Abraham Ben Ezra, who rebuilt it around the year A.D. 1100. The *shammas* said the congregation has forty-two member families.

The synagogue interior was attractive, but was so covered with dust, sand, and dirt that it looked pathetic. It was hard for me to believe any Jews would permit their sanctuary for worship to God to be so unclean. Some soap, water, and dust cloths would do wonders. On the other hand, with all their troubles in the past thirty years, these Egyptian Jews probably had all they could to stay alive while worrying about the safety of their families.

The Ben Ezra Synagogue is where the famous Genizah (Safekeeping) was discovered. It was rediscovered in 1896 by Rabbi Solomon Schechter. A veritable treasure trove of over 200,000 pages from sacred Jewish books, scrolls, literary works, and historical documents was found in the attic. The oldest document is dated in the year A.D. 750.

I checked my *Encyclopedia Judaica*: "This synagogue was originally built in 882 on the ruins of a Coptic church which was sold to the Jews." Ancient Cairo was called Fostat, which was where the great sage Maimonides and his family lived.

We were told the Ben Ezra Synagogue was built on the very site where Moses was found in the Nile River bulrushes. Our guide took us down some steps on the outside of the buildings where we saw an old wall. This was the remains of the earlier house of prayer. Alongside, to the right, was a small branch of the Nile. In that water, at that spot, the founder of the Mosaic religion was discovered. The Egyptian Jews believe that is so. And perhaps it is. Why not?

We were also told that the main synagogue of Cairo is open but not functioning, and that some of the other old synagogues have become mosques.

The spectacular sight of the Giza (land of Goshen) pyramids and sphinx on a moonlit night at a son et lumiere performance is truly awe-inspiring. The Cheops pyramid is one of the Seven Wonders of the Ancient World. It is about as tall as forty-eight-story skyscraper. Each stone is as high as a man. They say it took three million such stones weighting five million tons, and 100,000 men working twenty years to build it, five thousand years ago. *Some tombstone!*

When Menachem Begin was in Egypt for the peace treaty talks, he said to Mr. Sadat that some of our ancestors helped build the pyramids. With all due respect to Mr. Begin, I doubt that there were any Jews in Egypt at that time. Jewish history is definitely intertwined with Egyptian history going back a long, long time, but not five thousand years.

Egypt's current guidebooks have practically no mention of Egyptian Jews. I think the publishers deliberately omitted all references to Jews on instructions from their government, except as Jews are identified with ancient Egyptian history. The 400-page book I bought, under the caption "Population," said, "Lastly, Jews, who at all times formed an important minority in Egypt, have, for the most part, left the country and their community is on the way to extinction." To which I add: Perhaps this will be so in Egypt. But, if it is, it will be Egypt's loss. From what I saw of Egypt's economy, etc., it desperately needs Jewish ingenuity, intelligence, and vital progressiveness as well as Jewish ethical and moral values.

Egypt (Arabic name, Masr) has been called a gigantic open-air museum, the land of museums, mummies, and mosques. It has the longest river in the world, the Nile, and except for its palm-lined shores that form a band of fertility, the color of Egypt is sandy brown with very, very little green. Camels, water buffalo, and donkeys help work these narrow strips of green fields. The weather is extremely hot and dry, with only about five days of rain all year.

Modern Cairo is jam-packed with about nine million people. Some say it is on its way to becoming the Calcutta of Africa. The poverty of the city remains insoluble: unemployment and inflation are at terrifying levels, public utilities are temperamental servants, the cars you see are old and decrepit, the noisy, snarled traffic is unbelievable as it tries to get through the narrow streets; but the population remains cheerful.

There are some excellent hotels. The food is quite good. Prices are reasonable, one of the few places in the world where they are still so. The Egyptians were all very friendly even after they found out we were Jewish. They tried hard to make us welcome. We experienced no rancor. They seemed very anxious for peace. The veiled woman has almost vanished from the streets. Generally speaking the country and the people look impoverished. Children are constantly harassing you on the streets, begging for *baksheesh*, money.

There are young and old peddlers everywhere, plaguing the tourists with junk jewelry. In Cairo and throughout Egypt, near the tombs and museums, they hawk their wares, calling out, "One dollar for the whole *schmeer*—five pieces." They also sell postcards, film slides, etc. To get along you need to know two words: (1) *showkrun* (Thanks) and (2) *Lah-ah* (No).

The most impressive feature of Egypt is its fantastic five thousand-year-old history of civilization and art, a great deal of which remains. It is thrilling to know that it can be seen and appreciated by those of us who live in the 20th century. The mighty tombs of the Pharaohs and their queens, the massive temples which they built as tributes to their gods, the reliefs, the colorful, detailed paintings and the hieroglyphs that line many walls and ceilings of the tombs have been preserved for about five thousand years! It all sounds impossible and improbable . . . but, thank goodness, all still exists.

Egypt is for the serious tourist rather than the frivolous. It is a strenuous trip but truly memorable, enchanting, and exciting. If you like antiquity, you'll love Egypt.

Red China

In the way the Chinese greet each other, I say to you, "Nee-how," or "Hello" as we say in America, "Shalom" in Israel. Speaking for my fellow China traveler and Temple Beth El member, Dr. Milton Lipson, it is a pleasure for us to be here today and to share some of our impressions of Red China with you.

First of all, let me tell you that I have a twenty-minute talk on Mainland China, and forty-five-minute talk, which is the same talk . . . I just lose my place a lot.

How I became a *maven* (an expert) on Red China in sixteen days can be explained in one word: pretend. Pretend you know more than you do.

Actually it is much more than that. You read everything you can about the country before you leave. You attend meetings where speakers tell you about their experiences in the places you are going to visit. You see slides of the sights, the scenery, the historical places, the people, and then you go to see for yourself . . . providing you can get an invitation from the People's Republic of China.

As the Chinese say, one picture is worth a thousand words. So, when I finish, Milton will show a few of the seven hundred slides he took, and he will talk about his pictures. Milton takes great pictures. Me? I did not take a camera because I take what are called "Marie Antoinette pictures." I usually cut off the heads.

There were a great many things that impressed me about the Chinese people. Some of my thoughts will be serious— and some not so serious. For instance, when we got off the plane in Peking, I could swear I heard one Commie say to another, "Well, there goes our neighborhood."

My wife Harriette and I tried for three years to find a way to visit Mainland China, with no success. Luckily, Pres-

Talk given at Temple Beth El, sponsored by the Sisterhood, October 1977.

ident George Gullen invited us to become members of the Wayne State University Study Mission when Wayne received its invitation from the People's Republic of China. With the approval of the U.S. State Department, twenty-one of us left Detroit on the April 6th and landed in Peking on April 8, 1977 in China, during the Year of the Snake (each year is named after some animal or reptile).

It was the start of one of the most exciting travel adventures I have ever had. This opportunity to visit one of the world's oldest civilizations, even if only to catch a brief glimpse, is something I will never forget.

Visitors are honored guests. All Chinese try to give favorable impressions. They are truly pleased that you have come. The country is not interested in large-scale tourism; it is too busy trying to raise the standard of living for their people. You are advised in advance that you will be propagandized, you will be shown one point of view—the party line. But, it is a soft sell. If you are upset by ideas different from your own, stay home.

There are no night clubs, no foreign movies, no escapist TV. You are up at 6:30 A.M., on the busses by 8:00, and sightseeing morning, afternoon and evening with time our only for meals. Then early to bed. Every visitor is directed toward schools, factories, communes, hospitals, and, of course, the Forbidden City, the spectacular Great Wall of China, the Ming Tombs, and the Canton Trade Fair.

The Chinese Travel Agency—called Luxingshe—had our tour completely arranged for us, based on the information they had about us from advance questionnaires. We had told them what our interests were, and they tried to accommodate our requests.

Our tour guides all spoke English quite well and were pleasant, polite, and articulate. Some were men, and some women. They knew their history and the thoughts expressed by the late Chairman Mao.

Luxingshe picked the five cities we visited and the length of time to spend in each one. Thank goodness Peking was a six-day stop, and, to quote from my wife's diary, "If we see no more than Peking, the trip was worthwhile."

As I think back about the Chinese, most of their faces were tanned, and the girls had rosy cheeks. The Chinese women were among some of the most attractive I have seen any-where. I was particularly impressed by their complexions and bone structure. All the men and women have short noses, and you rarely see a man who is bald; they all had a good head of hair. And that, of course, made me kind of jealous. The Chinese have a saying: "Man who is bald in front—great thinker; man who is bald in back—great lover; man who is bald in front *and* back—thinks he's a great lover."

The Chinese wake you in the morning with a tremen-dous thermos of hot water, left outside your door, so that you can make your own tea in your room. Then they serve you tea, and tea, and more tea, all day long, every place you visit. You drink a little, and they immediately refill your cup. But, they do not give you any time to go to the "john." That is how I discovered the modern-day "Chinese water torture."

When we visited schools, factories, hospitals, and com-munes (communes are something like a gigantic kibbutz), we sat down with the officials and were immediately offered cig-arettes, in addition to the tea. It seemed to me that all the Chinese smoke. When you are on their planes, you are offered cigarettes free of charge. I had a rough time with my asthma.

When our doctors asked their doctors if they believed there was any relationship between smoking and cancer, as publicized by the U.S. Surgeon General's Report, they said their studies did not confirm that smoking induces cancer or that smoking is hazardous to your health. Maybe they are using cigarettes to try to control their population growth.

We also learned that when a Chinese motorist has an accident, and if it is his fault, he loses his driver's license *for life*.

As I said, we were in Peking for six days—and we used the same sheets and towels during the entire time. After we bathed the first day, we threw our towels on the bathroom floor, expecting to receive clean towels the next day. But they just hung the same towels back on the rack. The second day, my wife tied her bath towel in a knot and threw it on the floor. That night, when we got back to our room, the knotted towel was back on the rack.

Generally speaking, I would describe China as being N.B.N.C.—*Neat But Not Clean.* I guess the fact that the Chinese do not believe in God makes the old saying, "Cleanliness is next to Godliness," meaningless to them. Or, at least, let us say cleanliness is not high on their priority list.

Chinese men have a habit that annoyed me. I have come to the conclusion they are not only the world's champion ping-pong players but also world's champion spitters. They spit any time, any place. We could be sitting in the theatre listening to a Chinese opera or watching acrobats, and suddenly you hear people in the audience clearing their throats and coughing and spitting. There was one guy right next to me who just missed my shoes.

There are few opportunities for spending money on entertainment or recreation. Movies and cultural events are ideological facts, set to song and dance, but they provide the only public exhibition of young women in feminine dress and colorful costume.

The biggest impression I have of China is the fantastically large number of people I saw everywhere. Eleven million people in Shanghai (with six million in the city alone); nine million in Peking (with four million in the city); and the rest in the suburbs. I have never seen as many people, or as many bicycles, in my life. It didn't make any difference whether it was six o'clock in the morning or late at night, there were always crowds, not only on the main arteries but on the side streets as well.

I was told the Chinese work three shifts a day to accommodate all these people. The street scene can best be compared to that when the crowds leave the Ann Arbor Stadium after a Michigan-Ohio State football game. The street traffic continues to be mainly bicycles. Vehicular traffic is all commercial or public transport or military. And they do have their parking problems, too.

So far as large cities are concerned, China is organized bedlam. What noise! All day and all night; you actually need ear plugs. The bus and taxi drivers lay on their horns constantly trying to move the cyclists out of their way. And the cyclists keep ringing their bells to get the pedestrians out of their way. There are almost two million bicycles in Peking alone. The barges and ships keep tooting and blasting their horns all night long. The atmosphere is like New Year's Eve in New

York's Times Square. Only the young, and the sound sleepers, should come to China's big cities.

Everything seems incredibly well organized from the top echelon and universities down to street committees. Everybody has to belong to something so he can be given consideration if he has problems of any kind.

Family life seems to be very close; the children are loved and cared for, as they should be. The kids were animated, attractive, well mannered, and well disciplined. They demonstrated their skills with enthusiasm. They recited for us; they sang and danced and played musical instruments. They showed us their artwork, clay modeling, and decorations. We were fascinated. We enjoyed being with the children. The boys were cute, and the girls looked like little China dolls. In contrast to the adults, most of the very young wore colorful clothes.

The people are trying to create a society where police are unnecessary, and lawyers and judges not required. Today in China, crime has been virtually eliminated. I asked about this because I did not see any policemen. They said all arguments and litigation are handled by conciliation and mediation at the commune or neighborhood level. When you are finished, you are supposed to go "sit in the corner" and criticize yourself.

As you walk the streets you cannot help but realize that most of the people are young: two-thirds of all the people are under thirty, and one-half under eighteen. Among the elderly are many women whose feet were bound in the barbaric old Chinese custom. It is pathetic to see them hobble as they try to walk. Incidentally, you will like the name they give to their homes for the elderly. They call them "Houses of Respect."

All the schoolchildren are taught English. After Chinese, it is the No. 1 language. They still have not seen many Caucasians; wherever we went we were surrounded by people staring at our faces; they wanted to see what we looked like. Now I know what a panda bear feels like.

There were no restrictions. We could go where we pleased, but very few people spoke English, so it was not a good idea to go exploring on your own. I was told that only twenty-five hundred Americans will be invited to China this year.

We did not see any churches, but I was told the people have freedom of religion, because there are about fifty-four minority groups in China. Some of them, I feel sure, have some religious beliefs.

The Chinese have some beautiful museums pertaining to their history. When going through one of them, the guide pointed out that the Chinese invented gunpowder and then showed us a picture of Dr. Pian Cheh. The guide said he was world-famous because he invented the theory of doctors "feeling the purse." Everyone roared, of course, and then she realized she meant "pulse."

Everything is owned by the government; everyone works for the government. And the government takes care of everybody. So it must have been some frustrated Chinese would-be advertising man who came up with the slogan "From the womb to the tomb." Which is more rhyme than reason, because they no longer use tombs in China; the dead are cremated. Land is too precious to be set aside for the dead. Incidentally, there is no demand for my kind of work in Red China. They need advertising men like Israel needs hog callers.

The people definitely are honest. We were leaving one of the towns, and I had forgotten to pack a dirty handkerchief. We were on the bus when suddenly a boy came running out of the hotel shouting, "Room 406, room 406, you left this in your room." And in front of everyone, I had to take the soiled hanky.

The written language is the same everywhere. But in the northern part of China, the pronunciation is Mandarin, or Peking dialect. That is the official language of the country and understood by about two-thirds of the population. However, as you begin traveling south, by the time you are halfway down the country some people do not understand the Mandarin language unless you pronounce the words differently. Finally, in the lower southern part of China, you run into entirely different words having the same meaning; that dialect is called Cantonese. One of these days, they are going to try to standardize on one national language.

I learned a few Chinese words like *Nee How* (Hello), *T'sai T'sien* (Good-bye), *Ching* (Please), *Shay Shay* (Thank You), *Hi*

(Yes), *Tang You* (Candy), *Bing Bang* (Ice Stick), *May Lee* (Very Pretty). And when you want to know where the bathroom is, you say, *Wishy Washy*.

From behind, most men and women look alike because they all wear the Mao jackets and baggy pants and drab colors: blue, gray; and some khaki. However, farther south, in Canton, the men and women discard their Mao jackets because of the heat and switch to white shirts. That makes it easier to separate the boys from the girls.

The women wear their hair short, with one or two pigtails, about three inches long. They wear no cosmetics of any kind; neither do they wear jewelry. And this means no wedding rings.

The average family has a bicycle or two, a sewing machine, wrist watches, a clock, a transistor radio, and a few people have a TV set. But most of the TV sets I saw were in public places.

In some cases, the people actually live in cave houses, which seem to work out nicely; they are cool in the summer and warm in the winter. In fact, they are proud of the fact that Mao formerly lived in one of them.

Automobiles are manufactured in Shanghai. They ride beautifully, although they are old-fashioned in styling. But no individual owns one; they are all owned by the government, as are the busses and all businesses.

Everywhere you look, you see soldiers, men and women, but not with guns. Some are army and some navy, but from what I heard, the country is actually run by the army.

Everyone in China is not Communist, per se. However, unless you join the Communist party, and are accepted by them, you do not get into positions of leadership, which they call cadre. They have schools for cadres. If you want to be a doctor, you are not chosen on your ability or intelligence or aptitude alone; first consideration is whether you are a good Communist. If you are not, you are not even allowed to be recommended for the school examinations.

Men and women work in the fields, side by side, with their animals, including camels and water buffalo. Machinery and draft animals are scarce. And you may be a leader in the big cities, but still you are supposed to go out and work in the fields about one week, or one month, of the year so that you do not forget that even though you are a so-called big shot, you are no better than the peasants. You must get your hands dirty by working in your country's soil, side by side with the peasants, to learn from the peasants (farmers), workers, and soldiers. This rule is designed to guard against arrogance.

Because my audience today is primarily female I assume you would like to hear some things about women living in China. Women are treated as equals in everything, including marriage. Since the founding of the People's Republic, this has been the law.

Women work in jobs and hold positions not previously open to them. They manage factories, sit on the Central Committee of the party, and work in the fields. Recently a China ship with a woman captain and an all female crew called at a port in Canada. A much-publicized railroad is run completely by women and is also maintained by them. More than one-half of all Chinese doctors (including surgeons) are women. The same holds true of the paramedics, the unique "barefoot" doctors.

Regarding marriage, all that is required is for two people who want to marry to register with the government office in the district where they live. The law states that both husband and wife enjoy "equal status at home." It also guarantees each "the right to free choice of occupation and free participation in work and social activities." The law allows for divorce, although it is rare and considered not to be in the interest of China. Women have more protection in divorce than in the United States.

In an attempt to control the growth of the population, which has increased 60 percent in the past twenty-seven years, China encourages people to wait longer before marriage. The government recommended age for marriage today is about twenty-six for women and twenty-eight for men. It is also requested that each family not have more than two children. Birth control clinics are abundant; pills and contraceptives are free. Before marriage, sex, to a certain extent, is also "free," but there is no prostitution. It seems that Chairman Mao found a cure for nymphomania.

The country has a national fitness program which you can see every morning, that is, if you get up about five or six A.M. Men and women exercise in the public parks, and it is very interesting to watch. They do the very graceful and athletic Tai Jai exercises. Countless thousands get up early every morning all over China, so they tell me, for exercise. Me, every time I thought of exercise, I would lie down in bed and do some serious reconsidering.

There was no rubbish in the streets. We saw very few birds and none in the large cities. I was surprised that we did not see any dogs in China, with the exception of a few German shepherds out in the country. When I asked about this they said it was because dogs eat food, and they do not have food to spare for animals. The truth of the matter is that people eat dogs there, so I read recently. They do have a lot of cats; they are kept in houses and factories to kill the rats.

There are no flies to speak of, and no mosquitos, except in Canton (just eighty miles from Hong Kong). For some reason, Canton is headquarters for mosquitos and is loaded with them. The hotel rooms had forty-two yards of mosquito netting around each bed, and it worked just great. Not one mosquito got out.

Our guides could not have been nicer. They were very concerned about our health, and if any of us had a cold, they wanted to rush us to the hospital immediately, because, they said, "It is the law."

Our doctors visited several hospitals, of course. This was an important part of their trip. Chinese medicine combines ancient herbal treatments and Western modern medicines. They watched an eye operation on a soldier, in full uniform, with acupuncture as a local anesthetic. The soldier was so friendly that he even smiled for the X-rays.

Talking about acupuncture in China reminds me of a dream I had over there. I dreamt I was ill during the night and had to call the doctor. I said, "I am in pain." The doctor said, "It's OK. Stick a pin in your ear and call me in the morning."

One of our doctors asked the director of a large hospital how many stabbings and shootings they have handled in the past year. The answer was "none." Then our M.D. asked, "How many in the past five years?" And again the answer was "none." Wouldn't that be utopian if we in the U.S. could some day have that kind of peace of mind, too?

One of my Hong Kong friends said, "They do not have

holdups or robberies or theft for a very simple reason: nobody has anything to steal." Incidentally, the Chinese pay no income taxes as individuals.

We stayed in some of China's best hotels. The accommodations in Peking and Canton were new wings of existing hotels and were quite satisfactory. But there is no air conditioning. There is none anywhere in China. Chinese food, in my opinion, is excellent. We had some great dinners, several mind-boggling Chinese banquets, multi-course meals overflowing with fish, fowl and meat, with hot rice, beer, wine, and delicious teas. There is no chop suey or chow mein. These are American dishes.

They have one local version of hard liquor called Mao-Tai which has a real kick to it. But it must be too expensive for the natives because I never saw anyone drunk.

The only Western style cuisine we saw was at breakfast, when you could order eggs. There were no hamburgers. They served a nice, mild beer and bottled orange pop with every meal. You could get coffee at breakfast only.

Talking about food in China, I would like to quote a part of the diary my wife Harriette kept on the trip concerning food in China. Tuesday, April 12th:

> Back to the hotel; 45 minutes to get cleaned up and dressed, to go to dinner as guests of the China National Bureau of Travel. The Peking Duck Restaurant has been open for business for 125 years, without missing a day; Peking's best. (It is supposed to have been started by a tailor shop that merged with a restaurant and that is how they became famous for pressed duck.)
>
> We had a half hour of welcome by the chairman through our interpreter—very formal, place cards and everything; 8 courses of everything made from duck; liver, gizzard, wings, soup, one clear and one creamy, thin-sliced cucumber, and the duck itself served in slivers that you ate in a sort of rolled taco or biscuit with onions dipped in plum sauce. For dessert there was red wine, clear brandy.
>
> Every ten minutes there was a toast to something or somebody, clinking glasses and saying "Gombay" or "Gombee," which means "bottoms up." The meal was absolutely sensational—delicious! As close as I can figure out, they serve the skin and throw away the duck meat. LNS said it was the first time he ever had *gribbonees* for a main course.

You sense economy and conservation everyplace. Nothing is ever thrown away or wasted; an old piece of rubber, a wooden board, an old nail, everything you can think of is saved because someplace down the line they feel it might be needed.

On a few occasions we invited our guides to have a meal with us, and when the meal was over, carefully wrapped packages were made of all the leftover food and taken home by the guides.

No tipping is allowed. If you try to tip, you risk offending because they claim you are depriving them of their pleasure in serving you.

You could get your laundry done in one day and very inexpensively, if you like your laundry gray. In fact, everything was inexpensive. Our cost for the entire trip in China, for everything was, about $600 for the sixteen days and seventeen nights.

Pictures of Chairman Mao are everywhere. And, usually, alongside his picture is that of the current party leader, Hua Kuo Feng. On the larger walls are also pictures of Lenin and Stalin, or Karl Marx and Friedrich Engels, the so-called Fathers of Socialism. In some places, you would see all six pictures. There are also statues of Mao everywhere, of all sizes—busts and full length—some thirty feet or so tall.

While we were there, the Chinese were just completing a gigantic memorial building in Peking housing the mausoleum of Mao. It was started in November 1976 and finished in six months, in May 1977. An estimated 700,000 Chinese worked day and night around the clock, most of the time in the winter weather, to finish it on the first anniversary of his death. The building is magnificent and houses Mao's body in a clear crystal sarcophagus.

I suppose you ladies are interested in the kinds of bargains to be found in China? The answer is, very few. There are some stores called Friendship Stores, where everybody speaks English. They are like small department stores. The best prices are for antiques, jade, ivory, oriental wood carvings, paintings, and silk scarves. There is no bargaining.

If you were to ask me why I was so anxious to visit Mainland China, I guess curiosity would be my answer. I saw what I believe is one of the world's most extraordinary social experiments; possibly there has been nothing like it in the long history of human society. When I try to imagine what this world is coming to, or how the world is going to be able to cope with the tremendous population explosion in these coming years, my mind turns to the unique experiment in human relations that is taking place in China. It deserves study, recognition and understanding. Perhaps they have some answers we have yet to discover.

Bear in mind that China covers 3.7 million square miles, compared to our 3.6 million square miles. China, then, is just a little larger than our own area. So try to imagine what we would do in the United States if, all of a sudden, 25 percent of the world's population (over 800 million people) were living here instead of a little over 200 million. I shudder to think of the problems we would have.

China today is struggling to become modern, while still trying to hang on to her heritage and civilization, which go back so many thousands of years.

In China, everyone has some place to live. Every Chinese has a roof over his head. There are many places far superior to some of our slum areas in Detroit.

All have clothes to cover their bodies and everyone has medical care; while not the finest, evidently it is adequate.

Everyone has food to eat; there are no beggars on the streets. Every able-bodied person has some kind of work to do to keep him or her occupied.

From what I saw behind the Bamboo Curtain, the results are amazing, but still not something for which I would willingly trade the type of existence and freedom I have in the U.S.A. I do not think we Americans would trade our individualism just for built-in security.

There is much more I could relate about my visit to China and her people, but my time is limited. In fact, I could not have talked this long, if I were not wearing Supp-hose.

But one more matter: Are there any Jews in China? The answer is no. Phil Slomovitz of the Detroit Jewish News told me that a Jew from Brooklyn named Sidney Shapira is the manager of the State Book Edition in China. He translates books from Chinese into English for the Chinese government. The history of the Jews in China goes back about fifteen hundred to two thousand years, and at times there were many thousands living there. But, as an article I read in the January 1977

Jewish Digest states, "It is extremely unlikely that today there are any Jews in China."

I would like to mention one more story I heard before I close. In Red China, many husbands and wives live apart, in different cities, because of their jobs. The government sends them where they can do the most good for China. Sometimes they are separated for months. There was a family named Wong, and the husband worked in Shanghai, but the wife lived in Peking. After a long separation, the husband came home and found his wife had given birth to a baby during his absence. He was surprised, but even more so because the baby had white skin.

He said, "Mrs. Wong, how come our baby not look Chinese?" The wife replied, "I do not know, but he is your son Mr. Wong." And the husband answered, "No way. Everyone knows two Wongs don't make a white."

The Oldest Synagogue
in the New World

Interior of Congregation Mikve Israel-Emanuel

*D*etroit *advertising executive* Leonard N. Simons joined in an appeal to help save a synagogue on the Caribbean island of Curacao which has been in use since 1732. A magazine that Simons receives reported that the three-hundred-member synagogue is faced with a $150,000 restoration bill to fix balconies, wooden supports, and the roof.

The synagogue was modeled after the "Portuguese" Synagogue of 1675 that still stands in Amsterdam. Jews began

From the *Detroit Jewish News*, February 1975.

settling in Curacao in 1651, after fleeing the Portuguese Inquisition.

The Curacao synagogue has a floor covered in white sand, as a reminder of the Spanish and Portuguese ancestors who covered the floors with sand to muffle the footsteps of forbidden worship.

Persons interested in helping the synagogue can write the Cong. Mikve Israel, P.O. Box 322, Curacao, Netherlands Antilles.

General "Mad" Anthony Wayne

Philip Mason and the author with the portrait of General Anthony Wayne

In Detroit, interest in General Anthony Wayne is genuine and sincere. Wayne's name is proudly worn by the county, the historic fort, a suburban city, and a great university. It was and is a personal association because here Wayne lived for a portion of the year 1796 while commanding the entire United States army. Wayne should be con-

Article in *Detroit in Perspective*, winter 1975.

sidered as the man who was responsible for bringing Detroit under the American flag as an American city for the first time in history. His smashing victory at the Battle of Fallen Timbers (near the present city of Maumee, Ohio) confirmed American possession of this critical western part of the continent.

This western campaign, of which the occupation of Detroit was the climax and goal, was not of local importance only. In 1776, thirteen states declared their independence from the British sovereign. The War of Independence was fought to establish that separation. The Treaty of Paris in 1783 defined the boundaries of the new nation, but for a decade after Yorktown, British soldiers held Detroit and from it ruled the old Northwest. Wayne's campaign, which raised the American flag over the frontier village in 1796, was thus the final campaign of the war. The American Revolution began in 1776 but ended in Detroit in 1796.

We knew a great deal about Wayne as a general and as a leader, but those facts of personality which a portrait would reveal were lacking because we had no likeness properly authenticated. There was no lack, we soon discovered, of pictures carrying his name. Which was the accurate one?

I first checked with one local history authority, the staff of the Burton Historical Collection of the Detroit Public Library. They had several photographs of paintings, etchings, pencil drawings, and so on, but each differed in appearance. Some shared a certain similarity, but others were radically different. I wrote letters chasing down other leads to portraits of Anthony Wayne. I wrote to historical societies, universities, libraries, private individuals, anyone and everyone who could be supposed to have had an illustration of Anthony Wayne. Here is what I found.

There is, of course, that remarkable work of Colonel John Trumbull, the historic scene depicting the *Surrender of Cornwallis at Yorktown* which hangs in the Capitol in Washington, D.C. Colonel Trumbull had served under General Wayne. Fordham University has a pencil sketch of Wayne, done by Trumbull, one of a series of studies made by the artist to be used at a later date when he was ready to create the large painting; Wayne appears among the important military personalities in that historic picture. Trumbull's likeness of Anthony Wayne was copied by many artists, including Benjamin

Tanner, and also by E. Prud'homme after an intermediate drawing by James Herring. The Trumbull likeness was also copied by Peter Frederick Rothermel.

From the State Historical Society of Wisconsin I obtained copies of three engravings. One was made after a portrait by Alonzo Chappel; one by J. J. Headley from the book *Washington and His Generals*; and one from Thomas U. P. Charlton's book *The Life of Major General James Jackson*. There was another illustration based on Trumbull's painting by Theodore Bolton in his book *Early American Portrait Draftsmen in Crayons*.

From a private collector (he requested that we not mention where I obtained the prints, or in whose collection the portrait is), I secured a photograph of the Charles Wilson Peale portrait of Anthony Wayne. This appeared in the book *The Peale Family*. From the New York Historical Society I had a portrait of Wayne that was made by Edward Savage. This was used on the cover of *American Historical Illustrations*. The Henry Francis du Pont Winterthur Museum had five portraits of General Wayne, plus two stipple portraits engraved by David Edwin of Philadelphia. These last two were definitely made after Anthony Wayne's death. The New York Public Library also gave me a photo of a painting by F. Kemmelmeyer.

Nicholas B. Wainwright, director of the Historical Society of Pennsylvania, gave me our first authentic Wayne portrait. It was an original painting by the French artist, Jean Pierre Henri Elouis, made in Philadelphia during the early months of 1796. Quite certainly, Anthony Wayne posed for this portrait; he was resting in that city after his western campaign and before he returned to his army command in Detroit.

Unfortunately, the Society said it had no information about the painting's present whereabouts. I was told that it had disappeared. Fortunately, an engraving of that portrait made by a George Graham had been published in June 1796. I was delighted to find that one of the few remaining copies of that engraving was in the Pennsylvania Historical Society's possession. It was only a black-and-white copy of the original portrait, but its history was complete.

It would have been wonderful if we could have secured an original print, but the Pennsylvania Historical Society, for obvious reasons, did not choose to part with their only copy.

They reminded me that Anthony Wayne was as much a hero in Pennsylvania as he was in Michigan. He was born in Pennsylvania, in the town appropriately named Waynesborough. The Wayne homestead, built in 1724 by Captain Anthony Wayne, grandfather of the General, is still standing. The original engraving was unavailable, but I was delighted to receive a reproduction, obviously also in black-and-white.

This Elouis portrait, of which I had the copy, was the portrait of the mature Wayne, and the fact that he posed for it can be documented. It could be that the Trumbull portrait and, more importantly, the pencil sketch on which it rests, were made from memory, though the sketch at Fordham University has a matting attached on which someone unknown has written "sketched from life." The Peale portrait is contemporary and could also have been done from life, but that cannot be stated as a fact. *The Wayne family has assumed that the three portraits, by Peale, Trumbull and Elouis, were all from life, but without attempting documentation. All may be authentic, but the Elouis is the one confirmed in origin and related to the period which associated Wayne with Detroit.*

It seemed appropriate that the university bearing Wayne's name should have a picture of the man, an acceptable likeness. The Elouis portrait was, for obvious reasons, the one chosen. I decided to copy my copy of the copy of the lost original. The first step was to get an artist who could give me what I wanted. A local artist named Arnold Livshenko whom I knew to be an excellent copyist was contacted. I wanted a painting which would be an exact copy of the likeness as shown on the etching, except that the painting would be in color.

Henry Brown, director of the Detroit Historical Museum, and I worked with the artist step by step to make this replica painting as close to perfect as possible. Henry Brown took him over to the Detroit Institute of Arts to show him the types of colors used in paintings that artists made in the 1700s. He gave the artist an actual Revolutionary War officer's uniform to copy. We ordered a close-up photograph of the emblem of the Order of Cincinnati which General Wayne wears in the Elouis painting.

We insisted that the artist show us his canvas in the various stages as he was completing the assignment. The first thing finished was Anthony Wayne's head. When we looked at it we said: "What's that long white gash in his cheek that you show on your painting? We don't remember anything that looked like that when we saw the etching." The artist replied: "Oh yes, it's in there. That's an exact copy." We said: "Show us where it is in the picture." So he took out the blow-up photostat and showed it to us. Where the stat had been folded, it had cracked the paper. Our perfect copyist had copied the crack in the paper!

In 1949 the painting was finally finished and framed. I wanted to turn it over to Wayne University, but the university decided it should be formally presented at a special reception held in one of the university's auditoriums. I was asked to present the portrait of Anthony Wayne to the City of Detroit, under whose auspices the university was then operating. Everything was proceeding with a certain amount of solemnity and dignity. Then, when the agenda called for the presentation, I handed the portrait over to a handsome young man, the president of the student body, and said: "It gives me a great pleasure to present the City of Detroit and Wayne University with this portrait of General Anthony Wayne, as a *genuine imitation*." Thus ended the solemnity.

This seemed to be the end of the story. For a decade this picture of General Wayne has hung in appropriate places in the University, most recently on the walls of the office of the president. But those of us who had worked on the project, including the staffs of the Burton Historical Collection and the Detroit Historical Museum, naturally remained alert to anything additional about the true likeness of Anthony Wayne.

Unexpectedly, but most fortunately, we discovered that our original information was incorrect. The portrait by Jean Pierre Henri Elouis was indeed *not* lost, though it was not in public possession. We made contact with a descendant of Anthony Wayne, in whose hands the portrait remains. This Pennsylvanian was most understanding of our interest in Wayne and was most sympathetic. Generously, he allowed us to secure and reproduce a color print of the original. This is the last picture in the series in this article, and in all ways the most important. It answers the question: "What did he look like?"

Detroit owes a second debt. The year 1976 is just ahead, and with it a most significant centennial. To our great delight, we were allowed as a distinguished feature of the first Detroit

Historical Museum exhibit keyed to the bicentennial, to borrow and show this significant portrait. It was a loan, for a limited time only, but we are delighted that "Mad Anthony" was thus again recognized in the City which owes so much to him. We venture to hope that he will come again.

Have we satisfied your curiosity about what Wayne looked like? After some twenty-five years of investigation, we have satisfied ours!

Notes

In the course of the correspondence we were informed that the Wayne family has always believed there to be two other authentic portraits of the General, painted from life, in addition to the one by Elouis. The Charles Wilson Peale (1741–1827) portrait until recently was in the possession of a descendent, Bessie Wirgman. (The present owner of the Peale painting also insisted upon being anonymous.) This likeness shows Wayne as he looked when he served in the Pennsylvania General Assembly and the Council of Censors. The Colonel John Trumbull portrait is the one more familiar to us. The artist had served under Wayne in the U.S. Army. The late Dr. Theodore Sizer of the Yale University Art Gallery spent a lifetime researching Trumbull and his art. He was the author of a couple of biographical accounts of Trumbull and considered this small sketch to be the original study, as does the family of General "Mad" Anthony Wayne.

Cadillac: A Retrospective View

*D*uring *my thirty* years of tenure as a Detroit Historical Commissioner, I assumed the responsibility for reading all available literature on the life of Cadillac. The more I read, the more fascinated I became because of the conflicting stories of this man's life. I visited the "Cadillac country" in France twice, and I met and corresponded with those who shared my interest, as a nonprofessional historian, in France and America. With the help of my friend, Philippe Wolff, retired professor and chairman of history at Toulouse University, and supported by the Detroit Historical Society, Rene Toujas, archivist of the department of Haute-Garonne (France), was asked to undertake research on Cadillac and his family to verify the accuracy of previous reporting and to attempt to locate new documentary evidence. Through the good offices of Mathieu Meras, the director of the Services d'Archives de Tarn-et-Garonne (he is also president of the Archaeological Society of Tarn-et-Garonne), I met Dr. Henri Negrie, a physician in the service of the French navy who had spent the last ten years of his life studying and writing on Cadillac. (I must report, sadly, that Dr. Negrie died last year at the age of eighty-five.) Hence my involvement in the career of Cadillac is long-standing. Here, I offer my personal, but I trust objective, view of the founder of Detroit.

After careful readings of the life and career of Cadillac by past historians of the City of Detroit—Levi Bishop, Silas Farmer, Clarence Burton, Milo Quaife, and George Stark, and many other commentators, including the Jesuit priests Jean Delanglez and George Pare—it was inevitable that I, too, should reconstruct a picture of Cadillac the man. I am convinced that Cadillac was not as great a man as many historians have described him, or was he as bad a personality as other historians have claimed. The truth, as it often does, lies somewhere in between. On balance, I view him as the type of 18th-century

From a chapter in *Cadillac* (Detroit 1976).

military man that one would expect to find as a servant of his government, a soldier sent to open unexplored lands in a new world, to find ways to control the Indians there, to fight the enemies of his country—particularly the British—and, quite naturally, to create a reputation and fortune for himself.

What was Cadillac really like? We may never have the definitive answer. But I try in this retrospective view, after having read the many accounts and documents available, to picture the man.

I visualize Cadillac as a pioneer adventurer with the courage, fortitude, and stamina to tackle any assignment. In his efforts to accomplish that which he had set his heart and mind on doing in North America, for France as well as for himself, he would tolerate no interference from any group or individual. In his fight for survival among the natives, as well as in his dealings with his contemporaries, who, like Cadillac, were also opportunists, he lived by his wits and by his audacity. He played for the greatest of stakes, his own survival.

One can understand why a man in his situation may have considered necessary the taking of liberties with truth and the exploiting of some people in order to reach his goals. Those were hectic days in the New World. Cadillac was striving to plant a new civilization in an ancient wilderness. Certainly he made many enemies, chiefly because he would not let others force their will on him, or because he had deprived others of making money at posts he commanded. Some were jealous of his authority and his contacts with the top echelon of government in Old and New France. Ambiguous, often slanderous or libelous, comments were written about him by those who disliked him for a variety of reasons. But even those contemporaries who criticized his actions found him keen and cautious, resolute in holding his ground. He would yield neither right of judgment nor his prerogatives as commandant. His position of leadership made him vulnerable to accusations of wrongdoing, but his loyalty to king and country was never in dispute. He was strong willed, but perhaps without such men in the New World at the beginning of the 18th century, there may not have been a United States of America today.

The official correspondence of the government of New France in Canada records valuable information about Cadillac that shows him to have been of great assistance to Governor

Frontenac. A solid friendship was created between these two men. Count Pontchartrain (Louis Phelypeaux), secretary of state of the French department of Marine in Paris, was another valuable friend of Cadillac. Such friendships indicate the confidence the top-level men of France had in Cadillac and are a measure of his ability and the respect it commanded. A man in Cadillac's position usually makes friends and enemies, and Cadillac had no interest in attaining popularity at the price of his goals. He had duties to perform that unquestionably would irritate many, but he accomplished that which his superiors expected of him.

When Frontenac appointed Cadillac commandant of Michilimackinac, confident of the latter's ability to cope with Indian opposition, he wrote to Count Pontchartrain that Cadillac was "a man of rank, full of capability and valor . . . we could not make a better choice than to appoint Lieutenant de Lamothe Cadillac, captain of the troops of the detachment of the Marine, whose valor, wisdom, experience, and good conduct have been manifested on several occasions." When Frontenac died in November 1698, Cadillac's proposed arrangements to establish a post on the Detroit River were interrupted. Undaunted by Frontenac's successor, who did not approve of the idea, Cadillac went to Paris for an interview with Count Pontchartrain and a personal examination by King Louis XIV of his project to establish a colony at Detroit. He was successful: "The King granted every request and returned Cadillac to New France with a commission signed by Count Pontchartrain to establish a trading post wherever he desired."

Thus, Detroit came into existence. Cadillac picked the spot on which to build a village called "Fort Pontchartrain du troit" in honor of his friend and benefactor, Jerome (son of Louis) Phelypeaux, Count de Pontchartrain, who was the colonial minister of Marine when Cadillac sought permission to establish the colony. The count, head of colonial affairs for fifteen years, was bitterly criticized, as was Cadillac, by his enemies. In Cadillac's day, both Old and New France were governed by cabal and intrigue. Officials, priests, and traders competed with each other in devising schemes for personal and churchly aggrandizement. Hundreds of old letters show how these various groups were divided by jealously and distrust.

In Detroit, Cadillac was lord of all the property, millions of unclaimed and uncultivated acres. Even the church buildings, with their vestments and paraphernalia, by a decison of the King belonged to Cadillac. The first settlers in Detroit obviously were not a simple, contented, Arcadian folk. The wilderness village was a place of tension, nervousness, and unrest. The Jesuit order was the dominant power in the New World. Cadillac inherited the power conflict between the Jesuits and Governor Frontenac. Contemporary correspondence clearly shows how they hindered Cadillac's projects and how he in turn opposed their plans.

Thus, it is understandable that the Jesuit priests wrote disparagingly about Cadillac, with whom they were continually quarreling. He would not take their orders; it was as simple as that. "In matters pertaining to the civil state, the responsibility is mine, and I will decide what I think is in the king's best interest," Cadillac announced. Under these circumstances, Jesuit historians could not be expected to compliment Cadillac. But the Jesuits were not wrong in their attitudes and viewpoints, nor was Cadillac in his. It appears to me that the best judges, those in the position to evaluate Cadillac's actions, were the king of France and his deputies, the colonial minister and the governor-general of New France. History records that these men agreed that Cadillac was serving France properly and that he should continue to be the head of the village he founded.

The love and affection of a wife and children are some indication of a man's worth. Cadillac's marriage was happy. His wife followed her husband from Montreal to Detroit, traveling a thousand miles in open canoes, over all kinds of terrain and in all weather, to reach Detroit, traveling with the tough *coureurs de bois* and Indians. Cadillac must have had many redeeming qualities to deserve this tribute. His wife was his companion during those long and difficult years in the wilderness, and she bore him thirteen children.

We have the story that when Madame Cadillac was preparing to leave Quebec to join her husband at Detroit in 1701, several ladies said to her, "It might do if you were going to a pleasant country where you could have good company, but it is impossible to conceive how you can be willing to go to a desert country where there is nothing to do but die of ennui."

She is said to have replied, "A woman who loves her husband, as she should, has no stronger attraction than his company, wherever he may be; everything else should be indifferent to her."

I do not want to cast Cadillac as a hero but only to base my opinion upon the accumulated reports. They show him as a courageous young soldier who sought adventure and money in the wilderness of the New World. Courage was required; what he accomplished was not the reward of a coward.

Much comment has been stimulated by the fact that Antoine Laumet took the name of Lamothe Cadillac when he came to Canada. Accusations have never been specific. I am not convinced that there is any truth to the intimations that he "had to leave St. Nicolas-de-la-Grave (in France) for some undisclosed reason." Of what was Cadillac guilty in taking a new name at the age of twenty-five? Countless Europeans did that in those days. (My own relatives adopted new names when they came from Europe many years ago, and not to conceal some dark deed in the past.) It was not unusual for French families in the late seventeenth and early eighteenth centuries to have several sons with as many different surnames. Each chose the name he wanted, for whatever reason. Cadillac's oldest brother changed his name to Francois Laumet Lacousille. The practice is common today in America and, of course, quite legal. Clearly a name change does not infer wrongdoing, although the possibility remains. But in the case of Cadillac, without a shred of supporting evidence, we must dismiss the accusation as simple malice.

Finally, in an evaluation of Cadillac the man, we must remember that our historical record does not begin until he is nineteen years old, still unmarried, living in a tiny farm community, with no promise of a future. In this there is reason enough for Cadillac and his two brothers to have joined the French army. Cadillac soon left France for adventure in the unknown, the largely unexplored New France. Young people dream of thrilling lives, as Cadillac must have; but Cadillac made his dreams come true in spite of all opposition. No matter his motives, he made a significant and permanent contribution to history, establishing the first important outpost of European civilization west of the Alleghenies, the oldest city in the Middle West. Above the flood of controversy, one fact remains secure: Cadillac founded the city of Detroit, and for that he deserves our respect and the honor we accord his memory on this, our 275th anniversary.

Postscript

In the spring of 1971 my wife and I visited St. Nicolas de la Grave, a small town in Gascony, in southern France. I contacted the mayor of St. Nicolas and explained that for many years citizens of Detroit had dreamed of preserving Cadillac's birthplace as a museum, but the owners of the property refused to sell. I had learned that the present owner no longer wanted the house. I asked the mayor how much it would cost to buy the dilapidated structure and give it to St. Nicolas. We would then have an architect restore it as closely as possible to its appearance in 1658, when Cadillac was born.

The mayor was enthusiastic. "One hundred thousand francs" was his answer. I quickly did some mental arithmetic. "You have a deal," I told him, "providing your municipal council provides written confirmation." I also wanted the town to agree to maintain the house as a museum once it was restored.

Back in Detroit, I formed a committee with Walker Cisler and Glen Coulter as cochairmen. Eighty-four of our friends responded to our appeal with the twenty thousand dollars we needed. My friend Nate Goodnow sent a note along with his check: "I cannot turn you down, but I've come to the conclusion that knowing Leonard Simons is an impoverishing experience."

The agreement with St. Nicolas was completed, the property purchased, and the restoration work begun. In May 1973, the Cadillac house was ready to be dedicated. About twenty-five Detroiters made the pilgrimage. French dignitaries and representatives from the American consulate in Bordeaux joined us in a series of dinners, parties, and champagne receptions. We cut the ribbon across the entrance to the Cadillac house and read Mayor Coleman Young's resolution in French and English to be hung there. Photographs and movies of Detroit were deposited for viewing by future visitors to acquaint them with the city that a son of St. Nicolas de la Grave had founded in 1701.

The French minister of cultural affairs had confirmed the

Detroit Historical Society delegation at the restored Cadillac birthplace

Detroit Mayor Coleman Young witnesses the author receiving the
Order of Merit from French Ambassador Jacques Kosciusko-Morizet

authenticity of the house as Cadillac's birthplace, which now was recorded as a historic monument. The restoration had been accomplished with the use of building materials salvaged from other buildings in the area of similar vintage, and the house was furnished with items typical of Cadillac's era.

A farewell dinner was held for the Detroit delegation, an elaborate gastronomic delight with the leading townspeople as our hosts. We ate and ate and ate in the great banquet hall of the 11th-century Chateau Terrides. After the speeches confirming the friendship between our two cities, I was asked, as president of the Detroit Historical Commission, to say a few words in response. In my awkward high school French, I thanked our hosts for their hospitality and the sumptuous French cooking. I closed my talk with the stirring words, "I regret that I have but one stomach to give to my country," and sat down.

On July 24, 1976, I was greatly honored for my small part in establishing the Cadillac museum by the President of France, who nominated me to the rank of Chevalier dans l'Ordre du Merite, the second-highest French civilian award. The award was presented to me on that occasion, which marked the 275th birthday anniversary of Detroit, by Hon Jacques Kosciusko-Morizet, the French Ambassador to the United States.

Who Put Detroit on The Map?

The map drawn by Guillaume de l'Isle

Are you a history buff? Does curiosity always prod you? Do you gain much pleasure and enjoyment in having a great fund of what some people call "trivia" knowledge?

If you are one of these people and like to accumulate tidbits of researched local history, then this story is for you.

When the question is asked, "Who put Detroit on the

From the *Detroit News,* July 24, 1981.

map?" the answer is: it all depends on what we are talking about.

If we're referring to the person who founded our town, then, of course, the answer is that courageous French soldier, Captain Antoine Laumet de La Mothe Cadillac. He did it 280 years ago, on July 24, 1701, when he established Fort Pontchartrain and the trading post called the village of "le Detroit."

He made possible, for the first time, the right of any mapmaker to include the name of what would become one of the world's best known cities, Detroit. But that does not tell us who actually did put Detroit on the map.

We are not referring to exploration but rather to maps, specifically *a* map, the *first* map that mentions "le Detroit," as our French ancestors called our town for many years. (When first settled, the area received the name Ville de Troit, "the village of the straits." But, soon the Ville was dropped and the other two words were joined as one.)

As verified by (Mrs.) Alice Dalligan, director of the Burton Historical Collection at our Detroit Public Library, Dr. Douglas Marshall of the Clements Library at the University of Michigan, and Dr. Le Roy Barnett of the State Archives at Lansing, illustrated here is the first printed map showing "le Detroit" at the location where we live. It was published worldwide and is dated 1702, within one year after our town was founded. It carries the title "Carte du Canada et du Mississippi" (Map of Canada and of Mississippi).

The name of the cartographer who drew the map, engraved and printed it, is Guillame De l'Isle (1675–1726). He was the founder of scientific geography, the first man in France to be named "Premier Geographe du Roi" (first geographer to the King). We salute De l'Isle and thank him for being the first man "who put Detroit on the map."

A sequel: For many years my office wall proudly displayed a De l'Isle map. It is a large, handsome, original map of "Mexico and Florida and c" printed in 1722 and showing "le Detroit" in relatively large type. The 259-year-old map is extremely rare. It was made when Detroit had just reached the age of its majority, twenty-one.

One day, back in December 1972, Clement E. Conger, the curator of the White House in Washington, D.C., visited Detroit. He was seeking gifts of Early American furniture, maps, artifacts, etc. to enhance the White House interior. Interviewed by the Detroit newspapers, Dr. Conger appealed to our local community to donate some of its treasures to the White House as a patriotic gesture.

I offered my map and told them it dated back to twenty-one years after Detroit was founded. It was authenticated and accepted. The White House wrote that the map needed a new frame in keeping with the decor of its new home. I requested permission to pay to have it done, and there were no objections.

So today, the map hangs in the office of the vice-president of the United States at the White House. A little plaque declares it a gift of affection from Detroit to our First Families who live there.

David Heineman and the
Flag of Detroit

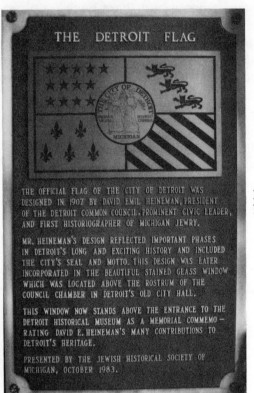

THE DETROIT FLAG

THE OFFICIAL FLAG OF THE CITY OF DETROIT WAS
DESIGNED IN 1907 BY DAVID EMIL HEINEMAN, PRESIDENT
OF THE DETROIT COMMON COUNCIL, PROMINENT CIVIC LEADER,
AND FIRST HISTORIOGRAPHER OF MICHIGAN JEWRY.

MR. HEINEMAN'S DESIGN REFLECTED IMPORTANT PHASES
IN DETROIT'S LONG AND EXCITING HISTORY AND INCLUDED
THE CITY'S SEAL AND MOTTO. THIS DESIGN WAS LATER
INCORPORATED IN THE BEAUTIFUL STAINED GLASS WINDOW
WHICH WAS LOCATED ABOVE THE ROSTRUM OF THE
COUNCIL CHAMBER IN DETROIT'S OLD CITY HALL.

THIS WINDOW NOW STANDS ABOVE THE ENTRANCE TO THE
DETROIT HISTORICAL MUSEUM AS A MEMORIAL COMMEMO —
RATING DAVID E. HEINEMAN'S MANY CONTRIBUTIONS TO
DETROIT'S HERITAGE.

PRESENTED BY THE JEWISH HISTORICAL SOCIETY OF
MICHIGAN, OCTOBER 1983.

Plaque in the lobby of the
Detroit Historical Museum

These days while auto manufacturers
are recalling more and more, I find myself recalling less and
less. But, I vividly recall standing here eleven years ago, in
this very room, paying tribute to David E. Heineman when

Talk given at the Detroit Historical Museum dedicating plaque given by Jewish
Historical Society of Michigan, October 1983.

we installed the stained-glass window above our main entrance. On that same afternoon, while we were honoring David Heineman as the designer of the flag of Detroit, three courageous astronauts were planting an American flag on the moon. I remember saying this might mean America had conquered the moon, and I wondered if that meant we would have to send the moon foreign aid?

Today, we again honor David Heineman for designing the official flag of our city with the placement of a bronze plaque in the foyer of Detroit's Historical Museum. It is a gift of love to the museum and a further recognition of David Heineman's creative talent by the Jewish Historical Society of Michigan.

David Heineman was a turn-of-the-century civic leader who played a very important part in our city's history. His parents, Emil Heineman and the former Fanny Butzel, came to Detroit, where he was born, in 1851, when the city's Jewish population numbered sixty out of a total population of twenty-one thousand. The Heineman and Butzel families enjoyed enviable reputations for integrity and philanthropy. With that heritage, it is no wonder David was such a splendid man. Tomorrow, October 17, is the anniversary of his birth date in 1865.

David Heineman had impressive credentials. He graduated in 1883 from Detroit High School, president of his class, and went on to finish his schooling at the University of Michigan, where he was later given an honorary degree also. Elected to Phi Beta Kappa and a graduate lawyer, he began his law practice in Detroit. A lawyer, you know, is someone who is dedicated to Life, Liberty, and the Law Suit of Happiness.

Heineman was a brilliant scholar. People said he was so bright, he could say "hello" in algebra. He also had a multiplicity of personal interest. He had an intense interest in books and libraries, and he loved music. Because of his vision he became one of the most active, most vocal, of the leading citizens behind the movement to build this great Cultural Center of which our Historical Museum is a part. He secured $750,000 from Andrew Carnegie to help build the Main Detroit Public Library next door to us. He helped to build the Detroit Institute of Arts and founded the Scarab Club of Detroit.

In addition to his own law practice and political undertakings, he found time to originate the city manager's plan of government for cities, was president of the State of Michigan Anti-Tuberculosis Society, and served under three governors as president of the Board of State Library Commissioners. While acting as chief assistant city attorney, he revised and codified all of the city's seven hundred ordinances. One of "Ping's boys," he so impressed Mayor Hazen Pingree that Pingree urged him to run for elected office. He did, becoming a state legislator, but after a couple of years in Lansing he decided he would rather come back to Detroit.

In 1903 he was elected alderman for the 1st Ward. That made him a member of the Common Council, where he served for seven years and was Council president. Mayor Breitmeyer appointed him city controller in 1910. At the end of his term he decided to quit politics, but World War I brought him back when he was appointed Food Administrator for Detroit and Wayne County.

I had seen David Heineman at some civic functions, but I never met him myself. He has been described as a gifted storyteller with a flair for the well-chosen word and with a sense of humor. A great debator, he was admired by all for his good common sense. An aristocrat, he associated with top Detroit society and enjoyed equally consorting with ward politicians. Here was a democratic man.

Let me quote from some of the editorials and obituaries written on his death in order to give you further glimpses into the man.

> He seemed out of place in the Council because he used four-syllable words. Sometimes he employed them in reference to his colleagues who were never quite sure whether they were being insulted or complimented.

> Because he was from the 1st Ward, he was always the first to vote when the roll was called. Two-thirds of the Council listened to see whether Heineman would say "Aye" or "No" so they would know how to vote. Not that they loved the highly educated, cultured Heineman, for they feared his tongue, but he was so often right that it was wise to follow his lead.

> To make his stand clear, he would explain why he voted as he did. This was a great help to those he had momentarily offended because they would then vote the other way.

He enjoyed using big words, like in later life when someone happened to ask how he was feeling, he is reputed to have said, "My physiology is catching up to my chronology," or "I'm deteriorating on schedule."

The passing of David E. Heineman takes memory back to the days when he was one of Detroit's first citizens, before he was defeated for Lt. Governor of Michigan and then seeking nothing further, retired from politics.

Heineman was just a dabbler in politics. It was not his profession. He would have liked to succeed in it but he would not pay the price. He would not make small surrenders or cultivate nit-wits . . . and in those partisan days, one had to do those things. So, he did what he could for Detroit and wished to do many things that were beyond his powers. He was too honest and too outspoken and too independent.

His caustic tongue spared neither friend nor foe. Because of his refusal to compromise, rather than any lack of knowledge or ability, he did not become mayor, governor, or senator.

David Heineman had many financial interests, including one of the original Detroit street railway companies. But there was something about his wallet you couldn't help liking, as his generous contributions to a long list of charities proves.

He was active in the Michigan Historical Society, the Masons and the Shriners, the Elks and Oddfellows, and served as president of Pisgah Lodge of the B'nai B'rith. President of the local chapter of the American Institute of Archaeology, he also belonged to the University Club, the Detroit Boat Club, and the Old Club of St. Clair Flats.

The one hobby which he frankly admitted held the highest interest for him was the study of the early history of the Jewish people of Detroit and Michigan. Much of what is now known about early Michigan Jewry was uncovered by him, which earned him the title of Historiographer of the Jews of Michigan by the American Jewish Historical Society.

Imagine the surprise of even his closest friends when David Heineman, a confirmed bachelor, at the age of fifty-three married the daughter of a University of Michigan professor. They had no children. He died of pneumonia on February 21, 1935, at the age of seventy and was buried in the Temple Beth

El Section of Woodmere Cemetery. Today's ceremony shows that we have not forgotten the man who, among many accomplishments, conceived of the official flag of the City of Detroit.

Three Hundred Years of the Jews in America

The 1954 International Convention of the Sigma Alpha Mu Fraternity

Ever since my youth, the initials S.A.M. have been playing an important role in my life. First, because of Sigma Alpha Mu and now because S.A.M. means "Simons and Michelson" to me.

Many happy years ago—thirty-three ago to be exact— almost all of my friends went to Ann Arbor for their higher education and at the same time they founded the University of Michigan chapter of the S.A.M. fraternity.

Unfortunately, I couldn't go anywhere, except to work. But, I was "one of the boys" just the same. I knew the handshake. I went to the S.A.M. parties. I ate at the fraternity house.

From a talk given at the Sigma Alpha Mu fraternity International Convention, Detroit-Windsor, September 1954.

I probably sang "Fast and Firm" the loudest at meal time, and I even went to some of the out-of-town S.A.M. conclaves.

So, meet Fra Simons, a "pseudo-Sammy" since 1921.

That's why it is a real pleasure and an honor for me to be here with so many of my old friends, and the fraternity that I love best, to break bread with you, and to speak to you.

When Dr. Maurice Tatelman, chairman of your Program Committee, invited me to address you men tonight, I immediately thought that the message might be in connection with the event which is being celebrated by Jews everywhere throughout America this very week. This is the 300th Anniversary of the establishment of the First Jewish Community in North America. And that is my subject. It is called the Tercentenary Celebration, or "Thank God Grandpa Didn't Miss The Boat."

To commemorate the Tercentenary, all five million Jews in the United States are being called upon by official proclamation to "participate in the observance of this anniversary—to offer thanks unto the Lord for the blessings bestowed upon us in America—to pray for the continued peace and prosperity of our country and all its inhabitants—and to rededicate ourselves to the ideals of our Faith within the Freedom of American democracy." The theme of the Tercentenary is "Man's Opportunities and Responsibilities under Freedom."

Our records tell us that three-hundred years ago this week, the first week in September 1654, twenty-three Jewish refugees from Brazil landed in Nieuw Amsterdam, the original name of New York City.

These twenty-three Jews, who were at sea for about three months, were to form the first Jewish community in North America in Nieuw Amsterdam.

It is interesting to know that sixty years before these same Jewish families had fled the Inquisition in Portugal. They had gone to Holland. But, because opportunity for a livelihood in Holland was scarce, some Jews moved to the Dutch colony in Brazil and established trades. Now they were again driven from their homes, this time by the Portuguese conquest of Brazil. So, for the second time they were being expelled because of their religious difference, and once more they were not able to worship God in their own way.

There were six-hundred refugee Jews from Brazil who

set sail to return to Holland in sixteen ships. Fifteen of these ships did arrive in Holland, but the sixteenth ship bearing the twenty-three future Americans was captured by Spanish pirates. The passengers had been robbed and were penniless when the French frigate, St. Charles, rescued them and deposited them in Nieuw Amsterdam.

Hard-headed, hard-hearted Governor Peter Stuyvesant and the deacon of the colony appealed to the Dutch West India Company in Holland for permission to order the Jews to leave. Our people spent the whole winter anxiously waiting for the company's answer to come from the other side of the ocean. In the spring of 1655, the Company wrote to Governor Stuyvesant and turned down his request. They said "the fulfillment of the Governor's wishes would be somewhat unreasonable and unfair—therefore—these people may travel and trade to and in Nieuw Amsterdam . . . and live and remain there." That was the first of a good many good breaks Jews got in North America.

The first blow struck for Jewish rights was in August 1655, just about one year after they had arrived in their new homeland, when all ablebodied Nieuw Amsterdam citizens were ordered to stand guard. The Jews were not included but were ordered to pay a special tax instead.

Our historians tell us there were two men, Jacob Barsimson and Asser Levy, who stood up for their rights. They demanded equality. They insisted on doing their share and serving in the Nieuw Amsterdam militia. They undertook a long legal battle. Asser Levy went before the Governor's Council and won for himself and all the Jews of the colony complete citizenship. There later followed the rights to worship, own land, travel inland, and trade; a great major victory for us but one which also established equality for all religious groups that were to follow us, such as the Catholics and the Lutherans.

Incidentally, these same twenty-three Jews immediately established a congregation in 1654 called Shearith Israel; it is still in existence.

The story I have just told you is the beginning of our history in this land. Following these courageous Jews came many more families from different parts of Europe as well as from the West Indies.

Upon the long record of our past three-hundred years

in America, we American Jews of today must build for the future.

How great a debt you and I owe to these Jewish men and women who preceded us in North America is beyond my ability to state. But, we should thank God for them, because they made it possible for the good life and liberty we Jews enjoy in the United States today. Their courage and their integrity made possible for us all the good things that we have.

Now, in return, on the eve of Rosh Hashono as we are about to celebrate the Jewish New Year 5715, let us be reminded of the fact that we, too, must have the same kind of courage and integrity so that our children and our children's children for at least the next three-hundred years to come will continue to share in the good fortune and all of God's blessings which are available today to the Jews in America in such abundance.

By our actions, yours and mine, by our activities in every day life, by our honesty and sincerity, by our generosity, by our courage and by our vision do we prove ourselves worthy of being custodians of such a great tradition, and of assuring the fact there will be future generations of American Jews.

We must plan for the next three-hundred years of the Jew in America by using our intellect and our hearts to help build a true brotherhood. The S.A.M. fraternity is a brotherhood. It is an organization founded chiefly to promote friendship and welfare among its members. That is essentially the idea I am talking about, but as we grow older and more understanding we can appreciate that this basic idea should be expanded to take in more than just a limited number of Jewish boys, in a limited number of colleges and universities. We must think in bigger terms; we must think *not* in just Jewish terms, but must include ideals to foster brotherhood and fraternity among Jews *and* gentiles. And I say this seriously and selfishly because I believe that the future happiness and welfare of the Jew in America depends so much upon our own attitude, as well as on the way we accept our responsibilities. We are proud we had such personalities in our American Jewish history, men and women who blended their Americanism with their Judaism to the benefit of all, men such as Louis Marshall, Justice Brandeis, Julius Rosenwald, Herbert Lehman and Detroit's own, the late Fred Butzel, as well as countless others.

Central High School's 100th Anniversary

Central High School 100th Anniversary Dinner

Thank you, Miss Robinson, for that nice introduction. It was much different from the one I recently got when I spoke before an advertising club. The chairman was having difficulty adjusting the microphone. He finally stopped trying to fix it, turned to the audience, and said, "It seems our speaker has a screw loose. I want to introduce Leonard Simons."

As you can see from your program, I am tonight's

Talk given at Masonic Temple, June 1958 on the 100th anniversary of Central High School (1858–1958).

97

spokesman for the classes of the Roaring Twenties. I was in school for only the first two years of this decade, but I am sure there were times when some of my teachers thought it would take me the entire ten years to graduate.

I finally graduated because, as my principal, David Mackenzie, once told me, "*one* of us had to go."

I vividly recall my four happy years at Central, and I remember well a lot of other things and people who were in the limelight during the '20s.

Detroit then had a population of less than 1,000,000. In 1920 there were 14,000 students in our eight Detroit high schools. Central had about 2,000. Today there are 55,000 enrolled in twenty-two Detroit high schools. Back then women had finally secured the right to vote; we had the League of Nations; and we had prohibition. I think it was the '20s that made popular the two-bathroom home—one was devoted to making gin.

Ty Cobb managed the Tigers, movies became articulate and Al Jolson wowed us with the talkie *The Jazz Singer*, a brand new Ford cost $395, the fire department still used horses, and radio was just coming into popular use and was called wireless telephone. I called my set a railroad radio because it had a whistle on every station.

Flappers was the name for our teenage girls, the clothes the women wore looked just like the sack dresses of today, we were dancing the Charleston and the Black Bottom, high school boys and their dads sported Norfolk suits with a belt in the back and bell-bottomed pants, and many boys still wore knickers on Central's campus. We used heavy pomade on our hair, and, when we went into the barber shop, the barber didn't know whether we wanted a hair cut or an oil change.

Believe it or not, *I* had beautiful wavy hair in those days, but the waves are gone now; it's all beach.

We had a lot of wonderful teachers whose ideals and advice did much to shape the future of youngsters like myself. Edgar Thompson was my Study Hall counselor, and when I came to Mr. Thompson with some of what I thought were my important problems, I remember his favorite answer: "Leonard, remember that no matter how much you worry, you're never going to get out of this world alive."

Then there was Katherine Conover, our art teacher. She

lives in California now, but I occasionally see her and we correspond. I remember those lovely ladies, Kitty Hine and Helen Wattles, who, I understand, are here tonight. How we all fought to get into their classes. Miss Hine was always smiling, and I'll never forget one bit of advice she gave to the boys: "When you get into the business world, forget the tricks of the trade; just learn the trade."

Then there was Miss Hull, who made history live, exciting and dramatic. She taught that life can be understood backwards, but it must be lived forward.

We had a French teacher—for obvious reasons I won't mention her name—but, because her petticoat always showed, we called her Mademoiselle Droopy Drawers. I thought she liked me because she used to bring me candied violets; but she still flunked me at the end of the term.

Remember Winged Victory? It stood in the front lobby. Both arms are missing from this world-famous ancient Greek statue. One of our school comics pasted a sign on it that read: "See what happens when you bite your finger nails?"

One memory of our annual school outing by boat to Sugar Island will remain forever. I was captain of our house baseball team. We were playing for the school championship. It was the last half of the 9th, we were one run behind, there were two out, the bases were full, and it was Heavy Hitter Simons' time to bat. Supported by the lusty cheers from all the kids of House 275, I strutted up to the batter's box. Here was the chance to be a hero by driving in the tying, or maybe the winning, run. Just as I had seen Ty Cobb do, I swung three bats and threw away two. I tapped the soles of my shoes, hitched up my belt, pulled the visor of my cap down over my eyes, dug my spikes into the dirt, took a few vicious practice swings, glared at the pitcher, and, with my heart pounding, dared him to put one over the plate. The kids were still screaming. It was the tense, exciting, big moment of the day. Then the pitcher spun around and picked off the runner at third base.

Yes, it was a flamboyant, flaming, glorious, scintillating, sophisticated, wonderful, wacky era. Grand? Yes, but it doesn't begin to compare with these fantastic days, and the future looks even more exciting.

On behalf of all the students who graduated from Central during the 20s, I want to say how grateful we are for everything that Central High School did for us, for the enthusiasm and effort our instructors put into teaching us how to think and to analyze things for ourselves, for all which was given us as a most precious heritage by the dedicated staff of the splendid educators that it was our good fortune to have at dear old Central.

Yes, I like to believe that this world is a little better place in which to live because of the understanding, the training and foundation given us by these splendid men and women who taught us to be good citizens.

Happy 125th Birthday to Detroit's High Schools

The date August 30 by itself is not especially important. But what happened on that day in Detroit 125 years ago is a very important part of our local history.

In 1858 education took a giant step forward in our town: *We opened the doors of our first public high school.*

The record books tell a fascinating story of those early days, worthy of being recalled on this 125th anniversary. Even if you are not a follower of Clio, the Greek goddess of history, you will enjoy this trip down Detroit's memory lane.

The student body on the opening day of our first high school consisted of twenty-three pupils, all boys. They were selected, after an examination of their scholarship, by one man, Professor Henry Chaney. He was their only teacher and the first principal of our first Detroit high school. Classes were held on the second floor of the Miami Union School, an old wood-frame building on the site of the then Board of Education office on Miami Avenue (now called Broadway). Some history books say that to get to their classrooms, these students had to use the wooden stairs on the outside of the building.

It was not easy to sell the Board of Education on the idea of going beyond primary education in Detroit's schools even though as far back as 1852, Francis W. Shearman, superintendent of Detroit's Board of Education, had made a speech stressing that the time had come when Detroit was ready for a public high school.

Arguments about education are nothing new; we still have them today, just as we did 125 years ago. Then Detroiters were arguing about the value of secondary education: Should we have a high school? Do we need one? A good many of our town's solid citizens were against the proposal. They thought a high school would be little more than an unnecessary expense. The opponents also stated the public should not and

Prepared for the 125th anniversary of the high schools of Michigan, August 1983.

would not support the idea of a high school, and certainly they would not support one that included girls. They said there was something un-American in teaching youngsters Latin and Greek. Furthermore, there was nothing in our laws that said we should or must provide such a frill as a high school. Therefore, to propose a high school was illegal.

But attorney Divie Bethune Duffield, better known as D. Bethune Duffield, a member of the school board since 1847, became the devil's advocate. He took the opposite viewpoint, arguing for a high school. A brilliant court lawyer, he used all his powers of persuasion to convince the rest of the school board to agree to "try the idea for a while to see how it would work out." He argued that a high school would offer boys of limited means the opportunity to prepare themselves for college or university without the expense of tuition. Duffield won out and pushed through the experiment five years after Superintendent Shearman had proposed the idea.

Incidentally, up to this time a Detroit youngster could obtain a secondary education only in private academies and, for a very short time, in the nine branches of the university. Most of those branches were abandoned in 1846.

Because there was only limited available classroom space, the Board of Education decided it would be necessary to exclude girls from the program. However, they added, this may be obviated if more space became available. The original three classes were planned to teach Latin, algebra, geometry, and arithmetic.

"D. Bethune Duffield," according to Detroit's early great historiographer Silas Farmer, "was so thoroughly identified with securing the establishment of the high school and with its origins, he was referred to as the Father of our High School." In 1866, the Duffield School was built and named in his honor.

In 1859, the year after the high school opened, the Board of Education was content to continue indefinitely the idea of a permanent Detroit high school. In fact, over the bitter opposition of many taxpayers, the majority of the Board had the courage to spend $2,000 on a one-story brick addition behind their present building.

January 1860: the new Detroit High School building on Gratiot opened with an enrollment of eighty-five boys and girls and a faculty of three teachers. The Board permitted girls for the first time to become students at the high school. Detroit's population had grown to 45,619, and the Civil War was on the horizon.

Before Duffield retired in 1860, after thirteen years on the Board of Education which included several years as its president, he was given the honor of delivering the commencement message to the first high school graduating class in 1860: two boys, Amos Chaffee and John Paul Swan. When Duffield gave them his message, he also gave them the Latin motto adopted by the high school and used to this day. It was *Carpe Diem*, that is, *Make the most of every day*. Duffield advanced the idea and exhorted the students earnestly to seize every occasion and diligently appropriate every hour for self-improvement.

By 1863 the high school once again had outgrown its space. The Board started looking for a new and larger location. It wanted to secure the vacant old State Capitol building located in Capitol Park.

In trying to get permission to use space in the building the Board was tangled in government red tape. No one in the state government would say no, nor would anyone say yes to the Board of Education.

One day a member of the Board walked in to a Board meeting, put a key on the table, and said, "Please don't ask any questions. Let's just move in and use the old Capitol Building." Which is what they did. And, believe it or not, to this day nobody has ever complained or asked for rent! Detroit just commandeered the building, took squatter's rights, and transferred the high school to the second floor, where it stayed for thirty years.

1866—The study of French and German was introduced.

1869—In October, blacks were admitted to all public schools in Detroit for the first time. All Detroit schools had been desegregated by law.

1875—A new high school building was erected in front of the old Capitol structure.

1878—By June, the regents of the University of Michigan decided that graduating students should be admitted to the university on the basis of their diplomas from our Detroit high schools, without examinations.

1893—The high school had grown to include eleven hundred students and thirty-seven teachers. More space was needed, and gingerbread-design additions were tacked on to the old building.

Hazen S. Pingree (whose statue is located in Grand Circus Park) was Detroit's great reform mayor. After a tour of inspection of the high school, the mayor declared that in his opinion the school was a fire trap. Pingree told a Board of Education member that "it is surprising that this building has never burned down." To which the Board member is supposed to have responded, "Mr. Mayor, this is the kind of a building that never does burn."

Unfortunately this was not the first, or the last, time a school board member erred in judgment, but it was amazing how quickly and how spectacularly he was proved wrong. That very night, on a cold freezing January 27, 1893, the old Capitol building with its school additions burst into flames. The high school was burned down, but without casualties.

The prompt handling of the disaster by the Board was not appreciated by some of the less eager students who were hoping for a long vacation from their studies. The very next day, classes were resumed in emergency quarters. The 9th and 10th grades went to the Sunday school classrooms of the Central Presbyterian Church located at Farmer and Bates streets; the 11th and 12th grades went to the classrooms of Temple Beth El on Washington Boulevard and Clifford. The old Biddle House Hotel on East Jefferson was leased in March of 1893 as a temporary high school.

Over one thousand youngsters had graduated from the old Capitol building school before the fire. The unfortunate burning now hastened the erection of a completely new high school. On November 13, 1894, the now historic silver spade broke the sod for the construction of a new high school.

The year 1896 saw the end of one era and the beginning of another; the last horsecar was taken off our streets; Charles B. King put the first automobile on Detroit roads. The King car, like that made by Henry Ford, was hand-built. And in 1896, a brand new high school was opened with 3,036 students.

The magnificent, all-new school building, with sixty-three rooms and parking racks for five-hundred bicycles, was called "the finest on the North American continent." The Board of Education decided the new building was too important simply to be labeled the Detroit High School, so they called it Detroit Central High School. The name was formally adopted in 1895 before the new building actually opened its doors.

The board also decided to name its school Central High School because it realized the city's population was on the increase. It was only a question of time, therefore, before additional high schools would be built. Detroit would undoubtedly have a high school on the east side and one on the west side of town, and probably more, as indeed we did. Western High School was opened in 1898. Eastern High School was opened in 1901.

Many citizens could not understand why the Board of Education built the new high school "way out in the country." But once again some Board members had the vision to realize that Detroit was growing, fast becoming a great metropolis. The overcrowding and the pressure of business in the downtown area would make necessary the move north to the wide-open spaces on Cass Avenue at Warren and Hancock streets. (Old Central High School is now the building sentimentally called Old Main of Wayne State University.)

Central High School was actually the same high school with the same student body as the former high school, only the name and location were changed. Therefore, it is fair to claim this year as the 125th birthday of Central High School. Old Central's greatest years of glory were the twenty years (1904–1924) under the guidance of its great principal, David MacKenzie.

January 1926 and Central High School, after thirty years on Cass Avenue (1896–1926), turned over its building to Detroit City College and moved to new quarters on Linwood Avenue and Tuxedo. That was over fifty years ago. Joseph Corns was its 8th principal.

Our story of the early years in our high school's history ends here except for a brief report of the 100th birthday, the "Centennial celebration."

Twenty-five years ago, in 1958, a tremendous affair was held at Masonic Temple to commemorate Central High School's 100th birthday. It was, of course, also the 100th anniversary of the forefather of all Detroit high schools. It was a sellout.

Over a thousand alumni, teachers, and city and state officials attended the banquet and the party that followed. Bertha Robinson, principal of Central, was chairlady of the evening festivities.

There were speakers, of course. Those on the program were Leonard Kasle, of the Kasle Steel Company (class of 1934), who, as president, spoke for the Detroit Board of Education; Dr. Sam Brownell, superintendent of Detroit Public Schools; Arthur McGrath, assistant superintendent of secondary education; followed by three alumni who told about some of their student day escapades and incidents which brought much laughter and nods of recollection from the audience.

Dr. Harvey Merker, retired vice-president of Parke, Davis Company (class of 1905), reminisced about the turn-of-the-century era "When Hearts Were Young and Gay"; Leonard N. Simons, of the Simons-Michelson Advertising Agency (class of 1921), carried the story into "The Roaring Twenties"; and Dr. Mel J. Ravitz, Detroit Common Councilman (class of 1942), brought the chronicle almost up to the present with his tales of "The Fabulous Forties." The mood was set.

An operetta, appropriately titled *Nostalgia Set to Music*, portraying Central's history was performed. The lyrics were written by J. Fred Lawton, an insurance man made famous as the composer of the University of Michigan's great fight song, "Varsity"; the music was written by Rowland Fixel, Detroit attorney. Both were from the class of 1907.

The director and narrator of the musicale was Richard Frankensteen, a vice-president of the UAW-CIO and one-time candidate for mayor of Detroit (class of 1926). All the members of the orchestra were alumni. The night belonged to the Old-Timers, and they made the most of it, a stirring chapter in the history of Detroit's secondary education.

That was a quarter-century ago. The report of that evening makes a pleasant finale to these reminiscences. I should add only that the Detroit High School of 1858 is believed to have been not only the first in Detroit but also in Michigan, as well as the first public high school in America west of the Allegheny Mountains.

Today, there are sixty-nine high schools in Detroit and Wayne County, the grandchildren of the original Detroit High School.

Remembering David Mackenzie

David Mackenzie

W*hen I was* told I had been elected an honorary member of the Mackenzie Honor Society, I was pleased beyond words, for I am one of the fortunate few still alive who knew Dean Mackenzie personally. When I say personally, I do not mean to imply that we were intimate friends: David Mackenzie was the principal of Central High School during the four years I attended as a student.

When I was asked to speak in an informal manner about David Mackenzie, I asked myself whether I really knew enough about the man, or if I had had sufficient contact with him some

Talk given to the Wayne State University Mackenzie Honor Society, June 1960; published in *Detroit in Perspective*, fall 1983.

forty years ago, to say something of interest. After all, I was only sixteen years old when I graduated from old Central High. However, before that I had been able to know Mr. Mackenzie somewhat better than most students in the school. Hence, I may be able to tell you something new about him, some things personal, and then finish up with some things about him I have learned subsequently by doing a little research.

I was one of Mackenzie's office assistants, although if David Mackenzie were here now he probably would take exception to the word "assistant." I worked in his school office between my classes, doing odd jobs, a little typing, mimeographing examinations, and running errands. Despite the years that have passed, I well remember this great man.

I still have the picture of my high school graduating class with Mackenzie's picture on it. Underneath him is printed his name *McKenzie*, which should give you some idea as to how good we were at spelling in the Central High of the 1920s. Certainly I was no better in that skill than anyone else at school. Once, when I had done some of my one-finger typing, Mr. Mackenzie came and stood next to my desk. He turned to his secretary and with a twinkle in his eye said, "F-I-R-E him; he can't S-P-E-L-L."

The way I became Mr. Mackenzie's "assistant" reveals another side of the man. The boys at Central were supposed to participate in ROTC (The Reserve Officers' Training Corps), which meant that each of us had to buy his own khaki soldier suit. My family could not afford to buy me one. But any boy without his uniform had to go up to the top floor of the school and do "fatigue duty"—march for one half hour carrying the heavy drill rifle—each day he was out of uniform.

When Mackenzie would make his daily rounds through the corridors, he would always see me marching. One day he stopped me. "What have you been up to that you are on fatigue duty every day? Aren't you behaving yourself? What's the matter with you?" When he learned that lack of money was the cause, he told me to come to his office the next day, and he would give me a job. I am not certain, but I think I earned less than a dollar a week. I never did buy the uniform because I needed the money for books and lunches more than I needed an ROTC uniform. But Mackenzie eliminated my fatigue duty penalty every day and helped me make a little expense money that would see me through high school.

Because I was working in his office, he was kept informed of whatever trouble I got into. While I'm sure he would never admit it, I think he kind of enjoyed hearing about the scrapes in which I was involved. There was a school regulation forbidding students to hang around a certain poolroom either during or after school hours. It was on Woodward Avenue just north of Warren. I was caught there and suspended from school until I brought my mother to talk to the principal of my House or study room. Of course Mackenzie found out what had happened because I did not come to work in his office during my suspension. When I did return, he honored me with a long lecture.

I was again suspended from school when I painted murals on the walls of the headquarters of the school paper, the *Student* magazine. I was its assistant art editor and much impressed with myself. The school did not mind the murals as much as they objected to the caricatures I had drawn of some of the teachers. Mackenzie, however, came to my rescue again. I was returned to classes, and the principal cheerfully took me back as one of his lesser "burdens."

During my senior year, I thought I should be appointed the Advertising Manager for our graduation book, the *Centralite*, because I had held that position on the *Student* magazine. But Mackenzie's assistant, William Stocking, gave the job to someone else, someone who had never worked on the advertising staff. Of course I decided that was unfair and argued my case with Mr. Stocking. "Why hadn't I been given the job and the title?" Stocking told me I was not qualified, in his opinion. I do not remember the exact words I used in rebuttal, but evidently my choice of rhetoric showed poor judgment because I was suspended from school once more. Mackenzie, however, arranged to have my mother come and talk with Mr. Stocking so that I could return and graduate.

Mr. Stocking was partially responsible for my choice of careers. Because he said he thought I was not qualified to be an ad-man, I was determined to prove him wrong. After graduation, I was going to become a big success in the advertising business. Then, one day, I would return to Central and fling his wrong judgment in his face. Now, after forty years in advertising, I am not so sure that he wasn't right.

One of the graduation requirements at Central High in the 1920s was passing the swimming test. Every senior had to be able to swim the length of the school pool and back. I never learned how to swim. I told Mr. Mackenzie I would never be able to get my diploma. He was adamant: "You are going to get out of here. *One of us has to go!* You figure out a way to pass your swimming test." Indeed I did. I got one of my best friends to go to the pool. He told coach Collins he was Leonard Simons and then passed the test for me.

But Mr. Mackenzie's burden still was not lifted from his shoulders. In adding up my credits, the office found that I was a few short for graduation. Mackenzie sat down with me and my House advisor. They gave me credit for ROTC, for art work, for working on the School magazine, for basketball, football, tennis, track, and baseball until I had the total number of 160 hours of credit needed. I will never know whether Mackenzie's kindness was because he was fond of me, or because he was truly anxious to be rid of me, but either way, these small deeds give the measure of the man. I was certainly fond of him.

I graduated in June 1921 and immediately went to work in an advertising agency. In a few years, I realized I needed more education. So, in 1925 or 1926 I decided to go to night school at the City College of Detroit in Central High. I went to register, standing in line with seventy-five or a hundred other students on the third floor, the same floor where Mackenzie's office was still located. Mackenzie walked out into the hall and immediately picked me out of the crowd although he had not seen me since I had graduated. In a loud voice that could be heard by everyone standing about, he exclaimed, "Oh no! Not again! Leonard Simons, I thought I had gotten rid of you for good." I was so embarrassed I could have fallen though that nonexistent hole in the floor, but inwardly I was very pleased he remembered me. He had an excellent memory for names and faces.

I have since learned that David Mackenzie was born in Detroit. If he were still with us, a week ago last Saturday, May 28th, 1960, would have seen him celebrating his 100th birthday. According to his assistant, Mr. Stocking, May 28, 1860, was a date Mackenzie's wife had picked out for him as his birth date because he did not know the exact date.

In my mind's eye, I remember Mackenzie as being taller than average, a rather thin, plain-looking man with pince-nez glasses. He was forever removing them from his nose and wiping them clean. He had a somewhat full mustache and usually wore an oversize bow tie—not those large ones affected by artists but larger than those ordinarily worn by other teachers. He had that full lower lip usually described as the Hapsburg lip. He wore high, starched collars. Most of the time, he wore gray suits, neat but always in need of a pressing. He was rarely, if ever, seen without his suit jacket, while on his vest he always sported his Phi Beta Kappa key. I remember his hair as dark gray and sparse.

I know some people said he had a choleric disposition, yet I never saw him excited or lose his temper. When he wanted to, however, he could cut you down handsomely with his magnificent command of the English language—and without raising his voice. I thought of him as a dignified man with great poise. His eyes impressed me the most; they usually seemed to be smiling even when his mouth was not. Indeed, David Mackenzie had a fine sense of humor.

I am certain he found his greatest enjoyment working with school youngsters. His associates felt he loved his profession. He was liked and admired by both students and teachers. My contact with him and his advice were instrumental in the formation of many of the attitudes I hold toward life, even to this day. Because Mr. Mackenzie was a teacher in the best sense of the word, I think he would be pleased that this one of his students has been selected for membership in the society that bears his name. I am sure he would be equally pleased and probably surprised, even as I was, that Wayne State University, the school which exists today because of his vision, honored that same student in 1957 with an honorary LL.D.—doctor of laws degree.

Lee White, who formerly worked for the *Detroit News*, told me that when Mackenzie found Lee had not earned enough money working all summer to pay his tuition for college in the fall, Mr. Mackenzie sent him a check each and every month to enable him to get his education. This was not an isolated instance of Mackenzie's generosity, for there were many reports of his helping Central students further their education.

In the 1920s, I knew only the man who stood before me;

today I know much more about his background and activities. His father ran a grocery store in what was then the Corktown area of Detroit. As David Mackenzie's name betrays, he was of Scottish ancestry, and he was called Scotty by his close friends. His mother was a cultured woman, a master of several languages who encouraged her son to be the outstanding scholar that he became. It was due to her example and influence that her son spoke eight languages, the last of which, Sanscrit, he mastered in his middle age. He graduated from the University of Michigan in 1881 with the A.B. and M.A. degrees. He was one of the first five students at the University of Michigan to be elected to Phi Beta Kappa. He began his teaching career in Fenton, Michigan, moved on to become superintendent of schools in Muskegon, and came to Detroit in 1904 to be principal at Central High School.

A man of strong convictions, he accepted the job of principal only after the superintendent of schools and the Board of Education agreed to give him a free hand in running Central High. Both superintendent and Board were too anxious to obtain his services to give him anything less.

Mackenzie had the vision to create the Detroit Junior College in 1915 using the facilities of Central High School. He was its dean. Eight years later, in 1923, he successfully petitioned the Michigan legislature in Lansing to change the two-year school into a four-year college under the new name of College of the City of Detroit, again as part of Central High School's space. He continued as dean. The junior college had begun with thirty-three students; ten years later, in 1925 when the first students graduated from College of the City of Detroit, enrollment stood at eighteen hundred students.

The main reason why Mackenzie felt so strongly about establishing the junior college, and then the four-year school, was his conviction there were a great many gifted youngsters in our community who would never have the advantage of a college education unless it were possible for them to get it here in their own city, where they could live at home and at less expense than going to school in Ann Arbor or elsewhere. Mackenzie worried that a lot of wonderful talent would be lost forever if the opportunity for higher education were not made available locally. It was often said that some part of his concern for other people's youngsters sprang from the fact that

112

he never had any children of his own.

Almost every commentator I read refers not only to the man as an intellectual giant but also as a man who was sensitive, and understanding of people and their problems. He seemed to have the gentleness and tenderness that are the mark of the very strong. He died suddenly on July 16, 1926, at the age of sixty-six.

David Mackenzie had greatness. He left his mark on the first part of the 20th century in Detroit as an outstanding scholar, teacher and gentleman. God bless his memory.

A New Art Discovery

by Mark Beltaire

Mark Beltaire

The hour was late and Lester Gruber, who bubbles with ideas as much as with appreciation for fine food and wine, suddenly proposed: "I'll bet you don't know, and most people don't, that Leonard Simons was once one of the most talented cartoonists and caricaturists in Detroit."

Fine advertising man, yes. Civic worker, yes. Leader in the Jewish community, yes. But artist? The question was put and Simons answered: "If Les told you I was a great cartoonist as a youngster, tell him this bit of nostalgia is no different than many other things we think we remember about the olden days, in this case the late '20s.

"The truth is, I was a very ordinary cartoonist. In fact, some folks, including my high school art teacher, Miss Kate Conover of blessed memory, once told me that I 'was a nice

From the Mark Beltaire column, the *Detroit Free Press*, March 1967.

Author's sketch of
George Bernard Shaw

boy but if you are considering doing art work for a living, you better switch to some other field of endeavor—or *you'll starve to death!*'"

But after some prodding, Simons looked, reported: "I couldn't find any except some prints I had made from letters that were sent to my wife when I first started courting her back in 1928–29. These were just little decorative touches to my letters as part of my 'direct mail campaign.' Harriette says that my advertising campaign by mail sold me to her.

"I also found one caricature—made many years ago—of the author of *My Fair Lady*. Recognize him?" (At least, George Bernard Shaw might be termed collaborator, since Lerner and Loewe draped their musical opus around *Pygmalion*.)

Simons continues: "In high school—old Central—I was the assistant art director of the *Student* magazine. Theodore Rogvoy, now a leading local architect, was the art editor. When he graduated I became art editor of both the school magazine and our graduation annual, the *Centralite*. John Held Jr. was my favorite cartoonist and I could copy his style perfectly.

"Most of my pals went on to college. One close friend whose last name also begins with *S* went to the University of Michigan. He liked to draw also but he was worse than I was. I drew some cartoons and he sent them in with no comment to the school humor magazine, the *Gargoyle*. Several of the drawings were used which made me very happy. This was my only claim to fame in the field of art, but I couldn't tell anybody about it until now."

There was another reason why Simons gave up pen and ink. "I really wasn't very good anyhow except at caricatures.

The author's handiwork for Central High's *The Student*, April 1921

Most of the people showed their appreciation of the way I pictured them in sketches by offering to punch me in the nose. Or, they would pass judgement with comments like 'Have you looked in the mirror lately?' . . . I decided this was no way to make friends in the business world, so I quit ridiculing and exaggerating people's peculiar features. In other words, a Hy Vogel I wasn't."

Simons has kept his affinity for art to the pleasure of observing: "My wife and I travel a lot. When we get somewhere, the first places we go to are the local art museums and churches. . . . The most unusual experience I ever had was when we visited the Church of Santa Croce in Florence where Michelangelo is buried. There it was, the tomb of the great one, alongside a couple of relatives including his favorite nephew, whose name was carved in the stone: Leonardus Simonius. As I read it, my stomach did a flip. An Italian version of my name! So far, I haven't located any Italian ancestors— so my affection for art cannot be attributed to heredity."

The Urban League

The Urban League awardees. *L. to R., front row:* Harold Ledford, Mrs. Harold Bledsoe, the author; *back row:* Ben Rubens, Remus Robinson, Ray Eppert

Ladies and Gentlemen, I am very proud to be one of those honored today by the Urban League. I'm happy to say I have always tried to identify myself in some way with the good work of this organization. The Urban League's accomplishments over the years have been nothing short of miraculous.

On various occasions I've been called upon to try to help get jobs for blacks. In some cases we had good results, in oth-

Talk given at the 29th anniversary luncheon of the Urban League, Cobo Hall, November 1966.

118

ers, discouraging. But, today, the same people who formerly would not hire a black are now pleading for qualified or educated blacks.

I remember a phone call I had from Francis Kornegay back in about 1952 asking me to try to get the E&B Brewing Company to hire a black as a salesman. I contacted the brewery president and gave him Kornegay's request. He said, "Tell Francis to find someone, and we'll hire anyone he says is OK." About a month later Kornegay called me and asked how I liked Isaac Steinberg? I asked, "Who?" He said, "Isaac Steinberg, your new black salesman at E&B." (I got a big laugh out of it, too.) It so happens that he was one of the best salesmen we ever had. He's a fine citizen and the son-in-law of my dear friend, Beulah Whitby.

On second thought, a Jewish name for a Negro shouldn't be so surprising. I read in the Jewish Bible that Moses, the Father of the Jewish religion, was married to a Cushite. *Cush*, in Hebrew, means black.

I just returned from visiting Japan, Taipei, Hong Kong, and Bangkok. I now know, more than ever before, how it feels to be a member of a minority group. I had three strikes on me in each of these countries before I started, being white, American, and Jewish.

But, everywhere we went the people were very nice to us. It made me realize again how unfair it is to generalize in a derogatory manner about any group of people, because most people are good and kind. No race, no religion, has a monopoly on ethics, brains, or integrity.

On our return to Detroit we stopped off at Honolulu, and I was pleasantly surprised at the harmony among the various races that live and work together without hostility or prejudice. One of their ministers described what I saw as the "Aloha Spirit" which Hawaii offers to the world as the answer to unity and harmony. I always thought "Aloha" was merely their word of greeting. But, I learned that it means graciousness, kindness, love, and understanding.

They compare the world to the ukelele. The four strings represent the races of man: white, black, brown, yellow. The strings also represent the Christian, Jewish, Buddhist, and Moslem religions. Each string has its own importance, its own identity. They do not look or sound alike. Without all four you cannot play the ukelele. But when they are strummed, a miracle occurs. These diverse individual strings working together bring about the Aloha Spirit of unity and harmony. Our older states can learn much from our newest, the 50th state, Hawaii.

I believe that there are more idealistic, fine people in this country of ours than you'll find anywhere else in this world. It gives you a nice feeling to know that, even though the progress may seem to be relatively slow. Day by day this is getting to be a better world. Those who help the Urban League are helping to make this world that much better.

St. Cyprian's 29th Anniversary

Reverend Canon Malcolm Dade, Sr.

I'm very pleased and flattered that Rev. Canon Malcolm Dade invited me to be the toastmaster at the 29th Annual Anniversary and Appreciation Dinner of the Episcopal Church of St. Cyprian. I don't know who brainwashed Canon Dade into asking me, but when he invited me to handle this pleasant task, I suggested that he get someone else. I told him, "You don't want me; I'm not very good at this stuff. Why don't you get Mr. 'So & So.' He's a fine speaker, a scholar and a gentleman. He'd make an excellent toastmaster." And Canon Dade replied, "We don't want a fine speaker, a scholar and a gentleman; we want you."

So I accepted. But, I usually feel a little awkward when I stand before an audience. I asked my wife what I should do with my hands while I'm up here. And she said, "Why don't you try putting them over your mouth?"

Master of ceremonies introductions at the St. Cyprian Episcopal Church dinner at the Cathedral of St. Paul, honoring St. Cyprian's 29th anniversary (1938–67), 1967.

This civic affair has become very well known, and the list of the people who have been honored over the years includes a great many of our most respected citizens. I know how gratifying it must be to our honorees tonight to know that people like those who comprise the St. Cyprian congregation have noticed and approved of the things these three nice people are doing and are attempting to do for their fellow man. When others agree that the things you feel are important are important to them also, then you usually are inspired by this recognition to try even harder to be of service.

Our three honorees tonight have distinguished themselves as "Citizens of Concern." This means they are people who care about the welfare of others. These are the kind of folks that celebrate Brotherhood Week fifty-two weeks in the year.

It is my pleasure to introduce the gentleman who will be making the first presentation, Dr. Lloyd M. Cofer, principal of Mackenzie High School. He will present the St. Cyprian Award of Appreciation to Dr. Norman Drachler, superintendent of Detroit's schools. Dr. Cofer, in addition to being a distinguished scholar, is also chairman of the Board of Trustees of Central Michigan University. When we asked him for some biographical material to use in this introduction, he said, "This is sufficient." So I will respect his instructions.

(Remarks by Dr. Cofer and Response by Dr. Drachler.)
As an old friend of Norman Drachler, and I do mean old, no one knows better than I how well deserved is this tribute to him. Detroit is truly fortunate, Norman, to have you as its superintendent of schools. You are a dedicated scholar, a true liberal, and a man with the disposition and patience of Job. That's the ideal combination for a superintendent of schools in a large city. Norman, you like everybody. You once gave me some advice: "Be nice to your friends. If it were not for them, we'd all be strangers."

And now it is my pleasure to introduce to you the man who will make the presentation to John Feikens. His name is Burton I. Gordin. He has a master's degree in Social Work, and during World War II, he was a captain in the U.S. Army Signal Corps. This man has spent his lifetime trying to prevent and eliminate discrimination on the basis of race, religion or nationality. His direction of the Michigan Civil Rights Commission, of which for the past three and one-half years he has been the executive director, has received nationwide acclaim.

You might be interested in a little experience I had at my office a few years ago. I was anxious to have some Negro people working for us and couldn't seem to get someone with experience for our bookkeeping department. So, I phoned the Michigan Fair Employment Practice Commission and asked them to please try to find a Negro woman for this job opening.

Do you know what they said to me? And this is a true story. "I'm sorry, we can't take a request like that. We don't discriminate against white people."

Captain Gordin, the floor is yours.

(Remarks by Mr. Gordin and Response by John Feikens.)
I can truly say from personal experience that no man in Michigan is more deserving of this fine tribute than is John Feikens. It's an honor to be your friend, John. Congratulations and keep up the good work. You are living proof that Republicans can be just as liberal as Democrats. You are a great American.

To show you what kind of a man he is: when John Feikens goes into a delicatessen store, he always insists on the frankfurters *on the bottom,* because, as he explains, he's always for the underdog.

We come now to the distaff part of the program. We have the unusual combination of a great lady making a presentation to another great lady. In introducing Dr. Marjorie Peebles (or Meyers), I can assure you that she is a doctor in the truest meaning of the word. She is a specialist in internal medicine. She is married to Canon F. Ricksford Meyers, which gives me the opportunity to say in jest that, because she is a doctor, her family can be "well for nothing;" and because he is a minister, the family can be "good for nothing."

Dr. Meyers is a graduate of Hunter College in New York, took her master's at Columbia University, and did postgraduate work at Howard University; our own Wayne State University graduated her in medicine. She's a board member of the Urban League and the Women's Committee of the United Community Services. She's associate editor of the *Detroit Medical News* and one of the finest physicians in this area. I should also say that she is a fine "figure of speech."

It gives me great pleasure to ask this lovely lady to make the St. Cyprian Award to Mrs. Claude E. Grooms.

(Remarks by Dr. Peebles and Response by Mrs. Claude E. Grooms.)

Mrs. Grooms, may I add my congratulations to those of Dr. Peebles? As a leader in the YWCA of Detroit, you might be interested to know that I have a life membership in the YWCA. Yes, you heard me correctly: not the YMCA, the YWCA. I was elected a YWCA Key Man. I was given a little golden key, and that sounds exciting; but so far I haven't found out what door it opens. My wife says that at my age, when girls flirt with me at the movies, they're only interested in my popcorn. At the office I am called "Old September Song."

And now, Rev. Canon Dade will introduce our principal speaker of the evening, but I introduce the introducer. He is my friend and yours, too.

There is very little about Canon Dade that I can tell to this particular group. You know all about him, and you love him as much as all do who have had the good fortune to be acquainted with him and his fine work in the community.

Canon Dade knows that while it takes courage to stand up and be counted, the true test of courage is to keep standing after you've been counted. That's why he has taken the lead for almost thirty years in saluting these courageous civic and spiritual leaders of goodwill from every race and religious group in our town.

The name Canon has always fascinated me. I never quite understood it. I've heard exciting people who are go-getters described as being "a pistol," so I have come to the conclusion that a pistol is a little shot and a Canon must be a big shot.

With great admiration and the utmost respect, I call on *Canon* Malcolm Dade to introduce our principal speaker of the evening, another distinguished Detroit clergyman, the Reverend Dr. Henry Hitt Crane, minister emeritus of the Central Methodist Church.

(Remarks by Canon Malcolm Dade and Talk by Rev. Henry Hitt Crane.)

United Jewish Charities of Detroit, 60th Anniversary

Time was . . . *at* the turn of the century when our town first sensed the stirring tide which has since carried Detroit to the eminence it occupies today among the great cities of the world. In 1899, Detroit had a population of less than 300,000 and was a tree-shaded Midwestern community where many of the faces one passed on the street were familiar, where the motor man held the trolley for the man who waved to it from his doorstep half way down the block.

A compact Jewish community of less than 5,000 lived in our town. Then, as always, the less fortunate could look to their fellow Jews for help, and received it through individual donation—charity was a personal thing in 1899—or through the synagogues, charitable societies, and fraternal lodges. No Jew ever went hungry, or had to brave the rigors of winter with inadequate clothing or without shelter, or was ever untended in illness or alone in sorrow if the Jewish community knew of the need. Each charitable group worked separately, and there was competition for funds and duplication of services.

Then, in 1899, the concept of social consciousness outgrew the well-intentioned but sometimes haphazard bounty it dispensed. Organized Jewish social service came into being initiated by Rabbi Leo M. Franklin of Temple Beth El, sponsored and implemented by the leaders of our community. They envisioned the broader aspect, the greater objective, the need for an intelligent approach to a problem with many facets. It was they who first enlisted the best Jewish brains in our city to form the United Jewish Charities.

Preface of the United Jewish Charities booklet prepared for the anniversary celebration, October 1959.

Time is . . . as Detroit burgeoned and its population, including Jews, grew, the United Jewish Charities kept pace. That the founding fathers of the United Jewish Charities laid a solid foundation and built well upon it to meet existing and as well as future needs is evidenced by the fact that most of our present-day institutions had either their roots in the United Jewish Charities or were in their plans for the future. On November 9th, 1899, two days after the organizational meeting of the United Jewish Charities, an employment bureau was established. A few years later, an office was set up to find employment for new arrivals to our city (now we have the Jewish Vocational Service). As early as 1900, a free dispensary was opened, which was the modest beginning of the North End Clinic. We find in the 1901 minutes of a board meeting, a discussion on the need for a Jewish hospital. Today we have the magnificent Sinai Hospital.

In 1903, the Hannah Schloss Memorial Building on High Street (now East Vernor Highway) was opened in the heart of the then Jewish neighborhood and became the teeming center of Jewish communal activities. Today we have four Jewish Community Centers, including the splendid new one on Curtis and Meyers. Besides being the headquarters for the United Jewish Charities, the Hannah Schloss Building made available recreational facilities, a library, sewing rooms, model kitchen and dining rooms, educational and holiday programs, social evenings, classes where immigrants learn English, homemaking for girls and a manual training school for boys. It also housed countless clubs where Jewish boys and girls learned the basis of good citizenship. Later, a new wing was added, and the enlarged building was called the Jewish Institute. New facilities included a day nursery and public baths, as well as facilities for a clinic and for relief. Many of today's prominent businessmen and professional men can look back with fond memories because of their membership in some club in the Hannah Schloss Building and the Jewish Institute.

The Institute was the forerunner of the Jewish Community Center, which grew out of the merger of the Jewish Institute, the Young Men's Hebrew Association and the Young Women's Hebrew Association.

A Jewish foster home was first housed in the Hannah Schloss Building to care for children whose parents were unable to give them an adequate home, and provided casework services for parents and children who were having adjustment problems.

In 1910, the United Jewish Charities gave its first support to Jewish education, granting the Hebrew Free School permission to use its meeting rooms on Sunday mornings. And the United Jewish Charities also made an annual allocation to the House of Shelter (the United Hebrew Schools, established in 1919, and the House of Shelter subsequently became member agencies of the Jewish Welfare Federation).

With the march of time, horizons widened still further. To trace the growth and the structure of the program is in itself a history of the United Jewish Charities in our city. One of the primary functions had been service to our community; Detroit Jews, always generous as individuals to the call of the distressed and of religious and educational centers here and elsewhere, began to give thought to a unification of the city's needs with those beyond our own geographical boundaries. The need for overseas aid arose following World War I, and Detroit Jews responded generously. A plan was evolved for the creation of a comprehensive federation to meet new and existing needs, and the Jewish Welfare Federation of Detroit was born in 1926.

The emergence of the Jewish Welfare Federation marks a new era in the history of Jewish social welfare, community planning, and fund raising for a broad array of institutions and services to meet human needs in Detroit and throughout the world.

Detroit's Jewish community can point with pride to an enviable record for planned philanthropy, and to the more than generous contribution of its members who have consistently given handsomely.

Time to come . . . Detroit owes a great deal to the thinking and to the foresight of the founders of the United Jewish Charities, Detroit's first central Jewish community organization. Their original goal began with the primary virtue, the age-old *mitzvah* of *Zedakah* (commonly referred to as charity but meaning righteousness). They originally recognized the wastefulness of a multiplicity of overlapping Jewish campaigns for funds. It was they who realized that while sentiment is important as inspiration, it can, and often does, run away with reason. And it was they who inspired sociological studies of the needs. They helped channel enthusiasm so that no separate pet project thrived while others fully as vital, but less articulate in the presentation of their needs, suffered. Today, because of what the fathers of the United Jewish Charities taught us, objective appraisal is made of, and thoughtful apportionment is made to, the hundreds of organizations and the thousands of individuals deserving of aid from our Jewish community. A realistic, well-considered, well-implemented allotment of funds is pursued for local, national, and worldwide causes.

With the growing perception of the community as a truly cooperative mode of operation, the Jews of Detroit reorganized their communal activities into the Jewish Welfare Federation and, as a reminder of the pioneering work of our elders, retained in the important function of a property holding corporation the name of the United Jewish Charities.

During these sixty years in the life of our local community the United Jewish Charities and the Jewish Welfare Federation grew consistently in size and service until today we are a Jewish community of approximately 80,000. Goals have become larger as causes and needs multiplied during a generation of worldwide upheaval. We have met magnificently the challenge of the past. We are meeting most generously the challenge of the present. We can look forward to the future with the full knowledge that Detroit is a good community, has always been a good community, and will always be a good community; Detroit Jewry has never failed the vision of the fathers.

It is altogether fitting that there be a record of these achievements on the 60th anniversary of the organization of the United Jewish Charities of Detroit. In picture and narrative gathered by Irving I. Katz, executive secretary of Temple Beth El, you will find in brief retrospect the analyses of these last six decades plus a hope and a pledge for tomorrow.

Temple Beth El's 125th Anniversary

W*hen Flora Winton*, the chairperson of Temple's 125th anniversary celebration, asked me to speak, she told me I should be brief—no matter how long it takes. And you can be sure I won't talk too long because I found out that the program planning chairman has an ingenious way to keep the speeches short. The drinking water up here came from Mexico.

Tonight, we are celebrating Beth El's 125th anniversary. One hundred twenty-five years of commitment to the perpetuation of the age-old, ever-fresh, Jewish mission of social justice. One hundred twenty-five years! Think of that number this way: Our country, which will celebrate its bicentennial next year, is only seventy-five years older than Beth El.

I am honored that I was chosen to reminisce a bit at tonight's celebration. It is a coincidence, but just the other day, I found a copy of a Beth El Young People's Society program published on Student's Day January 15, 1922, fifty-three years ago. I was in the cast of a play. I also designed and painted all of the stage scenery. I remember that last part very well, because I became so engrossed in working on the scenery I forgot about time and got home around 2:00 A.M. I could not get in because I also forgot my key. So I spent the next couple of hours shivering in the cold, throwing snowballs and little pebbles at the window of my mother's room to try to awaken her. My aim was not too good, and mother was a sound sleeper. When I finally did attract her attention, around four in the morning, did I catch the dickens! So, you can understand why I will never forget my first active participation in a Temple Beth El affair.

I was seventeen years old and had joined the Young People's Society about a year before that. Even though my parents did not belong to Beth El, all my close friends did. I

Talk given at Temple Beth El, June 1975.

had been bar mitzvah at Congregation Shaarey Zedek. The Hebrew I had learned was by rote. Their services were in Hebrew except for the rabbi's sermon. Frankly, I did not understand a single word of the service. So, every Saturday morning, when my grandfather asked me to go to synagogue with him, I used to tell him that I had a "psycho-Semitic" bellyache.

The first time I really became active in Beth El's affairs was in 1943. Joe Welt was president. He wanted to pay off the mortgage. Meyer Prentis and Len Lewis were cochairmen of the campaign. My partner, Larry Michelson, and I were asked to handle the publicity and do some soliciting. We went to work.

Rabbi B. Benedict Glazer announced on Yom Kippur that the fundraising had been successful. In January 1944 we had a congregational dinner and built a little bonfire, actually burning the mortgage paper. Meyer Prentis had photographers there who took some wonderful color movies of the occasion. We still have these in Beth El's archives. I suggest we wait to show them until we are able to burn the mortgage on this building, too.

Later on in the same year, Dr. Glazer phoned me and said he wanted to come down to my office and talk to me. He told me that he wanted me to accept election to the Temple board. I became vice-president in 1952, but actually it was by default. Jay Allen's father, my good friend, Sidney Allen, was vice-president but did not want to be president. My partner, Larry, who was treasurer, could not take the presidency because of his health. I did not want it at that time either, because I was president of Franklin Hills Country Club. I did not believe that I should be president of both Franklin Hills and Temple Beth El at the same time. I worried that it would be too much for me to handle.

But, Dr. Glazer convinced me that I could do it. Because, as he explained, he would be guiding me every moment. And then, catastrophe hit Beth El. Dear Dr. Glazer died just a few months later in May 1952.

Dave Wilkus was president. He immediately appointed a rabbinical selection committee. It interviewed many candidates over a long period of time. While we were trying to decide on Rabbi Glazer's successor, our president left for a trip around the world which he had planned many months earlier.

We convinced him not to postpone his trip. So I became president *pro tem* at a time when we had no rabbi and not even an assistant rabbi.

Rabbi Glazer had selected the president of the June class of the Hebrew Union College to be his assistant after graduation. That young, newly ordained rabbi was Minard Klein. When he did come with us, he did a great job, all by himself, serving our sixteen hundred families. Minard and I are still close friends.

The congregation appointed Dr. Hertz as senior rabbi in January 1953. We had a big installation sabbath service in April with Reform leaders participating, including Rabbi Nelson Glueck, president of Hebrew Union College-Jewish Institute of Religion and Rabbi Maurice Eisendrath, president of the Union of American Hebrew Congregations.

When I became president in May 1953 I promised myself I would take care of some of Dr. Glazer's unfinished business. Before he died, Dr. Glazer had given two Friday night sermons in which he said the time had come when we should have bar mitzvahs again. So one of the very first things I did was to see that the ceremony of bar mitzvah was reinstituted at Beth El, after a lapse of about fifty years. The majority of our members wanted it, and they got it in December 1953. Now, I think just about everybody at Beth El is happy we have bar and bas mitzvah.

I had one very unusual experience in connection with bar mitzvah. One of our members said that he wanted his dog to be bar mitzvah. I said to him, "Your dog? Are you nutty? Why do you want a bar mitzvah service for your dog?" He said, "Because he is thirteen years old." I said, "I still think you are batty. You must be kidding." He said, "Well, OK, if that is the way you feel about it. But I was going to donate $10,000 to the Beth El Building Fund in honor of my dog." At which point I quickly explained, "Well for goodness sake, why didn't you tell me your dog was Jewish?"

Before Dr. Glazer died, he also had spoken on several occasions, at board level, that we should be thinking about moving one of these days further north, where our members were beginning to live. He had the vision to anticipate what was going to happen in the near future. The board was startled when he first mentioned it. No one had been thinking along those lines. But, we realized he was right.

In March 1952, twenty-three years ago, we set up a survey committee to consider facilities in the northwest area. Jack Hopp and Arthur Rice were co-chairmen. We also had a site selection committee to start looking for land. I spent many hours driving all over. We found 22.5 acres at Northwestern Highway between Nine and Ten Mile roads. At my recommendation, the congregation bought it for about $145,000 in November 1952.

Frankly, everybody in the congregation was not anxious to move. I was not so happy about the idea of moving either. That old temple of ours was something that gave me a very big thrill. It broke my heart to think of giving up our magnificent sanctuary. I explored the idea with architect Albert Kahn's office and member Stanley Fleischaker, who is an architect also, to see if it was feasible to save our beautiful main sanctuary. I suggested moving it, stone by stone to the new site. They both stated emphatically that it was not practical.

The time finally came when just about everyone agreed we could not wait any longer. We had to move. The Northwestern Highway location, which many members originally thought was too far out, was now not out far enough. The congregation sold that site for approximately $1 million dollars. All I can say is I wish I had been smart enough to have bought the land for myself. What a fantastically large gift I would have been able to give to our temple building fund!

And now we are in this exciting contemporary temple. It is amazing what you can do with a little effort, a little imagination, a little creativity, and a great deal of money. We are afflicted with the current trend in synagogue construction. We, too, have what is called the "edifice complex."

We now find ourselves with a *gelt* complex, or, in other words, in financial difficulties. Our fund raising did not work out as anticipated. I won't say things are bad, but this is the first time I have ever seen vultures circling over a synagogue roof.

The other day, President Jay Allen was so worried about the temple's mortgage that he sought solace in the Bible. He opened the good book at random and guess what was the first thing he saw? Chapter 11. If any of you don't know what Chapter 11 is, ask your husband. It isn't good.

Jay Allen, president of Temple Beth El during the Temple's 125th anniversary

Tonight I want to talk about our Beth El history and heritage. One hundred twenty-five years ago there were only fifty thousand Jews in the entire United States. Detroit had a total population of twenty-one thousand people, of which sixty were Jews. On September 22, 1850, twelve German Jews in Detroit met in one of their homes at Congress and St. Antoine. They founded the Bet El Society (the House of God Society), the first Jewish congregation in Michigan. It was orthodox in ritual and observance.

Our first rabbi was Samuel Marcus of New York, and he was paid $200 a year to be rabbi, cantor, teacher, *shocket* (chicken slaughterer), and *mohel* (circumcizer). And some members thought he was being overpaid!

They used to tell the story that when the rabbi was asked how he could live on $200 a year, he replied, "It is lucky I am a very religious man. If I did not fast three times a week, I'd starve to death."

Our first rabbi is buried alongside many members of his congregation, in Beth El's first cemetery. It was called the Champlain Street Cemetery because it was located on Champlain Street, which is now known as Lafayette Street.

Our 125-year-old history as the oldest Jewish congregation still in existence in Michigan is replete with accomplishments. The oldest Jewish fraternal organization in Michigan, Pisgah Lodge of B'nai B'rith, was founded by Beth El members in 1857.

In 1861, eleven years after we started, the use of music and a mixed choir at worship split the congregation. Seven-

133

teen members resigned to start the Shaarey Zedek congregation.

In 1862, our revised bylaws now permitted men and women to sit together, instead of women sitting separated from the men in the gallery upstairs. The ceremony of confirmation for boys and girls was instituted with bar mitzvah continuing.

Our rabbis organized the Jewish Widows Aid Society in 1863. In 1869, Beth El's Hebrew-German-English day school was discontinued, and a religious school, meeting after public school hours, was opened. Later that year, the Beth El Hebrew Relief Society, Detroit's first centralized Jewish philanthropic agency, was created, as was the Hebrew Ladies' Auxiliary Relief Society (later known as the Hebrew Ladies' Sewing Society) to assist Russian-Jewish immigrants.

In the early 1880s, the appalling Russian pogroms and riots broke out on a large scale, and Jews were being killed or expelled from towns and villages. The head of the governing body of the Russian orthodox church expressed the hope that "one-third of the Jews will convert, one-third will die and one-third will flee the country." Mass emigration of Russian Jews took place, especially to the U.S. In America, Jews were paraphrasing Paul Revere's famous words, yelling, "The Yiddish are coming! The Yiddish are coming!"

In 1898, when we had grown to 5,000 Jews out of a Detroit community of about 300,000, Dr. Leo M. Franklin became our rabbi. I wonder how many of you knew this wonderful man? Frankly, he was the reason why I became a "convert" to Reform Judaism. I liked the way he talked. I understood the services he conducted. He was Beth El's rabbi for almost fifty years, from November 1898 until August 1948, when he died.

In 1899, Rabbi Franklin initiated the first organized Jewish Social Service in Detroit. He brought together some of the leaders of our Jewish community to form the United Jewish Charities. Up until that time, the concept of taking care of Jewish social problems in the community was too big for the amount of money the community could raise. The funds it did raise were dispensed in a haphazard manner. From that beginning by Beth El's rabbi, we now have evolved into one of the best organized and most generous Jewish communities in the world.

Many of us work in philanthropy. But, how many of us

truly realize that Jewish philanthropy is only an expression of what is our religious belief. Many of us work in communal agencies. The existence of these agencies is justified because they serve our religious principles and purposes. A lifetime of giving to worthy projects, and collecting for them, has brought me much satisfaction.

I will close with a couple of stories about Beth El's 100th anniversary celebration, in May 1950, twenty-five years ago. I will never forget the big celebration we planned in the main ballroom of the Book-Cadillac Hotel. Another Simons, no relative, U.S. Federal Judge Charles Simons, was the toastmaster. My pal, Nate Shapero, was president. We had a program with speaker after speaker after speaker, about a dozen of them. Our principal speaker for the evening was to be Rabbi Solomon Freehof of Pittsburgh. Finally we arrived at the point in the evening's festivities when I began to think of that old expression "the mind can only absorb as much as the behind can endure."

It was after midnight when Dr. Freehof was introduced and invited "to give his *address*." He did just that. He said, "My address is Congregation Rodof Sholom in Pittsburgh." Then he said something like, "My plane is leaving in a few minutes. I should just say goodbye and leave but. . . ." Then he congratulated us for about three minutes and was rushed to the airport.

Irving Katz, our fabulous Temple secretary, has given me some of my happiest moments. For over thirty-five years we have worked together as friends. We collaborated on *The Beth El Story*, the 100-year history of Beth El published by the Wayne State University Press. It set a new standard for congregational history books.

I see that my time is running out, in more ways than one. I hope you enjoyed some of my memories. I am sure I express the hope of all of us, that our congregation can continue to "go from strength to strength," as the biblical expression reads, for at least another 125 years.

Temple Beth El Mortgage Burning

Benard Maas who contributed $1,000,000 to the Temple Beth El Building Fund

Y_{ou} *have just* seen the movie made at the 1944 mortgage burning. I would like to ask whether you have ever seen so many somber faces? I'll tell you a secret: in those days, in 1944, if you were caught smiling in the synagogue, your dues were raised!

Dear friends, this is a grand moment for all of us. I am happy to admit this is one of the proudest days of my life because our mortgage will be paid off. And, I am seeing the fulfillment of a promise I made thirty years ago to Rabbi B. Benedict Glazer of blessed memory.

For the past thirty years, many of us have lived with the determination that Beth El would have a new synagogue when our membership relocated itself. We were also determined it quickly should be free of debt. Thank God, our congregation has completed its sacred project tonight. I cannot begin to tell you how proud I am to be associated with so

Presented at Temple Beth El, June 1982.

many wonderful, dedicated men, women, and, yes, children too, who worked so diligently for so many years and who gave so generously to make this moment possible.

I will reminisce for just a few minutes. I hope I tell you a few things you may not have previously known.

Let us not forget it was Rabbi Glazer who was the first person who had the vision to see what was starting to happen to Beth El. At a Temple board meeting, Dr. Glazer threw a bombshell at all of us when he warned us to start making plans to move Beth El farther north. He advised us to start a new building fund and to do research as to where and when the new temple should be built. He stressed that now is the time to buy a big piece of land for future use. This was one of the greatest things Dr. Glazer did for us. This counseling was a mark of true leadership. He put us on the right track. He gave us direction. It is a pity he did not live to see how well we followed his advice.

We did establish a new building fund way back thirty years ago. In the immortal words of Ann Landers—"Let me repeat"—*thirty* years ago, 1952. In 1972, after a wait of twenty years, we were ready to start building.

In spite of our good fortune with a very low interest rate, there were many times when temple collections were so slow many of us were plenty scared. We worried so much that our frantic calls overloaded the telephone lines of Dial-A-Prayer.

Some of our members were worried that our bank might end up in the synagogue business, not deliberately, of course. Somehow the corporate name of Temple Beth El of City National Bank did not sound kosher to us.

We Jews have an ancient saying, "God will provide." At Beth El we used to say, "First God—then City National Bank." CNB did provide, and we thank them most sincerely. With our mortgage paid off, we members will now have peace of mind and sleep easy, both at home and in the synagogue.

We will always be indebted to the Bank, even though in a few moments we will no longer owe them any money. We are writing the officers and board of the CNB expressing our heartfelt thanks and appreciation for everything they have done for us. No bank could have been more cooperative than the CNB was to us.

Thirty-eight years ago, I helped burn the mortgage on

Woodward and Gladstone—I'm helping to burn the mortgage tonight—and when Beth El builds its next temple—thirty-eight years from now—*in Flint* or wherever—you can call on me again.

And now it is my great pleasure to introduce an old-time friend, Tom Leto, a senior vice-president of CNB. Tom, will you please come up and permit me to exchange our final payment check for the canceled mortgage. We want to start a little bonfire of our own.

Hebrew Union College-Jewish Institute of Religion

L. to R.: Irving "Bucky" Goldman, Rabbi Hertz, Rabbi Alfred Gottschalk, the author

I can only add my layman's viewpoint to the eloquent report and appeal you have just heard from President Alfred Gottschalk. But first, I think I speak for all of us when I thank Irving L. Goldman—"Bucky" as he is affectionately called by everyone who knows him—for hosting this luncheon honoring Rabbi Gottschalk.

I have been very close to the Hebrew Union College-

Talk given before the local Reform Jewish leaders at the Franklin Hills Country Club, September 1981.

139

Jewish Institute of Religion for a great many years. During this time I have come to know many HUC rabbis. I am completely sold on the college and its staff of excellent teachers, rabbis who train others to be rabbis. This ongoing chain of educating new groups of young Jews into the Reform rabbinate assures us that our children and grandchildren will have fine guidance in our religion and in the history of our people. It is important to all gathered here that they be informed and educated in the ways of liberal Judaism.

When I think of Hebrew Union College, I think particularly of three rabbis there, warm and dear friends of mine, who have had a great influence on my life. The first who exerted his influence on my thinking was Rabbi Nelson Glueck, the predecessor of President Gottschalk. Dr. Glueck was a world-famous archaeologist, the discoverer of the lost mines of King Solomon that are mentioned in the Bible. But Dr. Glueck was also one of our great rabbis. I've never forgotten his words to me: "A rabbi can preach a better sermon with his life than with all the words at his command."

The second great influence was Rabbi Samuel Sandmel, provost of HUC and the world's leading Jewish authority on the New Testament. He was a sweet, gentle soul whose life was wrapped up in Judaism and its earliest history, especially as it involved Christianity. This giant of a rabbi died much too young also.

The third dear friend and rabbi is, thank God, still with us. Dr. Jacob R. Marcus, the leading rabbinical historian of American Jewry, who is the head of the HUC's American Jewish Archives, is eighty-five years old, but he retains the tremendous mind and great enthusiasm of a young rabbi of fifty. I think this brilliant scholar was vaccinated against old age.

These three intellectual giants of HUC make you proud to say you are a Jew. Their astounding impact on the minds of young and old makes you want to do all you can for the school they represented, Hebrew Union College-Jewish Institute of Religion.

There are about eleven hundred Reform rabbis in the United States today, usually the leading rabbis in their communities. Almost all were trained at HUC. We have about eighteen Reform rabbis in Michigan, and HUC-ordained rabbis serve in synagogues all over the world.

The Reform Jewish Movement is highly respected. It is the largest liberal religious movement in the world, mainly because the HUC has done its job well. It has sent well-educated rabbis from the three HUC schools in this country and the one in Israel out into the world to create new Jewish leaders. All HUC students spend their first year in Israel to enable them fully to understand and appreciate Israel.

The six million Jews in America are truly blessed. We are a part of the greatest Jewry of all time. We are the most affluent and most generous people in all Jewish history, contributing over $700 million in cash and bonds a year overseas. Culturally and intellectually, we rate extremely high. Most of our children go to colleges and universities. While we are only 2.7% of the United States population, we have won 15% of the Nobel prizes. Politically, we are a powerful group. We help keep Israel alive. We are the real leaders in world Judaism, and much of the credit goes to the HUC and what it has accomplished through the leadership training inspired by our Reform rabbis.

Now I know that hardly a day goes by that people like us do not get a letter or phone call urging us to give money to this good cause or that worthy project. And they are all valuable, of course. Unfortunately, none of us can afford to give to all of them; we try to be selective. For myself, after my family needs are met, I feel that financial help for my religion is of next importance. In addition to belonging to my own synagogue, I try to help some other Reform temples by belonging to four others in Michigan so that I can try to help them with my dues. But, I never forget HUC. Each year for over forty years I have contributed because I know how important our Reform rabbinical seminary is to all of us. If the Judaism of our preference is to continue to grow and thrive, we must support HUC. It is as simple as that. Rabbi Gottschalk came from Cincinnati to make this appeal.

And talking about "appeals," have you heard about the rabbi who opened his sermon by explaining that he was about to discuss sex appeal in today's society. One elderly lady immediately arose and started to leave the synagogue. "You need not leave," the rabbi said, suspecting that he had offended her. "I will not say anything embarrassing to the young or the old."

"Oh, it isn't the sex in your sermon that bothers me," answered the lady, as she walked toward the exit, "It is just that I am sick and tired of appeals."

We all happen to live in an age of appeals. In these days of inflation, the HUC, like all schools, is having its money problems. So, it is up to us to show our faith in and support of what HUC is doing for us and for our religion. We must see that HUC is free from financial worries. Dr. Gottschalk is appealing to us and other leading Reform Jews throughout America to see that their rabbinical programs and their school operating expenses are adequately financed. Part of the expense of HUC is funded by the temple dues structure deductions, but that is not enough. We, as individuals, have to make up the difference.

And that is why we are gathered here.

Sinai Hospital: I Remember It Well

What do I remember about the beginnings of Sinai Hospital? I remember many things, only a few of which I can relate here. There are memories of many people and events, memories that begin with a telephone call almost thirty-seven years ago.

Dr. Harry C. Saltzstein was on the other end of the line that day in 1941 which marked my first personal involvement in what was to become our Jewish sponsored hospital. "Dr. Harry" wanted to come over to my home to discuss a matter of genuine importance to our Jewish community. Of course I said I would be glad to see him, he was not only a longtime friend, he was also my surgeon. When we met, he urged me to help build a Jewish hospital in our city. He told me how he had dreamed about and planned for such a hospital for many years. He was thoroughly convinced Detroit needed it.

I knew such a project had come up in general discussions many times, but I thought no one was seriously considering it. I know I was not. There were many worthy projects that took my time during those days, but helping to plan for a Jewish-sponsored hospital was not one of them. My first question to Dr. Saltzstein was direct: "Why do we need a Jewish hospital? There are many hospitals in town. Jewish people can get into hospitals when they are sick. I don't understand what you mean."

Dr. Saltzstein answered, "Leonard, you are right. *Jewish people* can get into any hospital, but *Jewish doctors* cannot! You just don't know the facts of why Detroit must have a Jewish hospital."

So I challenged him to convince me of our need. Carefully and patiently he began to explain the main reason why Detroit must have a Jewish hospital.

Reprinted from the 25th anniversary issue of the Sinai Hospital *Bulletin*, May 1978.

I do not remember, of course, our exact conversation that evening, but I well remember the gist of our talk. Dr. Saltzstein was positive that now was the time, at long last, to get the local leadership to establish a Jewish-sponsored hospital. He had come to me well prepared; after all, he had had over a quarter of a century to study and research the subject which was so close to his heart.

The main reason we needed a hospital, Dr. Harry began, was to help our Jewish physicians realize their full potential as medical men. He explained how many of our Jewish doctors could not get appointments to the staffs of our leading local hospitals, despite claims made to the contrary, because of their religion. There was discrimination. Certainly there were the few exceptions. Some of the old-timers were given staff appointments, but such could be counted on the fingers of both hands. "Can I put it any plainer than that?" Dr. Harry asked.

He explained to me how more and more of our young men were graduating from medical schools, but their practices would be limited to a great extent to house calls and office visits and, for the lucky few, to a small amount of inpatient hospital time. It seemed quite clear how much frustration our doctors would face, how fulfillment as physicians would be sorely curtailed for them. Jewish physicians in many other American cities faced the same problem. They were caught in the same pattern of discrimination. And Jewish hospitals were being established in other large cities to provide Jewish doctors with the opportunities and satisfactions they had earned through ability, many years of study, and training.

Sponsorship of a Jewish hospital in Detroit had been discussed since the turn of the century. Up to now, Dr. Saltzstein continued, local leadership had argued the idea was premature: we had too few Jewish doctors, there was not enough money available in large sums, the community had more pressing and more important projects to consider, Federation leadership was still taking the matter under advisement, the leading Jewish doctors of our city did not feel the need, etc.

Dr. Harry read me the summary of the reasoning for a Jewish hospital in the 1936–37 reports of the Maimonides Medical Society of Detroit:

We need to develop better doctors. Most Jewish patients are served by Jewish doctors. A large proportion of the 350 Jewish doctors in Detroit spend most of their efforts in caring for the Jewish sick. Most of these doctors do not have the opportunity for maximum professional development which would be provided if there were a Jewish hospital in Detroit. Jewish indigent patients do not like to go to Receiving Hospital or to Eloise. We feel that a Jewish hospital would strengthen the philanthropic impulse.

Then I was shown the survey and report of Dr. Jacob Golub of New York. This had been ordered and paid for by the Detroit Jewish Welfare Federation in 1938. Dr. Golub recommended that Detroit build its hospital, but although Federation was sympathetic, it decided the community was not ready for it at that time. Dr. Saltzstein felt that these controversial attitudes were now changing. After fifty years of debate and foot dragging, a Jewish hospital in Detroit had become an idea whose time had finally come. He believed our leaders were ready to open their minds and pocketbooks to make possible a Jewish-sponsored, nonsectarian, hospital manned primarily by a Jewish medical staff and directed by a Jewish lay leadership.

I well remember this brilliant physician and surgeon speaking with heartfelt conviction of his concern, not for himself, but for future generations of young Jewish doctors who were to take their places as healers and life savers; men and women who wanted to serve mankind in the Jewish tradition, as "Messengers of God."

I wager few of our young doctors know the story or are aware of the main reason for the creation of Sinai Hospital of Detroit. True, it was not the only reason, but it certainly was the primary, motivating, force why a Jewish-sponsored hospital was built in our city.

Finally, Dr. Saltzstein told me the exciting news given him by Max Osnos. In the will of Max's late father the sum of $100,000 was set aside for a Jewish hospital in Detroit, if we could raise enough money to build one. When the good doctor finished talking to me, I was completely convinced.

A very short time after I had sat with Dr. Saltzstein, he

and Max Osnos invited me to an initial meeting at Max's home in the summer of 1941. Only a handful of men attended. Max informed us that the Jewish Welfare Federation was now very sympathetic to the idea of having a Jewish hospital in Detroit, and they encouraged us to get a group interested and a fund-raising campaign organized.

With the Federation's approval, we made plans for a kick-off meeting with a large group of community leaders. We invited many to that meeting in July 1941 at Maurice Aronsson's home, but only about twenty came. We unanimously agreed that a city-wide campaign be started to raise money to build a Jewish hospital. Attending that first meeting—in addition to Max Osnos, Dr. Harry, Maurice Aronsson, and me—were Charlie Agree, Sidney and Harold Allen, Irving Blumberg, Nate Borin, Irwin Cohn, Abe Cooper, Alfred Epstein, William Fisher, Nate Fishman, Harry Grant, Larry Michelson, Jake Neiman, Leo Siegel, Barney Smith, and Abe Srere. Larry Michelson handled the publicity.

Although their number was small, these men generated abundant enthusiasm for getting the campaign started. Federation seemed quite pleased with our progress and suggested we combine our efforts with other groups that had made their own valiant tries to get a Jewish hospital on the drawing board. A name was suggested, and the United Jewish Hospital Committee was formed. Incidentally, from this original committee we secured our president, two vice-presidents, secretary, and five members of the hospital's first Board of Trustees in 1952, some eleven years later.

Back in those days, the most influential Jew in Detroit was Fred Butzel, and deservedly so. The leading Jewish general practitioner, who was also chief of staff at Harper Hospital, was Dr. Hugo Freund.

In a city containing between seventy and eighty-thousand Jews, it is strange but true that the approval of these two men was needed before the community would accept the idea that a Jewish hospital was necessary. Even Henry Wineman, whose family gift was by far the largest annual contribution to our Allied Jewish Campaign, would not declare himself for a Jewish hospital without first being assured that Dr. Freund and Fred Butzel were in favor of it.

Dr. Saltzstein, who lived next door to Fred Butzel, spent

many hours walking with and talking to him about the idea. Butzel remained unconvinced because Dr. Freund was not convinced. When Butzel and Freund saw that this new group was serious about going ahead with a major campaign to build a hospital, they had a change of mind and gave their approval.

I remember a meeting held in one of the small ballrooms of the old Statler Hotel. We had invited a great many people; the ballroom was crowded with about one hundred interested men and women. We told the people what had been accomplished so far by the special group of hospital supporters.

I will never forget Butzel's choice of words when he spoke to the group. He had not previously been in favor of a Jewish hospital, he confessed; he did not feel it was necessary, and so on. But, now that the Jews are "moving all over town, like cockroaches," he had changed his mind. He now believed we should have a hospital of our own. While some of us in the audience may have resented being compared to a roach, we knew the path was now clear to see how good we were in completing what we had begun. At least, we knew now that no one would be harpooning our efforts.

We were moving along with the help of a constantly increasing number of interested men and women who wanted to give money and to participate in the fund raising. But abruptly, on December 7, 1941, only four months after we had started, our plans and work came to an immediate halt. Pearl Harbor had interrupted our lives, America was at war, and all of us wanted to be totally involved.

Not until the war was coming to a close in 1944 could we start thinking again about the hospital campaign. Max Osnos once more assumed the leadership with Federation to counsel, advise, and guide us. In June, at a Federation Executive Committee meeting, Max Osnos outlined the 1941 developments that had led up to the hospital project. Our plans met with J.W.F.'s complete approval. They endorsed the idea, in principle, of a $2 million campaign for a 200-bed hospital. They even agreed to underwrite up to $40,000 a year, if the hospital had a deficit. Federation suggested that a group be incorporated as the Jewish Hospital Association.

By November of 1944, the flow of money and pledges was terrific. If the hospital could have been built at the anticipated, original cost, we would have reached our goal. But, unfortunately, prices were on the rise. Federation helped us organize the second stage of our fund-raising campaign with Sidney Allen as campaign chairman. After about a year of intensive solicitation, we finally reached about $2,300,000.

Then in 1945, we were fortunate to receive $2,500,000 as our share of the money raised in the city-wide Greater Detroit Hospital Fund campaign for the benefit of all Detroit hospitals. But $5,000,000 was not enough. We now needed an additional one million for the kind of hospital we were determined to build. So, we borrowed $1,000,000 from a bank and thought our immediate financial problems were solved. Our original schedule called for "plans completed by May 1946; hospital to open, January 1948."

An exciting architectural design for the hospital was submitted by Albert Kahn, Inc. When the bids came in, the costs were well beyond our budget. We could not afford these plans. Our only alternative was to have the architects return to their drawing boards and come up with a new set of plans for a smaller, less expensive, hospital. By the time the new plans were ready and the new bids in, inflation had brought the price for the smaller hospital back up to the cost of the larger building that had been planned originally! We wrestled with this problem and finally decided to delay no longer, we must go ahead. We broke ground on January 14, 1951, believing, as Jews always have, that "God will take care. . . ."

Those who participated in the ground-breaking ceremony are worthy of mention. The invocation was given by Abraham Hershman, rabbi emeritus of Congregation Shaarey Zedek; followed by Max Osnos, hospital president, building committee chairman Nate Shapero, William Norton, who represented the Greater Detroit Hospital Fund, president of the Jewish Welfare Federation of Detroit Sam Rubiner, Michigan governor G. Mennen Williams, and Detroit mayor, Louis Miriani.

There were problems, other than financial, which arose as soon as we started to build. Let me select just one. Some Orthodox groups insisted that Sinai serve only kosher food. Our board of trustees believed that would be a mistake because Sinai was to be a nonsectarian hospital, under our sponsorship, as a Jewish contribution to the health care of our city. Despite many meetings with Orthodox rabbis and others, we could not settle the matter. But, at least all our discussions remained amicable.

I remember the dissident group decided to hold a mass-meeting in order to stir up action on their demands for *kashrut*. They insisted the board change its mind and give up the idea of having both regular and kosher food available to patients. Placards were put on bulletin boards and in store windows, advertising the date, place, and time of their meeting. Professor Ludwig Lewisohn of Brandeis University, the famous author, was invited, for a fee of $500 to come to the meeting and speak out for kosher food. Certainly the committee was sincere in its intentions. Some of our finest citizens supported the effort, including Rabbis Morris Adler, Isaac Stollman, and Joshua Sperka, but the board was adamant in its decision.

On my own initiative, because I was (and still am) a Fellow of Brandeis University, I phoned the school and explained the local situation. I said that outside interference would not be appreciated. I expressed my opinion that Professor Lewisohn's proposed visit to Detroit for the intended purpose would cause more trouble than good. Brandeis University could be hurt, if only to the extent of the loss of the support of some of its good friends. I asked that Ludwig Lewisohn, whom I knew, be informed of my feelings. He did not come, the rally was called off, and no other took its place.

We finally reached a compromise with the advocates of kosher-only at Sinai. A *mashgiah* (supervisor) was to be employed on a permanent basis. He would oversee and inspect all the food prepared in our kosher kitchen. But, we would also serve nonkosher food from our other kitchen. I have found when I have had to be hospitalized at Sinai that the kosher food tastes much better.

You have seen a large neon sign on the top of the Outer Drive hospital building above the entrance many times. It is made of individual letters: S I N A I Hospital. The day we opened the building, we proudly turned on the sign. All the letters lit up except the A and the I. The sign boldly proclaimed: S I N Hospital. Our Orthodox friends were convinced that God was trying to tell our board members something because we were not running a "strictly kosher" hospital.

Several names were suggested for the hospital. When Fred Butzel died in 1948, it was suggested the new hospital be named The Fred M. Butzel Memorial Hospital. After much discussion, it appeared we would use the name customarily found on Jewish hospitals around the country—Mount Sinai. However, our next door neighbor was Mount Carmel Hospital. To avoid confusion, as I remember, we decided not to use the Mt. or Mount. The name was to be Sinai Hospital. Yet, twenty-five years later, many people in word and print still insist on referring to us as Mount Sinai Hospital.

We found that many of our wealthy doctors had their "gentile hospital" affiliations and felt they neither needed nor would be using Sinai. They gave token amounts. The young physicians, on the other hand, were just getting started in building a practice, and so could not afford to give much money. Furthermore, nearly all the doctors said they gave a day or two of free service each week at clinics and hospitals. The giving of their time and talents in this manner was, they felt, their way of making contributions in lieu of cash.

Those were the very early days of Blue Cross-Blue Shield. And, of course, Medicare and Medicaid did not come into the picture until July 1965. Medicine is now the highest paying profession in the world, and probably should be. I have a great personal admiration for the medical profession, whose members work hard and long hours, devotedly helping the ill. Perhaps, if I could have stood the sight of blood, I might have trained for a medical career. Those who have watched me carve a turkey or a chicken understand why my wife calls me a frustrated surgeon.

In retrospect, the necessary "shot-in-the-arm" for us to begin the fund-raising campaign, clearly was the challenge given by the will of Sam Osnos, the late father of Max Osnos. His bequest had carried the stipulation that the $100,000 designated for a Jewish hospital in Detroit would go to another specified charity if the hospital were not built. I believe that Max Osnos talked his father into making the $100,000 gift to a then nonexistent entity because Max hoped it would accomplish exactly what it actually did.

As I go over the roll call of the thirty-five members who served as the first Board of Trustees of Sinai, I sadly note twenty-five have died. Of the ten of us that remain, seven have continued to serve over the years: Charlie Agree, Louis Berry, Irwin Cohn, Max Fisher, Max Osnos, Nate Shapero, and myself. No longer serving are Nate Fishman, who lives in Florida, Ben Silberstein in California, and Sam B. Solomon of South-field.

One man stands out in my mind as the outstanding leader in the planning for the future, as well as the actual construction of Sinai: Nate S. Shapero. He did the work of many men. He "put his money where is mouth is" and gave the hospital countless thousands of dollars. He seemed to watch the placing of every brick into the walls of the hospital. He even supervised the purchasing of all the furnishings. He gave Sinai its Shapero School of Nursing, without which we would have been hard put to provide our patients with the wonderful care they get. He raised, single-handed, a young fortune in gifts of money to the hospital from his friends and acquaintances. Among our lay leaders, Nate S. Shapero stands alone. No one can approach his dedication and continuous years of service since 1944.

These reminiscences would be incomplete without mention of my good friend, Dr. Julien Priver. I have worked closely with him on Sinai matters for almost thirty years. He taught those of us who have served on the board that life is much like wearing bifocals—there are two ways of looking at most everything.

I have never seen Julien lose his poise or his temper. He has the happy faculty of being able to disagree without being disagreeable. His intelligent understanding of people, his great deftness in dealing with the various temperaments and egos of the medical staff and businessmen on his lay board, his imaginative planning for the hospital's future, his anticipation of the hospital's needs, and his watchful supervision all mark him as a man of genius. He must be given the highest praise for having guided Sinai to the degree of national excellence it enjoys today.

Henry Wineman, as chairman, and Sidney Allen, as vice-chairman of the Selection Committee, were charged with the task of finding an executive director. To Sidney we must give credit for convincing Julien, who was with Mount Sinai Hospital in New York, to come to Detroit and join us when we were about to start construction. It has been our good fortune to have had Julien with us for almost twenty-eight years. As we now celebrate Sinai's 25th anniversary, he deserves our sincerest accolades. Julien has made all of us look good.

My active involvement with Sinai, that began with that first meeting with Dr. Harry Saltzstein and continued since the doors of Sinai opened to admit the first patient, has provided me with much satisfaction and some of my fondest memories. I was privileged to act as vice-president for several years. Over the first twenty-five years, I have watched Sinai Hospital magnificently meet its challenge to serve the medical needs of all people, regardless of race and creed. I hope I can continue to be a part of its wonderful history as Sinai goes on to even greater service to our entire community in the coming years of our second quarter-century.

These are my reminiscences, not a collection of facts and statistics that are the dry bones of history. It was my privilege to give personal kudos to some of Sinai's stalwart leaders. In honoring them, we honor ourselves. I congratulate the many thousands of men and women of Sinai—physicians, volunteers, and paid employees—for their many years of unselfish service to the community. Their devotion and generosity made a shared dream into an enduring reality.

How do I remember all these details? I should confess to having a *sui generis*—unique—type of memory, one that often prompts me to quip that I have one of the great funds of *unimportant* knowledge in town.

Sinai Hospital Recognition Banquet

Thank you, Charlie Daniels, for all those nice things you said about me. I really don't deserve getting such a fine introduction, but then neither did I deserve to get bald in my early 20s either. Actually, I am really *not* bald; I simply have an exceptionally wide part.

I am looking forward with you to a wonderful evening of fun and prizes. Because I am the toastmaster, no speaker is allowed more than just a few minutes to hear himself talk, except me, of course.

I bring greetings to all of you from the officers and board of Sinai Hospital. It is my special privilege to congratulate each one of the eighty members of Sinai's selection group of five-, ten-, and fifteen-year employees who are receiving their pins tonight. We are very proud of your consistency and your dedication. We are truly grateful for your loyalty. We number you among the most important of the approximately twelve hundred men and women who earn their livelihood at Sinai. We thank you for everything you have done and are continuing to do, year after year, to help Sinai carry on its services helping those who are ill. Without you we would not be very much.

All of us have an important part to play in the total operation of our hospital, whether we administer medication, cook meals, make beds, or mend pipes; whether you are a member of the professional staff, a volunteer worker, or, for that matter, an unpaid member of the board of trustees. Most times, through our joint efforts, we can save lives. In nearly every instance it is within our means to prolong lives through care, comfort, treatment, and day to day nursing. I know that none of you hospital workers want special thanks, and that all of you get your inner satisfaction from the knowledge that we are people trying to help other people.

By all of us sticking together, we can continue to work together not only to keep Sinai among the finer hospitals in

Presented at the 10th annual recognition banquet for personnel of Sinai Hospital, Raleigh House, April 1970.

153

Greater Detroit, but also help make Sinai a better and more satisfying place for all of you to work.

I'm one of three vice-presidents of Sinai. What I've never been able to figure out is, if the United States can get along with one vice-president, why does Sinai need three?

Our first brief speaker is a man you all know, Dr. Julien Priver, so it would be ridiculous for me to say that I am going to introduce him. (*Dr. Priver speaks.*)

Next you will receive greetings on behalf of the medical staff from Dr. Harry Saltzstein.

Dr. Saltzstein is currently listed in the Sinai family as being the editor of the Sinai *Bulletin*. But I wonder how many of you know that he was our first chief of staff. I've known him for many, many years. When he was in practice, there was no finer surgeon in town. He is the author of the book published by the Wayne State University Press on the history of Sinai Hospital and the history of medicine in Detroit under Jewish auspices. It was Harry who first got a group of us interested in the idea of a Sinai Hospital in town. He fought for many years before he convinced the powers that be that we should have our hospital. If any one man can be given credit for getting this hospital started, it is Harry Saltzstein.

The man I am introducing to you is also famous for that very profound observation: "Being a doctor is the world's greatest profession. In what other business can a man tell a woman to take off all her clothes, and then send her husband a bill! (*Dr. Saltzstein speaks.*)

One of my dearest friends of long standing is Louis Tabashnik. He is a man who prides himself on maintaining the highest standards of excellence. Everything he does, he does well. He is a man of lofty ideals. He has always shown a sincere interest in the welfare of other people. That's why he was selected to be the chairman of Sinai's Personnel Practices Committee. Mr. Tabashnik also has a fine sense of humor. So, I know, he won't object to my telling you a little apocryphal story about him.

It seems that it was one of those cold wintry Detroit nights, and it was time for the Tabashniks to go to bed. When Lou got under the covers, his sweet wife, Lee, exclaimed, "God, your feet are cold!" He replied, "Dear, when we're in bed it's OK for you to call me Louie."

It is with the utmost respect I give you Mr. Louis Ta-bashnik. (*Dr. Tabashnik speaks.*)

We have just concluded the so-called formal portion of tonight's affair. I would like to again extend my personal congratulations to all of you for a job well done. Our top administrators, as well as the Board of Trustees, are always thinking about what they can do for you. We appreciate and treasure the people in our organization.

The pay envelope falls short of explaining why men and women like you perform far beyond the call of duty. We know that deep down in every human breast is the desire to be taken seriously and to be respected by his fellowman. We know that to be good at our job means a long step toward earning respect for ourselves. And we also know that recognition of the human soul is the most important kind of recognition in the world.

So again, our sincere thanks to all of our new members of Sinai's five-, ten-, and fifteen-year groups. Please keep up the good work.

But in spending the time that we do around the hospital, it isn't only sickness that we hear about. Sometimes this experience has its lighter moments, and you hear some funny tales.

In the OB department, a husband waiting to register his wife for immediate entrance to the maternity ward nervously asked her, "Darling, are you sure you want to go through with this?"

I was visiting the Shiffman Out-Patient Clinic one day when a woman was being examined. She was asked if she had ever been X-rayed, and she replied "No, but I've been ultra-violated."

Then there is the story about one of our interns who was asked to make a preliminary examination of a lovely young lady and was heard to remark, "You're my first patient; do you mind if I rummage around a bit?"

I wonder if you folks recognize the tune that Dr. Rosensweig in Psychiatry keeps whistling and humming. It's his favorite: Tschaikovksy's *Nutcracker Suite*.

At one of the board meetings, I was talking to a friend sitting next to me about a certain obstreperous fellow board member who was usually sounding off about something or other that he didn't like. My friend observed that he didn't think we could put this man in "4-South Psychiatry." But, on the other hand, if Mr. "Hard-to-get-along-with" was already there, he didn't think they'd let him out.

I finally had a chance to sample Sinai care and attention. I was a patient for a few days last week. I was given a physical. I finally found out what the true definition of the word "sadist" is. A sadist is a doctor who keeps his stethoscope in the refrigerator.

When I asked my doctor what he thought about my physical condition, he said to me, after a few moments hesitation, "Well, Leonard, let me put it this way—if you were a house, I would say you should be condemned."

I asked him what he thought my chances were to live to be a hundred. He asked me, "Do you smoke?" And I said, "No." He said, "Do you drink?" And I said, "No." Then he said, "Do you chase around with girls?" And again I said, "No." So he said, "Well then, Leonard, why do you want to live to be a hundred?"

Incidentially, the doctor said I was to come back in three months. Then he said: "I want to see three-fourths of you back here for a check-up."

Say, did you see the letter in the medical column "Ask Your Doctor" that runs in the *Free Press*? You know, the one where you write and get free advice or a booklet on your problem. This letter said, "Please send me one of your free books on personal hygiene. I'm afraid I've got it."

And with that story, I'd like to close with a great big thank-you for allowing me to express Sinai's gratitude to all of you. And may I say that in America, where we spend so many millions of dollars each year just on health alone, is it any wonder that we have so many healthy doctors?

Before we start drawing for the prizes, I wish to recognize a wonderful man who has guided our hospital's relations with its staff of over one thousand loyal men and women, the people who make our institution run smoothly, and who have helped Sinai build its enviable reputation. I will let you in on a little secret that I found out about Charlie Daniels. Charlie plays the violin. He was a member of the Wayne State University orchestra. I won't say he played the fiddle badly, but he is the only one who played on "What's My Line" and stumped the panel.

Michigan Cancer Foundation

The author with Michael Brennan, president of the Michigan Cancer Foundation, *back row:* Murray MacDonald, treasurer; Edward Tuescher, executive vice-president; William Simpson, scientific director

G*ood evening and* welcome to the 1966 Annual Dinner Meeting of the Michigan Cancer Foundation. My name is Leonard Simons, and I'm chairman of the

Master of ceremonies presentation at the 1966 Michigan Cancer Foundation annual dinner meeting, Pontchartrain Hotel, February 1966

board; in the Orient I was also known as the "Happy Buddha." I asked Dr. Brennen if we should begin the speeches now or let you continue to enjoy yourselves a bit longer.

This has been a momentous year for the Michigan Cancer Foundation, a year of many important decisions. Last spring saw the culmination of many years of dreaming and planning: the merging of our four cancer organizations, the Detroit Institute of Cancer Research, the Cancer Detection Center, the Michigan Cancer Registry, and the Michigan Cancer Foundation. We are now one fully integrated organization working under the parent name of the Michigan Cancer Foundation. We are coordinating our efforts in all directions and working together as one unit, expanding our every area of research, education, and service to cancer patients.

We have now outgrown our facilities. Since the merger of less than a year, our research program has been stepped up tremendously. We want to tell you of some of our exciting plans to increase our cancer research activities.

But research, important as it is, is only part of our cancer control program. To save lives means not only working toward the day when we will find a cure but also to work with the people whose lives may be saved through factual information and the elimination of ignorance and fear. Public education is one of our most powerful weapons.

Service to cancer patients is another vital area of concern. Perhaps we cannot save the lives of those already afflicted, but it is within our means to prolong these lives through care, comfort, and the providing of necessities for treatment and day-to-day nursing.

The board expresses its profound thanks to you volunteers for your continued service. One way to acquire a real appreciation of your volunteer service is to compare it with what is done in other countries. Two of our volunteers, Alfred Glancy, Jr., and Dr. Jean Golden, will report on their trip to Tokyo to attend the International Cancer Congress. I attended this congress also. I do not want to steal any thunder from our speakers, but I would like to tell you a few things that happened to me on this trip to the Orient and Hawaii. For example—

I found a new perfume in the Far East that's driving the Orientals crazy. It smells like American money.

I was sold a little radio for three dollars at convention headquarters, but all I could get on it was Tokyo Rose.

After looking at Japanese products, I thought of a way to save the United States millions of dollars. Instead of making H-bombs and missiles, we could give one of each to Japan. In a couple of months we'll be able to buy all we want at about 25 percent of the cost.

I had dinner in Tokyo with a Japanese rabbi. He had his collar turned backwards. I asked him why he was wearing his collar that way. "Ssssh," he answered, "I'm moonlighting."

My wife bought some clothes in Hong Kong and discovered that the backless, frontless, bottomless, topless evening gown she bought is a belt.

A Taipei merchant tried to sell me a vase that he said was two thousand years old. But he couldn't fool me; I know it is only 1966 now.

We tried the Bangkok special drink made of Hawaiian punch and carrot juice. You get drunk just as fast, but your eyesight gets better.

When I asked a man, who was dressed like a native, how to pronounce the name of our fiftieth state, he answered, "Havahyuh." So I said, "Thank you," and he replied, "You're velcome."

But now it is time for me to introduce our new president, who is also the medical and scientific director of the Michigan Cancer Foundation, Dr. Michael Brennan. He is a man who does things in a big way. How many of you can match his family of eight children?

We are fortunate that Dr. Brennan accepted our call to head the Michigan Cancer Foundation. He had been at Ford Hospital for about seventeen years and served as chief of their Oncology Division for the past twelve years. He is a professor of medicine at Wayne State University Medical School, and his record in the medical profession certainly belongs in Who's Who in Medicine. He was president in 1965 of the American Society of Clinical Oncology. He has served on the Cancer Committee of the American College of Physicians, is a delegate of the American Association for Cancer Research to the National Council, National Society for Medical Research, and is the chairman of the Cancer Committee and the Cancer Coordinating Committee of the Michigan State Medical Society.

He belongs to several honor societies and, for a change of pace, is a former member of the Laborer and Hod Carriers Union. He is also a good Irishman. Mike says the Irish always fight among themselves in order to be sure to have worthy adversaries.

We are to hear Dr. Brennan's report, which I understand he has titled, "How to Give Mouth-to-Mouth Resusitation without Getting Emotionally Involved." But he will also tell us what impressive plans the MCF has for the future.

(Dr. Brennan speaks.)

I also have the pleasure to introduce the man responsible for the success of our annual House-to-House Educational Crusade. This year we were fortunate in attracting the interest and cooperation of a man whom I like to designate as one of Detroit's most useful citizens: Mr. W. Calvin Patterson, vice-president in charge of public relations, the Michigan Bell Telephone Company.

I have known and worked with Cal Patterson for over twenty-five years in behalf of worthy civic causes. He's a man who gets things done. He is president of Grace Hospital, past president of the Detroit Area Council of the Boy Scouts of America, past president of the United Community Services of Detroit and of the Detroit Convention Bureau, a board member of the Cranbrook School, of the Detroit Grand Opera Association, of the Detroit Day School for the Deaf, and of the Michigan Colleges Foundation. And those are just a few of his extracurricular activities.

(Cal Patterson speaks.)

Cancer strikes—not in the streets, factories, churches, schools, or clubs—but in the home. That is where the pain, frustration, and economic distress are felt. And so it is in the home where we feel we must come to grips with the disease. The report of the 1966 house-to-house crusade under Cal Patterson is encouraging. It would not have been so without the inspiration and incentive offered by our crusade chairman. On behalf of the MCF, its volunteers, and the innumerable persons of southeastern Michigan whose lives were touched by the efforts and results of our last crusade, I take great pleasure in presenting to you, Cal, these two tokens of our appreciation, one for you and the other for your associate at Michigan Bell, Don Gillard.

Another honor I have tonight is to introduce a fellow traveler to the Ninth International Cancer Congress. Alfred Glancy, Jr., the nationally famous real estate developer and railroad engineer, has agreed to tell us about some of his impressions of our trip. A moment ago, the photographer came and asked if he should take some pictures of Al while he is making his report; or should he shoot him before he starts? I told him that that was a very provocative question.

Alfred Glancy is "Mister Michigan Cancer Foundation." While there may be some of us who go back further in years of service, no volunteer has given more of himself, more of his time and money, more of his wife's time and ideas, than Al. He is a fabulous guy.

When this dinner comes to an end, we will have closed a good year and have begun an even better one.

(Al Glancy speaks.)

Simons Says at the Michigan Cancer Foundation Dinner

Brock Brush, president of the Michigan Cancer Foundaton, and the author

*T*hank you, Dr. Brennan, for presenting me with this citation from the Michigan Cancer Foundation. I don't deserve this memento, but then again I have alopecia areata and I don't deserve that either.

My service to the Foundation goes back to about 1945 when John J. "Cap" O'Brien asked me to be the fund-raising chairman of a campaign to secure enough money to buy the

Talk presented as retiring board chairman, Michigan Cancer Foundation annual dinner meeting, Book-Cadillac Hotel, December 1967.

grocery store and the garage at the corner of John R and Hancock. We wanted to transform it into a cancer-fighting building which would include service and research facilities. I insisted that he be chairman and I would be his cochairman. I did most of the panhandling, and we raised about a quarter of a million dollars, enough to buy the first building for our headquarters.

I have served on so many fund-raising campaigns that my friends no longer just say "Hello"; they greet me with, "Hello, Leonard, what are you collecting for today?" I have had many unusual experiences in the process. One of my favorites is the story of "Chocolate Pie." My prospect was a person rich but difficult from whom to get money. I had used all my skill as a fund-raiser, but to no avail. Finally I asked him why he didn't want to give to the cause that I had been sure would touch his heart and pocketbook. "I don't want to give you anything because of chocolate pie," he responded. Surprised, I asked, "What has chocolate pie got to do with charity?" "When you don't want to give money," he explained, "one excuse is as good as another."

Now I know that we are all volunteers for the Foundation, and that none of us wants special thanks for our continuing service. We get our inner satisfaction in the realization that we are helping other people, which is the way God meant us to live our lives.

Educational materials we create here are being used all over the world. Recently I was in Israel and visited with Dov Ben Meier, the head of the Israel Cancer Association. He said our film *Why You Should Stop Smoking* was the greatest they had ever seen, and they wanted extra prints because they are having so many demands for showings of the film.

Dov Ben Meier also told me that "the trouble is that you always need a cigarette to give you the courage to stop smoking."

He told me that they are working on a new male hormone that's good for what fails you. But I responded that criticizing a man's virility is hitting below the belt.

(Incidentally, when you see the initials TV in Israel, it doesn't mean "television"; it means "Tourists Velcome."

And one store had a sign in its window that read "We honor Visa, Diner's Club, Carte Blanche, American Express, and Money.")

Between my extracurricular activities and traveling, I don't spend as much time at our office as I used to. Recently, a piece of equipment at our company needed repair. The repairman came to the reception room just as my partner, Larry Michelson, was going out to lunch. The repairman asked him if there was something in the office that wasn't working. "Yes," answered Michelson, "my partner Simons." Well, that is pretty much true, but I want to tell you how I feel about the man who isolates himself from the community.

That man is selfish, an outcast of his own making. His penalty comes both during his own lifetime and afterwards. Alive, he knows none of the joy of achievement, the sense of identification with a cause beyond himself and which will live after he is gone, be it an organization like our own Michigan Cancer Foundation, a hospital, a school, a church, or an agency involved in the fight for justice and cultural progress. Life must mean much more than merely existing or it is worthless. We would all agree that life must have some meaning, a measure of satisfaction, if it is to be worth having.

I believe that we all have before us opportunities to help in the growth and perfection of our work in cancer control, better than we ever had before. We are anxious to serve our city in combating this terrible disease by having a cancer control program that will reflect favorably not only on ourselves but also on the entire community. We can look forward with hope, and I thank the board for the opportunity I have had to serve as its chairman for two years. I am grateful for the tremendous help given me by you, my fellow volunteers, by the executive committee, by the members of the staff, and particularly by our president Dr. Michael Brennan.

And that is what "Simons says." I take the things I do seriously, but I do not take myself seriously.

The Joy of Collecting Jewish Books

Larry Michelson and the author

Thank you, Rabbi Hertz, that was quite an introduction. But I must say that if you of the congregation believed that introduction, you would not be sitting: you would be kneeling.

I was invited to tell you about the important part books have played in my life, how and why I have spent so many years collecting books, especially Judaica. I call my hobby "The Joy of Collecting *Jewish* Books."

From talk given on Library Sabbath, Temple Beth El, December 1976.

Yes, I collect books. But, I do not keep them. I collect for a purpose. I read as many as I can, and then give them away so that a great many other people can have the pleasure of reading them. My homes have been libraries with living rooms attached.

I love books; I always have. When I was a youngster, I hung around the public library for the mental nourishment, knowledge and inspiration which have served me throughout my life. My appetite for reading is so great that I have the reputation of having the greatest fund of unimportant knowledge in town.

For example, do you know that there are about seventy thousand libraries in the United States, counting public libraries, school libraries, synagogue and church libraries, etc. . . . and, on the shelves of all these libraries there are more than 200 million books? Is that not important information to have at one's fingertips? Or, do you know that today, December 10, is National Human Rights Day? How, indeed, did we ever get along without such knowledge?

But, to be serious. I believe that everyone should have a good, basic library in his home, and especially a good library of books pertaining to his faith. For, with that home source, people can achieve a deeper understanding of their own faith; it provides, when needed, the answers about their religion.

My collection at home includes the Catholic and Protestant Bibles. I believe it is important to know our neighbors a little better, just as we hope they will learn more about us and our Judaism. This type of reading is called the study of comparative religion. Knowledge shared about the many different faiths may some day make it possible for all people to learn to live together in peace and with mutual understanding. And that is what the ultimate goal has to be. Don't you agree?

Reading Jewish books in particular has always been one of my great interests in life. It began when I was studying for my bar mitzvah. I will always remember the inscription my mother placed in the *Chumesh*, the Torah portion of the Jewish Bible, which she gave me on that great day. Inside the cover of the book was written "For Leonard. With the compliments of the author."

Our religion began with the written word. Our Bible tells us that the commandments were engraved by God Himself on tablets of stone. Throughout history we Jews have lived with our books, our Bible. When we are spoken of, we are called the People of the Book—*am hasefer*. Actually, Mohammed said that, not only of the Jews but of the Christians as well. He meant the Jews and the Christians are the Bible people, the people who gave the Jewish Bible and the New Testament to the world.

Our Torah, the five Books of Moses, gave us a permanent stature by having us emerge as the teachers of religion for all mankind. The result has been a spiritual activity that has influenced western civilization to this day.

I enjoy reading the history of our people. I believe that second only to our faith in God and His divine moral and ethical commandments is our Jewish history. Yes, our history has been the greatest factor in holding us together as a people, in keeping Judaism a vibrant, a vital, religion that reaches the hearts and minds of over fourteen million Jews in every corner of the world.

I read every chance I have. In fact, I usually read four or five books at the same time. I skip from one type of book to another, depending on the mood I am in at the moment. I rarely read the current best-sellers. But I always find the time to read books on Jewish subjects. When I come across an interesting article or paragraph, I write it down to help me remember it.

For example, Dr. Jacob Marcus, head of the American Jewish Archives, mentions these tidbits regarding Jewish books in America:

> The first book published in North America was the Bay psalm book in 1640. The actual title was *The Whole Booke of Psalms Faithfully Translated into English Metre*. It was a translation of the Hebrew psalm book.
>
> The first Hebrew book published in America was a Hebrew grammar by Judah Monis, a professor of Hebrew at Harvard College.
>
> David Franks, one of the richest Jews in America at the time of the Revolution, had such an extensive library that when the family decided to sell his collection of books, they first had to publish a catalog describing the library. His was the first large library owned by a Jew in America.
>
> The first public Jewish library in the United States was

called the Maimonides Library. The B'nai B'rith established it in New York City in 1850.

My own collection of Judaica, covering many years, and numbering over four thousand volumes, was my pride and joy. But, when we moved from our home to an apartment, it became a question of either me or the books. There was not enough space for both of us. Reluctantly, I gave most of the collection to the Brandeis University Library and cried as if I had lost some of my best friends.

However, I still have a very good collection which includes three different sets of Jewish encyclopedias and perhaps a dozen Bibles, including the Septuagint version. This book was translated into Greek from Hebrew and Aramaic by seventy scholars; that's where it got its name, the Septuagint. It is the oldest written translation of our Bible, dating back to 300 B.C. I have several Jewish Publication Society of America books of the Holy Scriptures.

For many years I served on the board of the Jewish Publication Society of America. I am proud to recall that I planned their national fund-raising program which secured sufficient money to publish their latest translation of the Torah. I am sure you can understand why I was thrilled to be a part of that Bible project.

We Jews are urged to read good books about our history and our culture. I assure you that if you read Cecil Roth's *The Jewish Contribution to Civilization* you will have a new pride in being a Jew. Every time you see your Jewish image in a mirror, you will tip your hat to yourself.

I knew Cecil Roth. My wife and I visited him in Oxford, England, and he came to our home when he spoke in Detroit. I had every book by this prolific writer. He was a magnificent Jewish historian; one of the greatest of all time. I have been fortunate to become acquainted with many such authors through my interest in collecting books. These lovely friendships were an added benefit I had not anticipated.

I may be what you would call a book *mashooganer* (a book lunatic) because books have been such an important part of my life. But, that is better than being called a bookie, isn't it?

I not only love to read and collect Jewish books, but I also love to preserve the old books which are very rare. Rabbi

Solomon Freehof wrote, "When Jewish books were first being printed, they were never published in large editions. Traditionally, Jews have had the troublesome combination of intelligence and poverty. And due to our poverty, our books were published in very small editions and in out-of-the-way places. The Jewish owners of these books wandered over the world, suffered successive expulsions, and often only two or three copies of Jewish books of a few centuries ago remain in existence. Sometimes there is only one book left. Such a book is called a 'unicum'." Although very, very few such unica are left in the world today, you can see examples at the Yeshiva University, the Jewish Theological Seminary, and the Hebrew Union College–Jewish Institute of Religion libraries.

To build a special literary collection—bringing together something that never existed hithertofore—is properly called creativity. In my small way I try to be creative in the collecting of my books. Such is my interpretation of a *hiddur mitzvah*, my attempt to consecrate or preserve in holiness and beauty the words of Judaism and our Jewish history.

I have all my Judaica books rebound in beautiful "old-world" leather bindings with handsome designs stamped in gold on the spines. Several binders in England do my work. They have complete freedom to use the designs and colors they think most appropriate, with one leather reservation. You have probably guessed what that reservation is: no pigskin.

They take these old books, some of which date back almost four hundred years, and trim the edges, repair the pages, rebind them internally, and then put them in their handsome leather bindings.

These books are collected primarily for their content, voices from the distant past that speak mind-to-mind, heart-to-heart. But now their thoughts are framed in magnificent bindings. New life is breathed into these old treasures that often were about to be destroyed or lost forever. With this loving care, these books will now last at least another one hundred years. I will have left a small, my personal, legacy to future generations of Jews to enjoy.

Beauty is a pleasure for most people, and I am no different. There is always room for a little more beauty in this old world of ours. I like to see lovely women beautifully dressed, precious gems deserve exquisite mountings, handsome homes deserve beautiful settings. In the same way, I feel that fine literary works should have beautiful bindings. In addition, I feel that old Jewish books should be honored and loved, and so I respect my old, old books.

That collection of Judaica I gave Brandeis University is different from the collection I am giving the Temple Beth El Prentis Library. The Brandeis books were published in the twentieth century, while the Temple Beth El books were published prior to 1900. The oldest book in the collection is dated 1600—*376 years ago*—and all the books are completely or partially in English.

The special bookcases our office has contributed to Beth El's library will accommodate one thousand books. I have about one hundred more books still to come in from the binderies: these will probably be the last of my efforts in rebinding. I know that I shall continue to collect books as long as I live, but now it shall be just a few for my personal library. I cannot easily give up one of my greatest satisfactions in life.

And the giving of fine books is as great a pleasure as the collecting. On my fiftieth birthday I gave Wayne State University Library a collection of over two thousand books, maps, atlases, and gazeteers, all pertaining to Detroit and Michigan history. I had this collection rebound in the same manner, fine leather bindings with gold designs stamped on the spines. The university faculty have often told me how much they enjoy this unique collection, housed in a special reading room in the library of the university (now called "The Leonard N. Simons Room").

It is a well-known fact that even the most technical-minded librarian is not above feeling delight in owning a unique collection and in being able to say about this particular collection that "our library now has something no one else has." For that is what can be said of the collections given by my partner Larry Michelson and myself to Brandeis University, Wayne State University and Temple Beth El: something no one else has.

My interest in books has also taken me into the field of publishing. For more than twenty years I have served the Wayne State University Press as a member of its Board of Advisors. Among the many important books we have published, one is particularly close to my heart. It is *The Beth El Story*, the history of the first one hundred years of our own synagogue. It was published during the year I served as president of Temple. A copy was sent to every member of the congregation. Irving Katz was the author, and it was given a national award as one of the best books published that year.

I am told my last name, Simons, derives from the word *Shema*, to hear or pay heed. The most important statement in Judaism begins with *Shema*—Hear." First and foremost we Jews are commanded to hearken to the call of God. We have caught the call of God in the written word. We identify learning with worship of God, for learning is as important as prayer.

If you do not already have one, have I encouraged you to begin a good collection of Jewish books in your home? I can promise you happiness, personal satisfaction, and fulfillment, such as I have had in collecting and reading books of Jewish content.

We Jews have always been the "People of the Book." If you need tangible proof of that assertion, note that 20 percent of the Nobel Prize winners in the sciences are Jews who live here in America, although we are less than 3 percent of the total population. You may draw from that fact the conclusion that if you read Jewish books, collect them, study them, and patronize the Temple Beth El Prentis library, you may hope to become a Nobel Prize winner, *Ala veye*!

I hope you will not consider me irreverent if I mention that one statement in the Bible confuses me. We read in Genesis that God said, "I will make man in My image, after My likeness." Each time I look in the mirror, I find it increasingly hard to accept that fact. I simply cannot see God as short, fat, bald, and wearing bifocals!

On that profound observation, I conclude by thanking you for listening to me.

To the Board of Advisers of Wayne State University Press

*A*s *I look* back on the little more than three years of our existence, I cannot help but feel pleased and proud of the part all of us who are lay people have played in the progress of the Wayne State University Press.

You have heard from the financial report that the Publication Subsidy Fund has almost reached its original goal of $50,000, and I am also pleased to report that as of the moment we have sixty-four members on the Board of Advisers, of which sixty are paid up. The four that have not paid as yet phoned to say that they wanted to continue on the Board and would send in their checks in the next few days.

I know under our newly elected leadership we can increase this to seventy-five members in the coming year without much effort.

Wayne State University has three major functions which are named in the following order of importance: 1) instruction, 2) research, and 3) public service. In a publication issued by the University, which I believe all of us received about a month ago, the title of which is *The Cutting Edge of Learning*, we read that the University believes that research is the function most in need of being strengthened. The report goes on to say that it's in the public interest that research findings be published promptly. Until a study is communicated, the work has not been carried out to completion. A most important avenue of publication is, of course, the University Press.

Research is viewed as covering all investigative activities carried on at a mature level, including inquiries in the sciences, studies in the professions and creative work in the arts, in sum total *any scholarly effort to advance knowledge, increase skills, and improve understanding.*

Report given to the Board of Advisers, December 1958, upon retiring as the first president of the Board.

You will be pleased to know that the Board of Governors of Wayne State University feels that our University Press is helping the University accomplish its goal in research and has complimented Dr. Basilius, our staff, and editorial board on the quality of publications which the Press is producing. These, in the minds of the board, are in their words, "projecting the reputation of the University."

To refresh your memory, I wish to remind you that when the Board of Advisers came into the picture, the Press in the fiscal year 1955–56 produced a total of six publications, of which two were hard cover, one soft cover, and three journals. The following year we produced fourteen publications. The third year sixteen, this year twenty-six, and our plans call for an output of approximately thirty units a year. So you can see, we are moving along in doing what the University said they would be able to do if it could find some financial support in the form of a Publication Subsidy Fund.

Books are becoming more and more important in the lives of all Americans. There's a hunger for learning and reading in spite of the competition of television, etc.

I recently read that in 1954 there were 587 million books sold in the United States of all types. The latest figures available for 1957 showed 657 million books sold. That's almost four books per year for every man, woman, and child in the United States. During this same period, libraries increased their circulation about 33 percent.

I can't make any comments on a breakdown on the type of books that are being read by the public except to say that in our own little way we know that what we are doing at the University Press level is something very worthwhile for the overall good of our country, and that, I am sure, is very important to all of us.

I also recently read in one of our leading national magazines of a comparison between the United States and Russia as applied to libraries and books, and I think these figures are worthy of a little discussion.

We have 25,000 public, school, and university libraries in the United States. Russia has 392,000 libraries.

The University of Moscow has eight million volumes in their library. Leningrad has six million in theirs. There are not over a handful of libraries in the United States with one million volumes. At Wayne State University, we have 630,000 volumes.

In 1956 Russia issued 55,000 new titles compared to 12,500 in the United States. But our variety is greater. Sixty percent of Russia's books were in the exact, natural, and applied sciences. These facts, if they are facts, prove the need for some action in our country if we want to continue to be the world's greatest power for good.

So much for that. I don't want to bore you with statistics, but I think that you will derive some satisfaction in knowing that of the 230 universities in America, there are only forty-two accredited university presses, of which the Wayne State University Press is one. We received our accreditation from the Association of American University Presses in May of 1957. The University could not have secured this without the financial support or the help of our Board of Advisers. You made it possible for our University Press to publish the calibre of books that we are now able to produce.

While we are not asking individuals to spend much time on Press activities, those of us who have been able to contribute something of our thinking and time, when called upon to do so, have been of invaluable service to the University Press . . . if I am to believe what I have been told by Dr. Hilberry, Dr. Purdy, Dr. Basilius, and many others of the University top echelon.

In closing, I want to thank all of you for your financial and moral support in helping me as your president serve our great University. In case you don't know, Wayne State University has over twenty thousand students and this includes, of course, both the undergraduate and graduate students. We also have approximately eleven hundred regular faculty members.

Wayne, for your information, is the thirteenth largest University in America in total number of students. It is a far cry from the small school that I first knew it to be when it was started as the Junior College of Detroit. And, as Al Jolson used to say, "Folks, you ain't seen nothing yet." Each year, more and more needed facilities are being built and expanded on the campus. One of these days, I hope we will all see the erection of a Press building on the campus similar to what they have at other leading universities. I would like to recommend to the incoming president that a committee be formed to explore with the University the possibility of having such a facility on the campus. If so, request they reserve a site for us and tell us how far we must go and how far the University is willing to go in contributing to the cost of such a building.

On *The Oppermanns*

Lion Feuchtwanger

Saturday evening, May 21, and again on May 28, at nine o'clock on Channel 56, our popular local public service TV station will televise a program of great interest to our Jewish community, as well as to the world at large. It is a two-part TV film; each segment two hours long. The film is *The Oppermanns*, based on Lion Feuchtwanger's book.

Many of us will recognize and remember this title because it is the same as that of the famous book written fifty years ago in 1933 by that great German-Jewish author and historical novelist Lion Feuchtwanger. Thomas Mann once said of him, "Lion Feuchtwanger, never a name more unpronounceable, yet never one more renowned in the literary world."

The film *The Oppermanns* is unique because for the first time in TV history the same program is being shown all over the world at practically the same time. The event is reported

Reprinted from an article in the *Detroit Jewish News*, May 1983.

176

as a sensation, especially in Germany and in England, but most of all in Israel. *The Oppermanns* happens to be the first TV film made in Germany to be shown in Israel.

Lion Feuchtwanger was one of the earliest German authors to recognize that Hitler was dangerous. He became a dedicated and effective anti-Nazi propagandist. He ridiculed Hitler in his speeches and in his books going back to 1930, when he attacked Hitler openly through his novel *Success*. He wrote *The Oppermanns* in 1933, while in exile in France, in reaction to Hitler's rise to power that year as *Reichkanzler*.

Feuchtwanger was proud to report that "for years, Hitler and the Nazis have been calling me their *Enemy Number One.* . . ."

The film, *The Oppermanns*, brings to the screen a vivid picture of life early in the Third Reich under the madman Adolph Hitler. It describes the downfall of an eminent German-Jewish family of Berlin at the beginning of the Nazi persecutions. It details the brutal pressures of the Gestapo on its victims; it portrays a fictional yet realistic representation of how the Nazi terror infiltrated all domains of the life of the Jews in Germany and especially how it affected every member of the Oppermann clan.

The book was one of the most widely read novels of the early thirties. It had tremendous sales throughout Europe and many other parts of the world. It appears that the TV film will have an even greater audience.

History tells us that in 1932 Prime Minister MacDonald of England requested Lion Feuchtwanger to prepare the scenario for an anti-Nazi feature film. Feuchtwanger accepted the assignment and did a screenplay in two months called *"Die Geschwister Oppermann"* (The Brothers and Sisters Oppermann), but by then His Majesty's Government had resolved on a policy of accommodation with Herr Hitler, culminating in appeasement. The film was never made in England.

In 1933, Feuchtwanger converted his dramatic effort into a novel which a Dutch firm published. When the book hit Germany, an important Nazi whose name was Oppermann contacted Feuchtwanger and threatened him. He said that unless Feuchtwanger changed the title of the book, Feuchtwanger's brother would be thrown in a concentration camp. Because of that Nazi, the title was changed to *Die Geschwister Oppenheim* instead of *Oppermann*. However, the American and British editions of 1934 remained *The Oppermanns*.

Luckily, during 1932, Feuchtwanger with his wife Marta had left Germany for an extended speaking trip in America. When Hitler came into power, the Feuchtwangers never returned to Germany. The Nazis took over their home and burned his very large and valuable library. Feuchtwanger spent the rest of his life in exile in various countries including France and the United States.

The Feuchtwangers were captured in France when the Germans took over France. They were thrown into separate concentration camps, in Marseilles, which were under Nazi-Vichy control. Mrs. Feuchtwanger made her escape. Because of her friendship with the U.S. consul in Marseilles and with the backing of President Franklin D. Roosevelt and Mrs. Roosevelt, Lion Feuchtwanger was issued an emergency visa under the name J. L. Wetcheek, which Feuchtwanger had used as his pen name on various occasions in his early days. Feuchtwanger, translated into English, is "wet cheek." In 1940, he was smuggled out of his concentration camp. Husband and wife went over the Pyrenees to Spain and Portugal. They had many cloak and dagger experiences, but eventually got to the United States and California.

Feuchtwanger liked to say he was a German novelist whose "heartbeat was Jewish and whose mind was cosmopolitan." He wrote sixteen novels and ten plays about French, Spanish, British, American history and Jewish history. His books were translated into thirty-three languages.

In 1963, the Wayne State University Press found that Feuchtwanger had been writing a scholarly textbook for schools about historical novels, but he died before he finished his manuscript. However, Dr. Hal Basilius, the Press director, flew out to Los Angeles, met the widow, and was given permission to publish the book which is called, *The House of Desdemona*. It is a popular book in the classroom. Unfortunately, the second half of the book was never completed, but there was enough in the unfinished manuscript to make its publication very worthwhile.

Feuchtwanger's widow, Marta, who recently celebrated her 92nd birthday, is still very much alive, with full command of all her faculties. She lives in their home, a Spanish-style mansion in Pacific Palisades, California, overlooking the ocean. She gave the twenty-room mansion and the famous Feuchtwanger library, which is valued at over $3 million, to the University of Southern California in 1959, a year after her husband's death. Five years later she willed the remainder of her estate, over $1 million, to the University of Southern California to build a Feuchtwanger Memorial Library on the campus. It is a fantastic library with over thirty-five thousand volumes, including thousands of priceless first editions from the fifteenth through the twentieth century. There are complete first editions of many of the most famous authors in the world, as well as fourteen incunabula (books that were printed before 1500), including a priceless Nuremberg Chronicle (dated 1493) said to be a source for the first book written about Faust.

Mrs. Feuchtwanger dresses almost exclusively in simple black Chinese attire. She lives in the mansion with her two-hundred-year-old turtle. She is still vigorous and athletic, swims in the ocean daily, climbs the mountains near her home, and is the curator of the Feuchtwanger Collection. She recently completed a two thousand-page transcribed version of her oral history, the story of her life with Lion Feuchtwanger.

Lion Feuchtwanger was the greatest, most influential historical novelist of the twentieth century.

Incidentally, this is the 25th anniversary of Lion Feuchtwanger's death. He died of cancer in Pacific Palisades, California, in 1958 at the age of seventy-four.

To Marta Feuchtwanger on Her 85th Birthday

Mrs. Lion (Marta) Feuchtwanger

January 21, 1975

Dear Marta,

*A*ccording to the Paris Gazette, the *Los Angeles Times*, the *Detroit News*, etc., *This is the Hour* when congratulations are in order because of your *Proud Destiny* in reaching the wonderful age of eighty-five years young. Harriette and I send our love and best wishes to you for many, many more years of good health and happiness.

To reach this milestone is a type of *Success* not given by the good Lord to many people. It certainly did not happen to *Raquel*, to *Simone* or *Josephus*. As you also know, *Jephta and his Daughter* didn't make it; neither did any of *The Oppermanns*. You reached four score and five and with your *Pep* and *Power* there's no reason why you shouldn't reach the proverbial,

A letter written to Mrs. Feuchtwanger on her birthday.

biblical, age of a hundred and twenty in continued good health and with *mazel*.

I won't play *The Pretender*. You know I have a great admiration for you. In fact, you are one of the most interesting and most wonderful ladies I have ever had the pleasure of knowing. And I have met a tremendous number of ladies and men in my travels around the world.

In your *Conversations with a Wandering Jew*—me—did I ever tell you *Stories from Far and Near* about some of my trips? For instance, the first time I went to Italy, my family called me *The Jew in Rome* because they knew of my great interest in your husband's books. I never knew where to look for *The House of Desdemona* in Italy, or I would have. When I was in England, I saw *Two Anglo-Saxon Plays*. There were scenes that reminded me of portions of Lion Feuchtwanger's *The Ugly Duchess* and *Odysseus and the Swine*, but then many authors tried to emulate his style.

When we were in *Moscow* we saw *Three Plays*, but none that I enjoyed more than the *Wetcheek* favorites: *The Widow Capet* and *The Devil in Boston*, and that's the truth.

So, while it has been said, *'Tis Folly to be Wise*, you know that if a person isn't wise, it can mean *Double, Double Toil and Trouble*. In your wisdom, you have made the most of your unusual life's experiences. You have tasted more thrills, excitement, honors, happiness, sorrows—almost the entire gamut of emotions—than any person with whom I am acquainted. Yet, in spite of everything, you do have so much for which to be thankful. Few people in this crazy world of ours have so many happy memories to treasure in their golden years as you do. These must give you much satisfaction.

It has been a pleasure for me to have known you for these many years, and to count you as a friend. Harriette and I wish you, dear lady, all that is good on your 85th birthday (which is also our 46th wedding anniversary), and, *B'ezrat Ha Shame*—with the help of God—many more wonderful years.

As Ever,
Leonard

The Senior Adults Writers' Club

Thank you for inviting me to talk to the Senior Adults Writers' Club of the Jewish Community Center. I like Senior Adults because I am one myself. And, I like to write. So we have a lot in common.

The trouble with all of us is that we have *cacoethes scribendi*. Sounds like we have some kind of a disease, doesn't it? Well, maybe it is. The dictionary says it means "The itch to write, or an uncontrollable urge to write." *Cacoethes scribendi* is the worst kind of disease that should happen to us. *Ala veye*

When it comes to creative writing, I've been doing it for about sixty of my seventy-five years. My first attempts were published in our high school magazine. At various times I was the literary editor, the art editor, and the advertising manager of the magazine. Sometimes I wrote the stories, drew the pictures, and wrote the ads, and sometimes I would sweep out the office.

When I graduated from Detroit's old Central High School in 1921, I went right to work for an advertising agency. After fifty-eight years I am still working at an advertising agency. So, you might say that I've spent practically all of my life as a pencil-pusher or a writer.

I have written copy for newspapers, magazines, billboards, radio, TV, and circulars that cost our clients many, many millions of dollars. Ad writers are supposed to have a way with words. You must choose the right words to attract people's attention and interest.

You should keep your words brief, simple, and to the point to help sell the product. That is pretty good basic training for all writers because the fundamentals of writing are pretty much the same. The only exception is for writers on highly technical subjects for an audience familiar with the special language and terms.

Excerpts from a talk given before the Senior Adults Writers' Club of the Jewish Community Center, May 1980.

Excluding commercial advertising, what little writing I've done for publication has been written in the natural style that sounds like me. When people read what I write, they usually say, "Leonard, that sounds just like you talk." That is because I use plain, conversational language that people can easily understand. I know a lot of long or big words, but I don't use them when I write. I always try to use words that are familiar. I use sentences that are not too long and paragraphs that are short.

Then I start making changes. I revise. I edit. Then I correct and condense, shortening and simplifying sentences. I usually do all this three or four times before I'm satisfied.

A young man who wanted to become a novelist asked Ernest Hemingway, "How do you write a novel? Do you just make it up?" Hemingway replied, "Yes, you make it up. You make it up out of everything you've ever learned, out of everything you've ever seen, out of everything you've ever felt. And then you put it down on paper, simply, as if you are telling the story to yourself or to a child. That's how to write a novel."

It's been said that writers need and receive sizable amounts of advice from other writers. They tell this story about Nobel prize-winning author Sinclair Lewis. He was asked by a young writer how to proceed in finishing a book he had started but couldn't seem to end. Sinclair Lewis said "You must remember two things. First, convince yourself that the book will never be finished. And, second, pretend that you really don't care." He said he meant in this way you'll stop fighting your project and the ideas should start popping into your head.

Another interesting idea was submitted by a leading New York newspaper editor to a young reporter. He said that the problem of transposing ideas into type was best solved by staring at a typewriter or a piece of paper and "Start talking to it. Just talk to the typewriter or the piece of paper. You'll find that you get a lot of good answers." I've done this on a few occasions and it works!

The late Dr. Sprague Holden, who was the head of the Wayne State University Department of Journalism taught me much about writing. He once wrote, "The older I grow and the more I learn, the more I admire simplicity, directness, completeness, accuracy, and understandability." These were his rules for writing. He taught it to all his classes.

Of course, all writing begins with an idea, hopefully a good idea. Then you strive for the words and the kind of writing that expresses effectively what you are saying, what you mean.

Never use a long or unusual word that requires the addition of more words just to make clear the preceding word or sentence. After saying that, I'm going to use the word "epexegesis" because as a writer you should know it, but not use it. Epexegesis is another fun word that only one person in a million might know. The dictionary says that it means "the addition of more words to make clear the preceding word or sentence." So stay away from words like epexegesis that need explaining. Words like that only increase your fund of trivia.

Mariners' Church

March 31, 1975

Mr. Lloyd Jackson
c/o Mariners' Church
170 E. Jefferson
Detroit, Michigan

Dear Mr. Jackson,

I read with interest the article in the Sunday paper in which it was mentioned that you are writing a book on the history of Mariners' Church. I want to tell you a little story, and you can decide whether or not it has any merit for your book.

I am president of the Detroit Historical Commission, with which I have been connected for about thirty years. I was brought into the picture by my dear friend George W. Stark, who, as you may know, was buried from Mariners' Church. I was one of the pallbearers.

Many years ago I used to take my family down to Vernor's when it was at the foot of Woodward Avenue. One of the things that used to irritate me when I made this trip was to see the front of Old Mariners' Church being used for a fruit stand. I kept talking about it to George. I wondered if a group of us could get together and raise some money to get the fruit dealer out of there, and allow Mariners' Church to be a beautiful old landmark.

If my memory serves me correctly, he told me that from the very beginning there was always some kind of a store on that corner because the church needed the income. Later on, when it became known there would be some changes made at the foot of Woodward, I made the suggestion to George that we find some way to move Old Mariners' Church to a better

A letter to Mr. Lloyd Jackson of Mariners' Church.

site; for historical purposes we should put on a city-wide campaign to raise funds for this, if the church didn't have enough money. He told me the church did not have enough money to do it by themselves. George got into the matter and found it was feasible to move the church and asked me if I would like to be the chairman of the fund-raising committee.

I told him I didn't think it was right for me to take this title, because I was Jewish. They certainly had enough talent among the Episcopalians to have their own chairman. But I promised I would work with him in some capacity . . . I don't remember now just what it was.

I designed a letterhead that was used for the fund-raising program, and it's very possible one of these letterheads is in the archives at the church. If you can find one, you will see that my name is on it, and then you'll know for sure whether or not I had a title.

I know I did work on the fund-raising campaign and did raise some money. I also saw to it that some money was given from my partner, Larry Michelson and myself. . . . Perhaps under the name of Simons-Michelson Co. And, I argued very strongly that after the church was moved it should not have any "grocery store" on the corner.

I don't know if this anecdote has any value to you, but if it does after you have checked it out, you are welcome to use it in any way you wish.

Good luck and best regards,
Leonard N. Simons

An Ancient Rite and Michelangelo's David

Michelangelo's David

It all began with an article by Harnes in the *Journal of the American Medical Association*. Comment upon it was made by Dr. P. Ciaglia of Utica, N.Y., in a letter to the *Journal*. The editors captioned the letter "The 'David' of Michelangelo (or, Why The Foreskin?)." Dr. Ciaglia's letter reads:

> The article by Harnes reminded me of a visit to Florence, Italy. In this city, famous for its art treasures, the

From the *Detroit Jewish News*, January 1972.

"David" of Michelangelo towers over all of them. Although I am far from a "conoscente," this 17-foot statue of "David" filled me with awe and admiration. Nevertheless, I immediately made an observation that aroused my curiosity and I whispered it to my wife—who was immediately outraged. I had merely pointed out that "David" was not circumcised. To me this detail was of great social, political, and religious significance. Was Michelangelo so ignorant that he did not realize his error? We think not! Michelangelo was thoroughly versed in the Testaments. Did he fear the displeasure of the Church, since the statue would bear a visible sign of Judaism? The ideal of manhood would be presented as not even being a Christian. Or was it Michelangelo's own willful omission? Was it that he meant to present the idealization of man without any particular identifying feature? Dear reader, take your choice or make up your own answer or forget it!

Three versions of Michelangelo's "David" exist. A colleague, a urologist, has a small reproduction of The David in his office which he was given as a gift. He reports that his David is indeed circumcised. This was completely unexpected and most intriguing, evidently he possesses the Judeo-American version. No doubt, some outraged Zionist had felt that 400 years was enough to suffer this indignity to the House of David, and therefore had acted to correct it.

The third version of Michelangelo's "David" is strictly early American. A fig leaf placed with Puritan strategy protects the beholder.

Nothing escapes our dynamic advertising executive and able community leader, Leonard N. Simons. He not only clipped this letter but also found a follow-up on the subject in the *Travel and Leisure* magazine which published an article on the subject by Aubrey Menen. A photograph of the David statue was appended to the Menen article together with this explanatory editorial note:

Michelangelo's statue of David is in the Galleria dell' Accademia in Florence. Carved from a single block of marble between 1501 and 1504, it stands 13 feet, 5 inches high, excluding the base. Michelangelo, 29 years old at the time it was finished, made two preparatory models, which are still to be seen in the Casa Buonarroti, a house the sculptor bought for a relative. A copy of the David stands in the Piazza della

Signoria, the main square of Florence, where the original once stood until removed to the Accademia for protection against the weather. The copy was made with the use of the sculptor's 'pointing' device, a measuring machine. But the final details were, of necessity, done by hand and eye, and are much inferior in execution.

Captioned "The incredible piece of sculpture that started out as Goliath and ended up as *David*," the Menen article reads:

The contract which the Florentines had signed with the young artist has been preserved. "1501, die XVI augusti," it begins. "The Lord Overseers have chosen as sculptor the worthy master Michelangelo . . . to the end that he may make, finish, and bring to perfection the male figure known as the Giant . . . already blocked out in marble by Maestro Agostino of Florence, and badly blocked." For this work, to be done in two years, Michelangelo was to receive "six broad florins of gold in gold each month."

It was an honest contract: "gold in gold" means that they were not going to fob him off with barrels of wine and measures of corn, as some patrons did, and it was a good, if not generous payment. "Badly blocked" meant that Agostino had been given a splendid piece of marble to make the statue of a giant. He had started on the block, and botched it badly, so badly that no other sculptor but this young man was willing to put chisel to it after him.

Unfortunately, Agostino had begun with the legs. The cuts he had made set the pose of any statue that could be made from the block. In the second place, he had been commissioned to make a giant: so it was a giant's legs that had been sketched out. Michelangelo wanted to make a David. But as all the world knew, when David killed Goliath with a stone from his sling, he was a young boy. Michelangelo's revered predecessor, Donatello, had made an exquisite statue of him: slender, fragile, and adolescent, bringing out beautifully the point of the story.

Michelangelo solved the problem by ignoring it. He decided to sculpt David as a stalwart young man. If he was criticized, we may be sure it did not worry him. And no objections were raised when the David was finished. The Florentines were overjoyed. Not only had they got what was plainly a masterpiece, but they had recovered their outlay on the marble. Florentines were businessmen, and a florin saved was a florin gained. They appointed a committee of the best artists in the city to decide where the statue should be placed. The committee chose a perfect site in the principal piazza, where the great pillar of white marble was set off against the warm brick of the communal palace. In the 19th century, it was moved from there to protect it from the weather, so now we must see it in a sort of Victorian glass conservatory. Even that does not destroy its astonishing beauty.

All the same, it remains that David was a boy when he killed Goliath, not a man. One day after looking at the statue, I returned to my hotel. Opening a drawer, I found a Bible inside. I thought I would read the story of David's fight, a thing I had not done since I was a boy. I turned to the 16th and 17th chapters of the first Book of Samuel. To my suprise, I found that Michelangelo was correct—or, at least, half correct. According to the next, when David threw the stone, he was both a boy and a man. We are first told how he was brought to King Saul as "one of great strength and a man fit for war." He joins Saul's entourage and helps him fight the Philistines. But by this time he has changed into a shepherd boy. Plainly, two stories, or perhaps legends, have been confused.

Like Michelangelo's marble, the Book of Samuel has been botched. But there was no genius to put things right.

Leonard Simons doesn't let matters end at that. He has a viewpoint, and an historic sense. He wrote to *Travel and Leisure* magazine:

Gentlemen:

Aubrey Menen's article on Michelangelo's *David* claims that the Bible stories regarding David were confused. I say, so was the genius of Michelangelo, because he certainly knew that all Jewish males are circumcised. This is the covenant between God and the Israelites, and David was a Jew who surely was circumcised or he never could have been King of Judah and later King of the whole of Israel.

So, how come Michelangelo incorrectly showed David as he might have appeared if he were not Jewish? Seems to me *he* botched this detail when he did not take this piece off this masterpiece! If he had, he would have "put things right."

P.S. Christ was circumcised, also. The "Festival of Circumcision of Christ" is January 1.

Historically, and for art lovers, the clarifications, especially the Simons' letter, have considerable merit. The Michelangelo incident has been noted in the past, but not as extensively as in the material we now share with our readers. And, to Leonard Simons, once again appreciation for not letting an historical dispute be buried without thorough clarification.

Lincoln Cathedral and
a 12th-Century Libel

To Jews, *the* cathedrals of Europe are associated with much suffering. During the Middle Ages, when the building of these churches was at its height, hatred of the Jews was evidenced in persecution and expulsions. Not the least of these were perpetrated in Lincoln, a village in Lincolnshire. Hence, my surprise when on a recent tour of the British Isles to find the following plaque in the cathedral of Lincoln, over the "Shrine of Little St. Hugh."

> Trumped-up stories about ritual murders of Christian boys of Jewish communities were common throughout Europe in the Middle Ages and even much later. These fictions cost many innocent Jews their lives. Lincoln had its own legend, and the alleged victim was buried in the cathedral. The shrine was erected and the boy was referred to as "Little St. Hugh." A reconstruction of the shrine stands near. Such stories do not redound to the credit of Christendom and so we pray "Remember not, Lord, our offenses, nor the offenses of our forefathers."

In a letter sent to me, in response to my request for information on the plaque, Stuart Gunnill, secretary of the cathedral fund drive, added that when the cathedral had to launch an appeal in 1963, "the first to contribute was a Jewish doctor from Bournemouth, on our South Coast, who wrote that whereas his ancestors were forced to give to maintain the cathedral it gave him pleasure to do so voluntarily."

In Cecil Roth's *History of the Jews of England*, reference is made to Lincoln Jewry as far back as 1159. Pogroms took place periodically, climaxing in a ritual murder libel in 1255, when nearly one hundred Jews were arrested and many put to death following a trial in London.

From the *Detroit Jewish News*.

In 1290, twenty-four years after crusaders sacked the synagogue, the Jews of Lincoln were expelled, along with the rest of England's Jews. From that day on, no permanent Jewish community has been re-established in the town. Simons estimates there are no more than a half-dozen to a dozen Jews there today.

The oldest inhabited house in England belonged to Bellassez the Jewess, of Lincoln. It is marked with a plaque, Jews House, and is located on Steep Hill. Bellassez herself, a wealthy woman, was among the 293 English Jews sentenced to die following a trumped-up charge in 1278.

University of Detroit Alumni

L. to R.: Rabbi Hertz; Fr. Malcolm Carron, S.J., chancellor of the University of Detroit; and the author

I am very flattered to become an honorary alumnus of the University of Detroit. Thank you very much.

Response given on election to the University of Detroit's Alumni Club, Roostertail restaurant, October 1981.

I've had a warm spot in my heart for the University going back a long time. For about forty years we lived just a few blocks from the University. Several of its presidents were my good friends, especially Fr. Celestin Steiner and Fr. Malcolm Carron.

Twenty-five years ago, I was Brotherhood Week Chairman for the Detroit Round Table of Catholics, Jews, and Protestants. Fr. Steiner, then president of University of Detroit, was sitting next to me at a Round Table dinner. I told him about my Brotherhood idea to help the U. of D. celebrate its 75th anniversary. He liked it. To be more accurate, he loved the idea!

My plan was to write to seventy-five of my Jewish friends and ask for $100 from each in honor of Leo, a Jewish member of the University's lay board. I wanted a $7,500 gift from the seventy-five Jews of Detroit for a 75th birthday gift to the U. of D. To play safe, I sent letters to one hundred Jewish friends, assuming some would turn me down. But, would you believe that I got one hundred checks! A fantastic achievement for any advertising man.

Leo Butzel had made me promise that I would not embarass him by a failure. I assured him we would succeed or I would make up the difference. So now I could breathe easier.

I was honored by the First Friday club. Fr. Steiner and I were interviewed on a nationwide ratio network. The Catholic newspapers across the country ran my picture and a story about the Jewish gift to U. of D. You would think we gave at least $750,000 by all the publicity.

Now, twenty-five years later, I'm honored again by U. of D. History, in a sense, is repeating itself, and I'm enjoying it.

A few years ago, I had helped the Brothers of the Society of St. Paul start a school in Dearborn. The head of the school brought me a large, framed parchment scroll beautifully illuminated in many colors, with a color photograph of Pope Paul. My name was hand lettered in old English type. It was a Papal Blessing.

Because this does not happen to many Jews, I showed a Polaroid photo of it to some of my friends. One said to me, "Leonard, you help the Jews, you help the Protestants, you help the Catholics. What are you doing, playing religion across the board?"

I said, "That's right. I'm trying to make sure I go to heaven."

And he replied, "Leonard, when you get to heaven, with your luck God will be an Arab."

Oneg Shabbat

Good Shabbas (Sabbath), ladies. It is an honor and a delight to be with you on your Chapter *Oneg Shabbat* celebration. May I also extend my congratulations to you on Hadassah's 65th anniversary as well as the 60th anniversary of the Metropolitan Detroit Chapter of Hadassah.

We all know that the words *Oneg Shabbat* mean "delight of the Sabbath." But did you ever stop to ask yourself where the expression originated? The question intrigued me. So I decided to find where it came from. I started with the Bible. I assumed that the words *Oneg Shabbat* came from the Torah. But I was wrong. I finally found the source of the reference to the Sabbath as a delight: it is in the Haftorah, the *Neviim*—the Prophets—in Isaiah 58:13, 14.

I will paraphrase the first part of the passage: If you refrain from working on the Sabbath or pursuing your affairs on My Holy Day but instead *shall call the Sabbath a delight* and honor, then you can seek the favor of the Lord.

And that is where the expression *Oneg Shabbat*—Sabbath delight—comes from.

From a talk given before the Metroplitan Detroit Chapter of the Hadassah on their *Oneg Shabbat* celebration, March 1977.

Simons on Religion

by Rabbi Samuel Silver

Rabbi Samuel Silver

*W*hen *a rabbi* talks about religion, it is what you expect. When a layman talks religion, it is news!

Leonard Simons is an articulate advertising executive, but he has a wide-ranging interest. Local history, the story of the Jewish people, books, and people all claim his attention. And he is also a devout man who knows that no one is alone in his accomplishments. Of this, his declaration that appeared in the Detroit *Jewish News* is a clear statement:

I Believe in God

In my heart and mind I believe there must be some Supreme Being who made possible everything I see around me. I don't

From a column written by Rabbi Silver and distributed by the Jewish Telegraphic Agency, 1967.

think these things just happened. I don't have to prove by my own experience that God exists. My heart, my faith, tells me there is a Supreme Being. I don't know what shape He takes. I am not referring to any special kind of God when I say I believe in God. I just believe there must be some Supreme Creator of everything in the universe, and I hope He is a personal God so I can pray to Him and commune with Him. Whether He listens to me or does anything for me is beside the point.

I believe there is a God, but I can't describe Him any more than anyone else can. I believe that somehow, some way, some people get divine inspiration from God and that God in His way, brings His message to the world. What powers He has, I don't know anymore than you do. But I believe He could do anything He wanted to do if He so desired.

Maybe all God does is to give us a chance by bringing us into the world, and then it is entirely up to us to make of our lives what we can or want to do. I don't think I can accurately explain my feelings when I discuss this subject. All I can say is that I am sincere in my belief that there is a God, and I will pray to Him as long as I live.

Everything becomes a matter of faith. As Maimonides expressed it in the First Principle of Faith, "God is the cause of all existed things—the Author and Guide of everything that has been created." And for that we must have faith in the existence of a Divine Providence. This I have.

The Mayor's Prayer Breakfast

When Chairman Virgil Boyd asked me to give a short commentary on a portion of the Hebrew Bible this morning, I worried that you might think that I am now appearing in the guise of a rabbi. Let me assure you that I am not.

I chose what are considered the two greatest sentences that the human heart and mind have conceived. These are: Deuteronomy 6:5 and Leviticus 19:18. These are from the sacred five books of Moses known as the Torah section of the Hebrew Bible, or the Old Testament.

I come from a long line of Simonses, none of whom, incidentally, was a bachelor. One, who might have been an ancestor, was an ancient Jewish worthy named Simon. He lived over nineteen hundred years ago.

During those very days when my forebearer, Simon, the son of Gamaliel, flourished as one of the spiritual leaders of Jerusalem, a Galilean teacher came to that great city. His name was Joshua, the son of Joseph. You who are Christians know him as Jesus, and you call him the Christ.

Then it was that a scribe came to Jesus and asked him a question: "Teacher, which is the great commandment in the law?" And the Galilean answered him from the only Bible that he knew, the Hebrew Scriptures, "Thou shalt love the Lord thy God with all thy heart, and with all thy soul, and with all thy might." This is the fifth verse of the sixth chapter in the Book of Deuteronomy of the Old Testament. You read this also in Matthew, Chapter 22, verses 37–38. Jesus went on to say, "This is the greatest and the first commandment."

The most important phrase in this sentence from Deuteronomy is that part which begins: "Thou shalt love the Lord

Talk given at the Mayor's Interfaith Prayer Breakfast, Cobo Hall, September 1968.

thy God." This is a simple pronouncement that all humanity has but one God. And if all of us have but one common God, one Creator, then it stands to reason that He is the Father of all mankind. We speak of this concept as the Fatherhood of God. This is a great commandment because it unites us all and makes us one. I was taught, and I believe, that God is one and humanity is one. God is every man's pedigree.

Then in the eighteenth verse of the nineteenth Chapter of Leviticus in the Hebrew Bible comes this injunction: "Thou shalt love thy neighbor as thyself." This is the second quotation that Jesus, the Jew, chose because it is the natural corollary of the first verse. And having quoted these two verses from the Old Testament, the founder of Christianity continued: "On these two commandments dependeth the whole law and the prophets." (Matthew 23:29–40). By this he meant, this is the sum total of biblical teaching, this is religion reduced to its prime essence. This is the golden rule of human conduct.

Now, if God is our common Father, then it follows that we are all brothers, and we should love our neighbors. This concept we call the Brotherhood of Man. And we learn that the Hebrew words *Ve-awe-hav-taw L'ray-ah-haw . . . Kaw-mo-haw* mean "Thou shalt love thy neighbor as thyself" and are also translated to mean "Let the honor and property of thy neighbor be as dear to thee as thine own." One of the greatest rabbis of biblical times, Hillel, paraphrased this rule into "Do not unto others what thou wouldst not have done unto thyself" and declared it to be the whole Law, the rest being commentary.

So you see, these two great landmarks of the human soul are the synthesis of what is noblest in Judaism and in Christianity.

Today, over nineteen hundred years after the scribe, a Jewish teacher of the Law, and the Galilean teacher nodded their heads in assent, we find ourselves in a world that at times terrifies us. Our fellow Americans, thousands of them, are dying by violence on foreign soil. Here, throughout this land we love— including our own city—there is suspicion and hatred and sudden death. Is it not time that all of us here, Jew and Christian, believer and nonbeliever, turn to the great teachings which chart our path and resolve to try to follow them to our goal?

If all of us who are here pledge ourselves to have faith in these Judeo-Christian teachings, then it is still possible that, in the not too distant future, the world shall witness that messianic moment when, as it is written in Holy Scriptures, "every man shall live in dignity and at peace under his own vine and fig tree." And so it may be.

The World We Want to Live In

Francis Kornegay

When I was invited by Francis Kornegay and Reverend Banks to come here today and give a little talk in connection with Brotherhood Week, which starts today, I decided to discuss brotherhood as it applies to the world we want to live in. But then I wondered what I could say to people who know from bitter experience what an empty phrase "Brotherhood Week" has been to the Negro people for so many, many years.

It's been one hundred years since the Emancipation Proclamation and one hundred seventy-five years since the Bill of Rights was passed by our government. But it certainly cannot be said truthfully that the American Negro has been able to get all the benefits of Emancipation and all of the rights to

Talk given at the Second Baptist Church of Detroit for Brotherhood Week, February 1967.

which he is entitled as an equal citizen of the United States.

How much longer will it be before the Negro does have equal status with every other American citizen? How does America go about making the words "Brotherhood Week" something meaningful rather than something shallow? And, why just Brotherhood Week? Why not fifty-two weeks of brotherhood each year in this great country of ours?

Who are the important people that can bring about the kind of relationship between whites and Negroes that God intended when this world was created? The lawmakers in Washington and in our own state capitol cannot do it. They've tried for one hundred years or more and accomplished only a small part of the job. You cannot legislate brotherhood. The people that can bring about the kind of relationship between whites and Negroes that God intended are the American people. They alone can do it. And they can do it only if one by one they will all recondition their minds and their hearts to believe and accept the changes that must come about if we are ever to have true brotherhood, true democracy, and peace in this land of ours.

And I believe that that day will come. Maybe not in our lifetime but as sure as there is a God in Heaven that day will come. It has to.

There is no question but that we are living in a brave new world, in the best sense of the word, which promises to become the kind of world we want to live in.

And, we Americans can take a certain amount of pride in what we are doing to try to help make this a better world. We have accomplished a lot in recent years, but there's still so much more to be done, a great deal more. The American way of life, the principles which we have established, must be proven to the world. We must prove that we actually live by these principles and that we don't just talk about them. We can do this by making sure there are no second-class citizens in our country. It is not enough to be known for our tremendous production records, for our luxurious automobiles, for our color television sets, for our abundance of nearly everything. We must be known for our sense of justice, decency, tolerance, freedom, and courage. It is good to be able to boast of our high standard of living, but far more important we should be able to boast of our high standard of values also.

Unless we all face up to the hard-core problems of the Negroes that exist in our communities and try to solve them with integrity, the talks and the dinners and the meetings are only mild brotherhood gestures.

On this, the first day of Brotherhood Week, 1967, let's think about our daily pattern of life. Each day as we go to work we become so engrossed in the problems of making a living that there is little time for deep reflection on the human relations problems of our country. Brotherhood Week suggests that we think about these things and, after reflection, determine what each of us, in our own way, proposes to do about the brotherhood of man during the days to come. This is a time to stop and take stock of what's going on all around you as it affects you and your family. Brotherhood Week is a good time to reflect upon your own personal code.

When we think about such advances as supersonic jets, space travel, and autos, we realize that we are no longer isolated from how our fellow man thinks and acts. Today we realize that if for no other reason than self-interest and self-preservation, we have a spiritual and moral collective responsibility toward each other and toward our neighbors because we are more than neighbors—we are brothers.

"Getting To Know You" is the name of a popular song, and it also sums up the meaning of genuine dialogue: getting to know each other as individuals instead of as stereotypes.

So it must be one day within the larger family of mankind. We will come to see each other not as so many symbols, not as representatives of a certain group, but as human beings without labels. The world has grown too small for men not to reach out to one another. Distrust, prejudice, hate, and fear are human things which must be overcome by human intelligence and love.

Brotherhood is born in the home, made wise in the school, strengthened in the church and reaches full flower only when each of us tries vigorously to implement it in his own personal life.

I believe that the people who can help most to bring about what all decent people hope for someday are the ministers, the priests, the rabbis, and the other religious leaders.

I believe that organized religion has *not* been doing all it can to educate the people, both young and adult, to the true meaning of brotherhood.

And this is not just a personal opinion. All one has to do is make an objective study of the role religion has played in bringing about harmony or discord in our world over the past two thousand years or so. The record speaks for itself. I don't mean by this to condemn all religious leaders. And I don't mean to give the impression that all religion has failed in its purpose. Over the years many ministers, many priests, and many rabbis have done an excellent job of teaching and educating people to the true meaning of brotherhood, but unfortunately they have always been in the minority. I believe that religion is meant to be bread for daily use, not cake for special occasions. Our churches and synagogues know that they cannot hold themselves aloof; they must reach deep into the human situation, and they are doing more and more these days to help draw mankind closer together. The churches are rebuilding themselves around man's problems.

Theologians are speaking out against prejudice and poverty. Timid pastors, priests, and rabbis have come down from their safe pulpits to march with Negroes, to fight anti-Semitism, to try to see that all people regardless of race, color or creed are treated equally well. The church is again irritating man by revealing the wide gap between what he ought to be and what he is. This is the true Christian way; this is the true role of Judaism.

I am convinced, as are millions of others like me, that the churches and the synagogues, and *not* the welfare state or the unions, will provide the Negro with his honest-to-goodness chance to find and get justice in this life.

All these new forms of religious restlessness, these intense religious activities to help our brothers regardless of race or color or creed, are benefiting religion and the churches. I think the way churches are beginning to march into the stormy center of American life is actually saving our churches and our religions from irrelevancy. It is saving the churches from being much less than what they are supposed to be if they are to have any meaning in our lives.

The United States Constitution adopted in 1788 is the most important document given to the world in thousands of years. For the first time anywhere, because of the United States Constitution, *any* free man, at least in theory, could become a citizen of this country if he lived here. On July 4, 1788, in Philadelphia, the American people put on the first great Independence Day parade in which a Protestant minister, a Catholic priest, and a rabbi marched arm-in-arm. This came about because all the great universal religions have the same basic ideas. All have developed the same concepts because of the same psychological needs. No religion has a monopoly on the truth.

Clergymen and lay people have learned to be concerned not only with their immortal souls in the world to come but also about the perishable bodies of people here on this earth. They have learned to concern themselves with the meek and the humble and the poor, with the widow and the orphan, with social justice and equity in our society. We all now realize that there are vast areas of an economic, social, moral, and ethical nature where people of all religions can and should work together. All this has brought about the improvement that we have today in Jewish-Christian relations, in what could be called brotherhood. It is making possible much of the good that we in America are accomplishing, we who are of different races, colors, and creeds working together.

I believe that the people of my faith, the Jewish people, can be of much help to the Negroes in their attempt to get a square deal in America. The Jews are also a minority group and can understand and appreciate exactly what the Negro is feeling because they have gone through the same experiences themselves. In addition, the Jews are taught that they must never compromise on what they believe to be the goal of human life.

I would like to mention a quotation from the teaching of our Midrash, the rabbinical commentaries on the Hebrew Bible. In regard to the creation of the first man on earth, the Jewish people are taught, "Then the Lord took dust from the four corners of the earth and in equal amounts. Some of the dust was red, some black, some white and some yellow as sand. These He mixed with waters from all the oceans and seas to indicate that all races of mankind should be included in the first man and *none* shall be accounted as superior to the other."

The Book of Numbers also tells us that Moses, the founder of the Jewish religion, was married twice. Moses' second wife was a Cushite, and *Cush* in Hebrew means black. Some Bibles use the word Ethiopian instead of Cush.

Whatever else may be said about Judaism, no one can deny or ignore its ethical teachings. It was this faith which gave to humanity what many consider to be the most significant religious contribution made by any religion, the concept of ethical monotheism. This asserts that there is one God for all mankind, and that this God requires of all His children, regardless of race, color, or creed, to live together in understand, justice, and peace. This is the doctrine of the fatherhood of God and brotherhood of man. It is a compelling fact that we Jews cannot be true to Judaism if we are false to the endless striving on man's part for social justice and brotherhood.

Not that all the Jews have been good friends of the Negroes; we've got good members and bad, just like all other groups have. But, with few exceptions, Jews are your friends and are anxious to see your efforts for equality succeed.

As Baptists, you'll be interested in this brotherhood story I found in the American Jewish Archives. It goes back to 1788. I read some correspondence which showed that Jews during the 1700s were active in raising funds for the completion of America's greatest Baptist church and that the Jews also made substantial contributions toward the establishment of Rhode Island College, the Baptist-sponsored school which later became Brown University.

Five days before the battle of Bunker Hill during the Revolutionary War, Jacob Rivera, a Jewish merchant of Newport, Rhode Island, wrote to Nicholas Brown giving him some money to help complete the Baptist meeting house in Providence, Rhode Island. That church, originally established by Roger Williams in 1638, the first of its kind in America, is still standing today. And, five years before the dedication of the Baptist meeting house, Rivera and his son-in-law, Aaron Lopez, the famous New England merchant shipper, also contributed ten thousand feet of lumber for the first building of the college that is now called University Hall at Brown University.

Several years ago I became interested in the United Negro College Fund for the simple reason that the southern American Negro boys and girls are not getting a square deal when it comes to education. I served as Michigan chairman exactly ten years ago. Like all good Americans (and remember I said like all good Americans), I believe that our country was founded on the principle of equality for people of all colors, races, and creeds. And this means that educational opportunity should be given to the Negroes, the Catholics, and the Jews as well as to others on an equal basis. I also believe that education for all people, both Negro and white, can be and probably will be the salvation of the world we live in. In fact, if the young generation makes the cause of brotherhood its own, the world has a chance.

Francis Kornegay can tell you that down through the years we have worked together in trying to help get jobs for Negroes. In some cases we had good results, in others discouraging. But today the same people who formerly would not hire a Negro are now pleading for qualified or educated Negroes. What the Urban League has accomplished over the years is certainly another great milestone on the road toward brotherhood. When white people come in personal contact with Negroes by working with them on the job, both groups begin to appreciate each other's good points. Brotherhood begins with personal contacts, not hearsay reports or opinions.

I'm proud to tell you that I sponsored the first Negro who was accepted for membership in the Adcraft Club of Detroit. And you'll be interested in hearing this little story. One of our civic clubs whose membership is open to everyone had a big social affair planned for the Grosse Pointe Yacht Club. Invitations were sent out in the mail. When I saw where the affair was going to be held I called and said that I thought the affair should not be held there because Negroes and Jews were not welcome in the Club, and I didn't like to go to places where my people aren't welcome. I'm proud to tell you that the affair was transferred to a downtown hotel, the old invitations were recalled, and new invitations were printed and sent out so that Jews and Negroes could feel comfortable at this party. I've done this on several occasions.

I try to be helpful wherever I can. I like to say that there's a great deal of difference between sticking your nose into other people's business and putting your heart into other people's problems. I believe that we must all devote our energies to the ideals of democracy and a concern for a better understanding among all people. All Americans should strive for the rapid elimination of enforced segregation because enforced segregation cannot be tolerated on any religious, moral, or legal basis. The decision of the Supreme Court of the United States must and will prevail. Bigots are trying to argue with history. It takes courage to stand up and be counted, but to keep standing up after being counted is the real test of courage.

I would like to finish by reminding you that we are all equal citizens in the eyes of our American Constitution. Racial and religious bigotry must be recognized for what it is . . . blasphemy and contempt for God. To think of people in terms of white, black, yellow, or brown is more than an error, it is an eye disease, a cancer of the soul. Race prejudice is a treacherous denial of the existence of God.

That equality is a good thing, a fine goal, is generally accepted. What is lacking is a sense of the monstrosity of inequality. The plight of the Negro must become one of the most important concerns of the white man, and his concern must be expressed literally, not symbolically, not only publicly but also privately, not occasionally but regularly.

I was taught and I believe that God is one and humanity is one. God is every man's pedigree. He is either the Father of all men or of no man. The image of God is either in every man or no man.

The world we want to live in is *not* a white man's world. It is *not* a black man's world. It *is* God's world.

Thank you.

The United Negro College Fund

L. to R.: Louis G. Seaton, vice-president, General Motors; Judge Wade McCree; the Author; Anthony De Lorenzo, vice-president, General Motors

When I was asked to accept the chairmanship of the 1957 United Negro College Fund for Michigan, I was proud to accept the honor and the responsibility for raising the $175,000 which is the Michigan quota for this year. I accepted because, in my heart, I believe most sincerely in the many important contributions to the future welfare of America that these thirty-one Negro colleges are making.

Recently, one of my friends said to me, "As a Jew, haven't you got enough fund-raising campaigns of your own

Talk given at the United Negro College Fund dinner, Veterans' Memorial Building, spring 1957.

to keep you busy? Why do you spend so much time on this particular campaign, especially when none of the schools are located in Detroit or Michigan? Why don't you just give them some money and let the Negroes run their own campaign?" I answered this man by saying, "I could give more than a dozen reasons why I want to help in this campaign. But, basically, my reasons for wanting to do more than just give a little money to these Negro colleges come from the Bible.

In the Old Testament, we read in Amos these holy words, *Are ye not as the children of the Ethiopian unto me?* This means to me that we are all, regardless of race, color, or creed, one brotherhood of man under the Fatherhood of God, in the eyes of God; that we must all help each other regardless of color, creed or, for that matter, even nationality. And the Bible also teaches us that God also told Moses that this, too, was part of His law to all mankind, *Ye shall have one manner of law both for you as well as the stranger.*

That, to me, applied to education, means equality of *opportunity* for education. But until that day comes, it is up to all good people, both black and white, to help finance the Negro youth of America in their search for higher education. By so doing, we can help the entire Negro race in creating educated leadership, and we will all be making another investment in democracy to help assure the future of our beloved country.

In accepting the chairmanship for this year, it was my feeling that this campaign for funds should not be so overwhelmingly a campaign for funds from white people. I said that I would accept this chairmanship if my very dear friend, Judge Wade McCree, would be my cochairman. I am very proud to be able to say that Judge McCree did accept this position of leadership and is spending a great deal of time to assure the success of this year's campaign.

Judge McCree is a man who is a fine example of the type of Negro leadership that it is possible for Detroit and America to obtain through the educational facilities of any one of these thirty-one Negro colleges because, as many of you know, he is a graduate of one of them, Fisk University of Nashville, Tennessee. From there he went on to Harvard.

I could talk for a very long time about this wonderful man, but he is a very modest person, and I don't wish to embarrass him. It is a pleasure for me to classify him as one of our outstanding citizens and a man who has the respect of the entire community because of his intelligence and integrity.

I want also to say that, even when the day comes that Negroes have the opportunity to go to any school of their choice, there will always be a need and a place for private colleges and universities in the American scheme of things. With the tremendous growth of population of America year after year, America needs all the schools that are now in existence and many more schools if it is going to try to meet the tremendous demands for higher education that will be necessary because of the great increase in the number of young American boys and girls who want to go to college, who want to help better themselves, and who want to be in a better position to contribute something worthwhile to the future success and welfare of the United States.

There will always be a need for private schools like these Negro colleges as well as for schools like Yale, Princeton, Harvard, Notre Dame, Brandeis, and hundreds of other private colleges and universities.

So that's my message to all you nice people.

Thank you.

The Detroit Round Table:
An Open Letter

L. to R.: Thomas Murphy, chairman of the board of General Motors; Nate Shapero, the author

I've long been identified with the work of the Detroit Round Table of the National Conference of Christians and Jews, both as a volunteer fund-raiser and as a contributor for about twenty-five years. I do it because I believe that the Round Table of NCCJ is an important force, working for the great good of all people. This organization merits all the financial support we can give it. This report will tell you about some of the good things it does with our money.

The purpose of the Detroit Round Table, one of sixty-

Talk given at the annual dinner of the National Conference of Christians and Jews, Cobo Hall, December 1973.

two regional operations of the National Conference of Christians and Jews, is to help us gain understanding and respect for each other. As people of different religious and racial backgrounds, we share a lot of tough problems as well as a lot of great opportunities. The Round Table creates opportunities for genuine dialogue which makes it possible to get to know each other as individuals instead of as stereotypes.

We live today in an age of easy communication, with more ways for people to communicate with each other than ever before. Yet, there is no way as effective and as meaningful as the simple act of talking together.

Throughout the year, week in and week out, in settings conducive to honest exchange of views and emotions, the Round Table has an ongoing series of programs to bring people together, to help find ways to solve many of the important social issues that confront us.

Here are a few specific examples.

From its beginning, NCCJ's Round Table has been Detroit's meeting place for priests, ministers, and rabbis—to talk together—to clear away misunderstandings. The Round Table serves as the communication center for their responses to community problems. These religious leaders are voicing their concern for the sanctity of human life in light of today's violence. They agree there are vast areas where all religions can and should work together.

They are also actively seeking ways in which congregations can assist people who have been in prison and returned to the community. And, they have put NCCJ's dialogue process to work to undo the alienation and to establish better relationships with members of the many Indian tribes in Michigan.

In the crucial area of police-community relations, the Round Table is the sponsor and partner of the citizens-police council of Detroit. Grass roots lay leaders and police delegates from the city's thirteen precinct associations meet regularly at the Round Table to iron out problems.

During the past three years, NCCJ has organized teams of informed key citizens and police, from Detroit and twenty other Michigan cities, to work as task forces on their local problems in the area of community relations and the administration of justice. This project has been co-sponsored by

Michigan State University's School of Criminal Justice, with backing by our governor. The Round Table provides workshop resources for the teams at MSU's Kellogg Center as well as consultant services in their various communities.

The teams' concerns include: relationships between our schools, our police and our youth; communication between the criminal justice system and minority groups; and the accountability of police and public to each other.

Through these and similar programs across the country, the NCCJ is helping to reshape and redefine the philosophy of law enforcement in a free society, which is their commitment to equal justice for all.

A crucial Round Table program emphasis is the vital need to "Rear Children of Good Will." Many of you have participated in the nationally acclaimed Border Cities Conference. Thousands of parents, young people, and educators meet together to find better ways to help children grow up with positive attitudes towards other children and adults of different backgrounds.

To this same end, Detroit and Michigan college youth are given opportunity for creative expression in NCCJ's annual Michigan college human relations conferences. This year the student teams from twenty-five Michigan colleges have been especially concerned with the increased interest in religious values demonstrated by college youth.

Our Women's Division involves over twelve hundred participants from city and suburbs. An extensive year-round program of events enlists women's leadership to build a wide base of interracial and interreligious understanding among women and women's organizations.

I would say that the Round Table is best known as a catalyst for local community people to meet and discuss their differences. It does this with groups whose leaders come together regularly. They use the Round Table for frank interchange of ideas on how to resolve tension-producing situations, how to dispel rumors, and how to build positive relationships.

The Round Table as a communication vehicle is backed by many publications and resource aids. These range from program guides for parents and youth, to extensive scholarship programs in cooperation with thirty-five human relations workshops across America, to NCCJ's Religious New Service (RNS). With its worldwide network of 950 newsmen serving the Michigan and national press, TV and radio newsrooms, RNS is the world's only interreligious news agency.

On national and local levels, NCCJ is building bridges in human relations which are vital to the future well-being of all American communities.

These are some of the reasons why we should enthusiastically endorse the good efforts of the Round Table. It is not a panacea for all our social ailments. A great deal of good has been accomplished by the conference, but there is still much to be done. We cannot sit on the sidelines and do nothing. We must continue to try. There's a big difference between sticking your nose in other people's business and putting your heart in other people's problems. That's exactly what the Detroit Round Table is trying to do for all of us because *we* are the other people. Please remember that.

Public Service Broadcasting

If we are going to be concerned about the future of our community and our country, we must decide what our priorities are to be. History has proved that joblessness and unemployment can, and do, create dangerous conditions in any country. The annual population explosion compounds our problems. Three of the main methods for dealing with potential unrest, etc. are (1) *educational opportunities* from the earliest age; (2) *poverty job training* by local and governmental agencies, especially among youths sixteen to twenty-one years of age, white or black; and (3) *employment opportunities* for people of all ages, educated and uneducated, in the younger than Social Security bracket.

Educational opportunities should be financed not primarily by property taxes but by local, state, and government income taxes, and these educational opportunities for youngsters should go much farther than just reading, writing, and arithmetic; they should include education and skill in various trades and fields of endeavor that appeal to the individuals involved.

When people reach adulthood, if they still are unemployed, regardless of being skilled or unskilled, organized job training, especially for those at the poverty level, should be available. Special tax benefits should be offered to business firms so that job training can be partially subsidized by business and partially by government.

I believe in more government spending constantly to stimulate our economy as conditions demand. If we can find money to put men on the moon, we can find money to see to it that every American can have adequate food, clothing, shelter, medical care, education, and employment. Americans of all ages must be able to live without fear, and with confidence that they can find gainful employment to protect and provide for themselves and their family if they are able and willing.

A public service announcement made on Station WQRS-FM, September 1977.

On the Word "Ethnic"

I always get a smile out of the definition of the word "ethnic" as the dictionary gives it to us.

The number one meaning, in *Websters Collegiate,* is "neither Jewish nor Christian; pagan."

In *Webster's Third International,* the first definition is "of or relating to the Gentiles or to nations not converted to Christianity: HEATHEN, PAGAN." (Gentile, in this instance, meaning non-believer.)

The secondary meaning of ethnic applies to *races* that have common physical or mental traits or customs—originating from racial, linguistic, and cultural tradition.

Jews, per se, are not a *race* of people. By the same token, Jews are not an ethnic group. Using the secondary meaning of the word, you could say Jews are a part of many ethnic groups, depending on the countries from which their families come. Again, using the secondary meaning, it is safe to say that everybody is a part of some ethnic group.

I'm explaining all this to show that I believe it is incorrect to just arbitrarily put all Jews into the category of one ethnic group. Jews from Russia may be one group, German Jews, another, and Spanish Jews, still another; Jews from India have many of their own exclusive ethnic customs and traits, and so on. So much for the word "ethnic," as the dictionary defines the word and as I think it applies (or does not apply) to the Jews.

Unfortunately, we all know that Jews believe a lot of different things about their identification with their Judaism. There are so many different opinions as to what it means to be a Jew, or what a Jew is, that we are anything but an ethnic group, all having common *traits* and *customs.*

I believe Jews are a widely diversified group of people who are members of one of the world's greatest religions.

From a reply written to Philip Slomovitz, publisher and editor of the *Detroit Jewish News,* May 1981.

We Jews do have something in common. We are bound together by a common history that goes back over four thousand years; we are bound together by our faith, which is belief in one God and His moral and ethical laws or commandments. We have some extraneous customs and rituals that are widely used nearly everywhere. These are not essential or vital, but are important. However, these facts do not make Jews an ethnic group.

And that's the way I see it.

Zedakah

Time and time again, I have had these or similar flattering words said to me: "You Jews are certainly the most generous people I have ever met."

Haven't you experienced this also?

A few years ago, a nun, Sister Mary Emil, the president of Marygrove College in Detroit, a Catholic girls' school, made the same statement to me. I acknowledged the compliment and then volunteered my interpretation of the reason why this characteristic is ascribed to our people.

I said, "Sister, *Jews are generous because philanthropy is basic to our religious beliefs*. It is the big, important, item in the Jews' philosophy of life." I went on to say that since biblical days Jews have been taught that money is only as good as the good it can do; that a shroud has no pockets; that there is no special honor in being known as the richest man in the graveyard.

I explained further that there is no word in Hebrew for "charity," and no word for "beggar." Actually, what we call charity these days was known in the olden days to Jews as *zedakah*, "justice or equity." It was also called *gemilut chasadim*," compassion, righteousness, loving-kindness."

Charity is something Jews have been educated to acknowledge as being our noblest tradition. In fact, when Jews specified the three most significant things in life, they said that in addition to belief in God and prayer nothing was more important than deeds of loving-kindness.

And then I concluded by saying that Jews originated tithing. The worthiness of Jews is judged by their willingness to share their possessions with those who have need for the kind of help we can give them. That does not always mean the giving of money. We have been taught, and we teach our

From the preface to a booklet published on the 75th anniversary of the United Jewish Charities of Detroit and the 50th anniversary of the Detroit Jewish Welfare Federation, October 1975.

children, that the highest degree of benevolence is the giving of a gift, a loan, a job, any kind of help that leads to self-support and independence.

When I returned home after this discussion, I decided to spend an entire evening studying the subject in greater depth. I read a number of passages from the books in my personal library; I read the Jewish encyclopedias; I learned much about charity that I had not known previously.

I made copies of some of the articles. I reread them many times and couldn't help but get a certain amount of pleasure. It made me feel good to realize that *the Jewish people have retained and enhanced the philosophy of love, consideration, and kindness for one another, particularly in times of distress, through all these thousands of years.* The principle of *zedakah* is preserved by Jews because we know it to be good and eternally true. It is one of the foundation stones of the goal of social justice and the key to the creation of a better civilization.

The thought occurred to me that you might be interested in reading some of these articles. I submitted the idea to the United Jewish Charities of Detroit. I suggested that this material be published as part of the celebration of their 75th Anniversary and the Detroit Jewish Welfare Federation's 50th Anniversary. They agreed.

Perhaps, after you have read these statements, you will have a little better understanding as to why you, and I, and most other Jews the world over, do the things we do. I am referring to our passion to aid others, our emotional and moral drive, and our sense of obligation to give generously of our worldly means and to participate in philanthropic projects to help our fellow man.

I am sure I now understand our Jewish heritage a great deal better than I ever did before.

After you read these excerpts I hope you will, too.

On Conversion

January 8, 1973

Dear Friends,

Thank you for your note suggesting that I "open the door to Jesus." I respect you for trying to share your beliefs. I can also understand that Believers are natural missionaries. But I am a poor prospect for your efforts because I believe in my heritage as strongly as you two believe in yours.

Christianity was founded by Jews. Jesus was a Jew. Mary, Joseph, Jesus's brothers, and all the apostles were Jewish. Christians obey Jewish laws, saturate their minds with Jewish biblical literature, and are influenced by Jewish thought in every one of its intellectual movements. So, in a deep sense, we are closely related.

As do you, I also believe in God as the Supreme Authority for all that exists in our lives. I have religious peace of mind. Let's all strive for the messianic ideal whereby all nations and individuals shall know peace, justice and neighborly love.

Incidentally, considering my age, I'll be knocking on God's door one of these days. When I do, I hope He will see fit to open it to me.

Stay well and happy,
Leonard

December 18, 1973

Dear Friend,

You are quite a person. To a certain extent, we are cut from the same pattern: we both do not easily accept no for an answer.

Two replies written to gentile friends who encouraged me to join their faith.

223

I'm certainly not "annoyed or angry" with you. In fact, I am flattered that you are so anxious to have me. I'll bet there are a lot of my fellow Jews who would be glad to give me to you.

I think I am a devout person. I believe in God, as I have explained my belief in the enclosed little statement I wrote several years ago.

I also believe that I am a Bible student to a certain extent. I am quite familiar with the Old Testament, the Jewish Bible, as we call it. And, I have read the New Testament many times over the years, bit by bit. I have several copies at home, including the Douay (Catholic), King James Version, etc. I have read the passages you refer to, and I don't want to argue the subject with you. Maybe you are right. Maybe I am right. But I am sure that I was born of Jewish parents, and I want to live my life as a good Jew, and to die when my time comes as a Jew. I like being a Jew and what it stands for, morally and ethically.

I understand life as a Jew, having lived almost seventy years as a Jewish person. I have the respect of my friends and relatives, "in spite of" being Jewish. I am happy to be Leonard Norman Simons, a Jew. I have peace of mind, a lovely wife, children, and grandchildren who are all Jewish and who love and respect me. Why would I want to change all that?

If I had been born a Christian, I'd be one of the best practicing Christians it would be in my power to be. But, I was born a Jew, and I have tried to be the kind of a Jew that would bring honor and respect to my people. So far, I think I have succeeded. I hope I have. What is so important about being a member of one religious sect or another, as long as you believe in God, obey His divine commandments, and do as Micah (6:8) said in the Jewish Bible: "What doth the Lord require of thee but to do justly and to love mercy and to walk humbly with thy God?"

The history of the world has been very sad, largely due to the so-called religions that are unwilling to let people of a different faith live-and-let-live, in spite of the fact that we are all God's children and should believe in the brotherhood of man under the fatherhood of God. There aren't enough true Christians in this world like you. You believe and practice the words of Jesus, but how many of your coreligionists practice Christianity honestly by following His words? No, there are not enough to convince me that your religion has more to offer me than does mine.

Stay well and happy,
Leonard

Dictionary Slurs

by Philip Slomovitz

Early in August this column in the *Jewish News* carried an item about the "suppression of anti-Semitic definitions in dictionaries," and emphasized the necessity for the removal of all anti-Semitic definitions in dictionaries and encyclopedias.

The item was based on recommendations that were made in Bogota, Colombia, at the congress of Spanish language academies of South America, that words and definitions that are anti-Semitic in nature should be suppressed in Spanish dictionaries.

We stated at that time: "Much remains to be done to remove anti-Jewish comments from textbooks, encyclopedias and dictionaries. Having attained that, we shall come much closer to assuring fairness in education and in human relations. Then, it will be perfidy to distort the true meaning of words and to instigate man against man hatefully."

It must have been telepathic that Leonard N. Simons, one of our most distinguished Detroiters, at the same time also should have discovered a number of insulting references to Jews in the Oxford University Press Dictionary. He then began the personal campaign to assure the elimination of insulting references from important dictionaries.

He wrote national organizations—the American Jewish Committee, Anti-Defamation League of B'nai B'rith, Jewish Publication Society, and others—presented the facts to them and urged that action be taken immediately to assure the elimination of references that are insulting in character and which misrepresent the status of the Jews and the Jewish people.

As a result of the action instituted by Leonard Simons,

From the *Detroit Jewish News*, December 1960.

both the B'nai B'rith Anti-Defamation League and the American Jewish Committee went into action. They began to correspond with other publishers of dictionaries and to indicate to them the injustice of using some of the terms that had been incorporated in their dictionaries. While the ADL reports "too small concessions," the effort is afoot to correct an injustice.

Prejudices and "Vulgar" Definitions

Cites Instances to Prove Bias Exists in Defining Many Terms

About a year and a half ago I had occasion to look up the definition of a word which started with *m*. I saw the word "Moses" and was shocked to see that the only definition they gave to the word was "nickname of a Jewish money lender." Nothing about the fact that Moses was the person who gave the Israelites and the world the Ten Commandments; that he was a great prophet and the Father of the Jewish religion.

The dictionary I was using, published by the Oxford University Press, is one of the most respected in the world.

Then, I looked up some other words. "Jew" . . . and on that same page I found "Jesuit." Here again the derogatory definitions astounded me. A Jew, spelled with a capital *J* had several definitions: "A person of the Hebrew race; (tranf. colloq.) extortionate usurer. Driver of hard bargains; rich as a; unbelieving, incredulous person . . ." The next definition of Jew, with a capital *J*: (colloq.) Cheat, overreach. (prec.)."

The next one is, "Jewing—Wattles at base of beak in some domestic pigeons. (*Jew*—from resemblance to hooked nose—*ing*.)."

I started to look up these words in several other dictionaries, and practically every one of them had similar definitions of the word "Jew."

The word "Jesuit" was defined, among other things, as "crafty people, intriguers, hypocritical people, liars."

As I gathered the definitions from approximately a dozen different dictionaries, I found only one dictionary that did not have any derogatory definitions of Jews or Jesuits, and also did not include any offensive words like Wop, Sheeny, Chink, Pollack, Dago, etc. This was the Thorndike-Barnhard dictionary, published by Doubleday & Co.

I then contacted the American Jewish Committee and

Written for the *Detroit Jewish News* and the Jewish Telegraphic Agency, December 1961.

the Anti-Defamation League of B'nai B'rith, to see what could possibly be done to clean up the dictionaries, not from a strictly selfish standpoint, of course, as applied to the Jewish people only, but also as applied to the Jesuits (an order of the Catholic religion), and as applied to any religious, racial, or ethnic groups.

A tremendous amount of correspondence has gone back and forth, between our Jewish defense agencies and the Oxford University Press, as well as many other dictionary publishers, some of which incidentally are owned by people of the Jewish faith. An attempt has been made to have some of these definitions changed, or eliminated.

The Oxford University Press, for instance, has agreed to eliminate their offensive definition of "Moses." They have agreed that in their next edition they will eliminate the statement that the "Jews are a member of the Hebrew race." However, on the offensive definition of the word "Jew" they have agreed in the future to insert "vulg." (mean vulgar) when they use the definition of the word "Jew" as meaning "an extortionate usurer," but they won't eliminate the definitions.

So far, each publisher insists on approaching the problem from a standpoint of what they call "lexicography." The fact that this permits them to include any inaccuracies, as far as modern-day definitions of words are concerned, is beside the point to these so-called scholars.

I cannot understand how intelligent people like the publishers of dictionaries cannot realize what they are doing to perpetuate derogatory definitions of words that no longer are in common usage, definitions which are offensive to people of various religious, ethnic or racial groups, definitions detrimental to a nation's future and to the relationship of one human being to another, definitions which should never have been included in dictionaries in the first place. These derogatory or vulgar definitions only perpetuate untruthful generalities and myths. Decent people will agree that this is a profanity against our fellow men, and that, in my opinion, is a profanation against God.

Definitions are certainly a part of our educational society. Recently President Kennedy said, "Upon the effectiveness of our educational system depends the future in this world." Anti-Semitic definitions in the dictionary are a part of the slow poison of hatred in our society. The dictionary is an important means of influencing the minds of men. It is another tool used to form and change people's minds. That is why it is so important to see that all definitions in current editions represent up-to-date thinking and up-to-date usage of words.

I feel that most dictionary publishers did not want to make these changes because of the expense involved in changing the type and plates in their books. If you take out a couple lines of type on a page, you leave a blank space in the plate. You then have to find some other definitions to fill up the space or the entire sequence of pages in the book is changed.

However, these changes shouldn't be too hard to do if they want to make them. They can merely include a few additional definitions of some of the words on that page, so that their problem would be eliminated.

Any dictionary publisher who recognizes his responsibility to advance life in this universe should, in good conscience, do anything and everything possible through his dictionaries to eliminate as much prejudice as he possibly can. He can do this by eliminating definitions which are today proven unfair and untruthful.

If responsible publishers, like Doubleday & Co., can arrive at the conclusion that vulgar and offensive words have no place in a modern dictionary, and can back up their judgment by publishing the kind of dictionaries that they get out, then why can't the publishers of the other dictionaries emulate their example, even if it does cost them a little bit of money to set some type and make some changes in their plates, before they go to press with their next editions?

New dictionaries are produced from time to time.

A new dictionary comes into existence because the publishers and the dictionary's editorial staff want to present a great many current or new words in the English language, which come into usage, as well as current definitions of some of the older words.

A new dictionary should eliminate archaic, obsolete definitions of words, which no longer are proper descriptive definitions.

I believe that if enough people of all religious denominations will express their feelings about these many vulgar and offensive words in the dictionary, to both the publishers of the

230

dictionaries and the retail stores which sell them, then perhaps the publishers will realize how much harm they are doing to so many of their fellow men by continuing to include unfair, offensive and untruthful generalization definitions of religious, racial and ethnic groups.

Postscript

After this article was picked up by the Jewish Telegraphic Agency and appeared in several papers in the United States and Europe, concerned Jewish and non-Jewish people and organizations wrote to the Oxford University Press. The American Jewish Committee also urged some positive changes. When another edition of the *Oxford Illustrated Dictionary* appeared about a year later, it contained many of the changes recommended by the AJC. To those definitions considered to be unfair and insulting, were added the words of explanation, "vulgar or approbium."

However, the victory was only partial. Only one of the several dictionaries published by Oxford carried the changes. Only the lexicographers who edit the one volume had been converted; the editors of the other volumes remained to be contacted.

I. Jerome and Diane Hauser

I. Jerome and Diane Hauser

I *feel* *doubly* honored tonight because this Jewish National Fund testimonial dinner is for two of our very dear friends, a husband and wife team that has earned the admiration of our entire community: Dr. and Mrs. I. Jerome Hauser.

This evening's large Jewish National Fund turnout should convince Jerry and Diane how appreciative we are of their lifetime of selfless service to others. They have proven that generosity is not just money. It is a matter of heart, a willingness to help on a nonsectarian and interracial plane of concern.

Introduction, Jewish National Fund dinner, Congregation Shaarey Zedek, June 1973.

232

Most of us know that these two wonderful people live their lives in the belief that God has granted them blessings to be utilized for healing as well as other worthy purposes. The Hausers have always believed that life means living, not escaping.

But, with your indulgence, I'd also like to talk about Jerry and Diane in a less serious manner. I'll tell you some stories about them that you will not find in their records.

For instance, did you know that the number seven is Jerry's lucky number? He was born in '07. He served as chief of staff at Sinai Hospital for seven years, and he has participated in seven UJA study missions to Israel. Of course, Diane was also a member of each of the seven missions.

Both Hausers love to visit Israel. They agree with Ben Gurion that in Israel, in order to be a realist, you have to believe in miracles. Jerry made his first trip to Israel as part of a Woman's Mission to Israel! The plane was packed full, loaded with about 289 people. This was the first plane in history with a hernia.

When planning one of their trips they told their travel agent they would like to get into China. The travel agent asked, "Which China do you want? There are two Chinas." Jerry said to him, "Why do people keep talking about two Chinas? What's so unusual about that? We've always had two chinas. One for meat and one for dairy."

Jerry is a most unusual doctor. I like the way he puts it: "Not every human being can be a doctor, but every doctor can be a human being." Every so often I have Jerry check over parts of me. Once he asked me to walk over to an open window and stick my tongue out. I said, "What for?" And he answered, "Because I'm mad at my neighbors."

Jerry is a specialist in Oto-rhino-larin-gology. Just pronouncing that word is enough to give anyone a sore throat.

Then, there's the story about a letter of recommendation that was sent to Jerry concerning a young, new doctor who wanted to become one of Dr. Hauser's assistants. The letter went on to say that "Dr. So-and-So is an outstanding young man. He is the son of Mr. Henry So-and-So, the philanthropist; the grandson of Peter So-and-So, the oil magnate; the cousin of Dr. Franklin So-and-So, the noted surgeon; and the nephew of Samuel So-and-So, Pulitzer Prize author." Jerry

233

wrote back, "Thank you very much for your letter recommending Dr. So-and-So. I must point out, however, that I am interested in him to assist me in taking care of my patients, and not for breeding purposes."

Dr. Hauser and Dr. Herbert Bloom became friends back in 1936 when they were students at the University of Michigan. Little did Jerry and Herb think that about ten years later they would become brothers-in-law by marrying the Davidson sisters, Betty and Diane. In fact, Herb claims he was the matchmaker. He says he was the "Hello Dolly" who made the *shiddach* (match) in 1946 when Jerry got out of the army. He introduced Jerry to the girl with the "patient eardrums"—Diane. It was instantaneous attraction because both of these lovely people had so many mutual interests.

They have been married twenty-seven years, and Jerry has this advice to give to all potential husbands. He says, "You'll never have any trouble if you'll think of your wife as 'fragile—handle with care.' "

Jerry and Diane recently became grandparents for the first time, thanks to daughter Margie and her husband, Michael Federman. Margie says she is now chief cook and bottom washer. Four-month-old grandson Robert is already being groomed for the medical profession. The Hausers love children. Jerry said to me, "Kids are so precocious these days. Remember when we had toy kits called 'Little doctor and little nurse?' Well I just saw one called 'Little gynecologist.' "

I tried to find out about their hobbies. It all seems to boil down to the fact that their hobby is people. They have great empathy for people, especially people who have need for the kind of help that they both can, and are so anxious to, give. They agree that you never work so hard as when you are not being paid for it. Jerry is definitely no athlete. His idea of roughing it is cutting a filet mignon with a dull knife.

Jerry is known as a "cool cookie." Diane was nicknamed in her youth "Dinny Din Din," but I haven't been able to find out why.

In this crazy mixed-up world of ours with so much free sex, pornography, and four-letter cuss words, it's a welcome relief to know that there are still some people like the Hausers who believe in the sanctity of the home and the family, and who still cherish the ideals of our ten commandments. You will never hear either of them use swear words, and they always show respect for the feelings of others.

And we now come to the climax of our Jewish National Fund tribute to Dr. and Mrs. I. Jerome Hauser. We all pray that they will be granted many, many more years of good health and happiness together with their loved ones. Another personal friend of the Hausers, and one of Detroit's outstanding Jewish leaders, will now make the official presentation to them of the Hauser Forest in Israel: Mr. Louis Berry.

Philip and Anna Slomovitz

Philip Slomovitz and the author

I am especially pleased to have this opportunity to introduce my dear friend, Philip Slomovitz, and also on behalf of the Jewish National Fund to make tonight's presentation to him. I have introduced illustrious personalities on many occasions. None of these honorees has been held in higher esteem by me than Phil Slomovitz.

To attempt a biographical sketch of Phil, and to give his

Introduction, Jewish National Fund dinner, Congregation Shaarey Zedek, June 1970.

career its just due, would take longer in the recounting than his response. You will find him listed in *Who's Who in America*. In tonight's program is a very brief resume of some of the highlights of his career. As you read it, you can appreciate how fortunate we are to have such a fine person living in our community as our friend, neighbor and teacher.

To encapsulate the life of a great man is not easy. Phil is unique. I have never heard anyone say an unkind word about him. He is a warm, gentle, soft-spoken, scholarly man, with a courageous, intense commitment to the welfare of his fellow Jews.

Phil was born in what could be termed Russian Poland, in 1896. He came from a large but poor family. There were so many kids—seven brothers and sisters—that he says he used to come home late so that he could sleep on top.

When Phil enrolled in the University of Michigan, he decided to study forestry. You heard correctly, forestry. He wanted to be a forester, a person in charge of the forests. He wanted to learn the science and art of caring for and cultivating forests. And he has retained that interest in trees and forests ever since, especially those in Israel.

The sequel to the story is that he did not get his degree in forestry. He changed his major subject at the University because he could not see through the microscopes he had to use in class. But, while at U. of M., he entered a contest for writing sponsored by Sigma Delta Chi, the professional journalism society, and won first prize. That showed him the power of the pen. From then on, there was no stopping him. Phil is a very prolific writer, as we all know. His writings often have been, reprinted in the U.S. *Congressional Record*.

Phil's greatest reason for feeling close to the Jewish National Fund goes back to 1924, when Phil and Joseph Haggai went to Cleveland to see if they could form an amalgamation of the Michigan and Ohio councils of the Jewish National Fund. They couldn't sell the Buckeyes on this idea, but he did sell the secretary of the JNF Ohio Council on the idea of becoming his wife. Anna and Phil were married in 1925, and on August 2nd this year, they will be married forty-five years.

For anyone to stay married to one woman for that number of years, during these days, is something to brag about. They have two sons, Gabriel and Carmi. Phil tells the story about Carmi coming home from Sunday school some years ago and saying, "Dad, you are a student of the Bible. Can I ask you a question?" Phil said, "Of course." Carmi continued, "I've just been thinking, the Bible says the Children of Israel built the Temple, the Children of Israel crossed the Red Sea, the Children of Israel did this, and the Children of Israel did that. Dad, didn't the grown-ups ever do anything?"

Phil and Anna have been to Israel over a dozen time. They go to Israel as you and I might go to Toledo. Phil, with his fine sense of humor, tells the story about the Jerusalem newspaperman who got a big news scoop, raced into the press room, and yelled, "Hold the back page."

In Israel, the government recently permitted television. Their TV stations are using some of the American shows, except that they are changing the titles. "Peyton Place," for instance, is called "A Shame for the Neighbors."

My own friendship with Phil goes back at least thirty-five years. I remember when Phil decided to leave the *Detroit Jewish Chronicle*, where he had been editor for about nineteen years, and go into business for himself, as most Jewish boys dream of doing some day.

I remember late in 1941 when Maurice Schwartz, the father of our Federation president, Alan Schwartz, called a meeting of a small group of us to back Phil in creating a new English-Jewish newspaper for Detroit. It was felt that the town needed what Phil had to offer. The Jewish Welfare Federation was anxious to have it, the leaders in our local Jewish community liked the idea, and so my partner, Larry Michelson, and I put up some money together with the others to get the paper started. We were paid back as Phil made good on his own. The *Detroit Jewish News* made its initial appearance twenty-eight years ago in March, 1942, and has been a tower of strength, information and education to the Jewish people in this area ever since.

Phil is a proud American Jew who is devoting his life to enhancing the prestige and dignity of the Jewish people everywhere. He has taken on many demanding jobs in the Jewish community.

Phil reminds me of the biblical David; he is constantly challenging the big Goliaths, some of whom are editors of our local daily papers, some of whom are so-called VIPs in the local Jewish and non-Jewish community. He is not afraid to tackle any person or situation if he feels that the Jewish people are being treated unfairly or without proper consideration. He has the God-given gift of being exceptionally articulate, and he has the instrument of his own newspaper to permit wide dissemination of his opinions and suggestions. He is a publisher who not only publishes the news but who also helps make it. He is personally deeply involved in it.

In spite of the fact that he is internationally famous. I know him as a very simple, unpretentious man. His friendly manner endears him to all with whom he comes in contact. He is a man of heart and conviction, of love and modesty, a devoted family man; in short, and I don't use this word loosely, Phil Slomovitz is a *tree-mendous* little guy.

The Jewish National Fund dinner and the establishing of the Philip and Anna Slomovitz Forest in Israel provide the friends and admirers of Phil Slomovitz with the opportunity to pay tribute to the man himself and his dear wife. And so Phil, in grateful recognition of all that you have meant to us and the Jewish National Fund since you established its Detroit Council, as well as for everything else you have done and continue to do to make this a little better world for all of us, I ask you to please come up to the podium and permit me to make this presentation.

Pontius Pilate is said to have told his prisoner, "This has nothing to do with the fact that you happen to be Jewish. Phil," this award is made because you do happen to be Jewish.

The plaque reads:

Keh'sir / shame tov / Hah O'skim / Beh-Tsor-Chai / Tzee-Boor / Beh-ehmoonah.

(The crown of a good name excels them all . . . those who faithfully concern themselves with communal needs.)

William and Fannie Haber

William and Fanny Haber

Thank you, Goldie Adler, for that very flattering introduction. I think some of the statements were overly generous, but as a golfer, I am always grateful for a good lie.

According to the Jewish calendar, today is June 7, 5732. The other night I had a wonderful dream. I dreamt that 5732 was not just the Jewish New Year, but rather the new Dow-Jones average, but that's another story.

Tonight is a very happy occasion for all of us. I am so pleased that our dear friends, Bill and Fannie Haber, are being honored in this unique manner, and that I have been given the privilege of participating in this affair honoring them.

Introduction, Jewish National Fund dinner, Congregation Shaarey Zedek, June 1972.

The name Haber is a transliteration of the Hebrew word *chaver*, which means "friend." Has any man every been more aptly named?

Many wonderful things have been said about the Habers over the years, by many great people. Their words of praise certainly need no confirmation from me. So, tonight, I want to talk about Bill Haber, the man who does not take himself seriously, but who does take his responsibilities seriously. And with that thought in mind, and because Bill has such a great sense of humor, I'll give this introduction in a light vein, with some levity.

If you want a sincere biographical sketch of Dean William Haber, take home the program on your table. You will find a most interesting story of this great man and his background. I do not intend to repeat what is in the pamphlet. But I will give you some inside information about the Habers, both apocryphal and factual.

As a youngster, he and his two brothers pitched in to help their widowed mother and two sisters take care of the hard work around the house. This included cleaning cupboards, washing windows, polishing floors, etc., the kind of work they would not let their women do because they did not believe in Women's Lib. The only thing Bill really couldn't do very well around the house was cook, and he still cannot cook. In fact, Fannie says he's the only person she knows who can screw up cornflakes.

Bill loves music and gets a great deal of pleasure doodling around at the piano. In his youth, he was called the Van Gogh of the piano—no ear.

The Habers have one of the oldest dogs in America. According to the vets, their French poodle, whose name is Robespierre, is about 126 years old—in dog years—computed in human terms. This is even longer than our proverbial biblical blessing. Of all the members of the Haber family, they tell me that Robespierre is the most thrilled because the Habers will have a forest of ten thousand trees in Israel. The dog would love to sleep in bed with Bill, but Fannie won't let him: Bill bites.

Most of the things I can tell you about Bill concern his activities as an economist serving the government, as a teacher at the University of Michigan for thirty-six years, and as the chief executive of several organizations that are today stressing technical job training for our youth, to include the new skills necessary for automation and computers. Bill says that working with youngsters helps keep him young. He says his definition of a Jewish dropout is a boy who did not get his Ph.D. Bill has written a lot of books on economics, social security, manpower, etc. (I once wrote a book, too, on a subject about which I am an expert: baldness. But the pages kept falling out.)

As president of the World ORT Union, Bill has traveled all over the world on many occasions. Some time ago, Bill told me a story about a youngster in an Israeli ORT School who wrote a letter to God asking for $20. The local post office detoured the latter back to ORT headquarters, who, in turn, thought it was a cute gag and sent the boy $10. Whereupon the youngster wrote a letter to God again: "Thanks for the money, but next time, God, please don't send it to me care of ORT; they take off 50 percent."

The Habers have a courageous, intense commitment to the education and welfare of the younger generation. They have empathy for people and understand their problems. The Habers are committed to the cause of justice for all people. Their services to their fellow man are nonsectarian and interracial, yet at the same time characteristically Jewish. And, they do all those wonderful things without thought of personal reward.

Fannie told me that Bill is an easy man to live with. He is never demanding. He is always helpful, always anxious to please. And, as a husband, he is absolutely superb. What a thrill it is, in this modern day and age, to have a wife say this about a husband. These are the kinds of people that give us some hope for the future of the world.

In my opinion, the Habers are the outstanding husband and wife team that we have in the state of Michigan. Speaking geographically, I could go farther. Every time the Habers are honored, it is not for expediency's sake; it is because they deserve it. Tonight is no exception.

Bill Haber is a very dear friend with whom I have shared many problems and satisfactions during our years of association. As old friends, there is nothing I wouldn't do for him, and there is nothing he wouldn't do for me. So, we go through life doing nothing for each other.

Bill Haber and I have worked together beautifully for a

great many years, on many projects. We recently collaborated to try to establish a course in Judaic Studies at the University of Michigan. And, I am happy to tell you that a $40,000 grant was just made by the Jewish Community Foundation of the United Jewish Charities of Detroit to the University of Michigan which, together with the money that the university has already appropriated, will make it possible for a student to select Judaic Studies as his major field of interest.

As we come to the climax of our tribute to Dean Haber and his lovely wife, Fannie, we all pray they will be granted many more years of good health and happiness together, so that they can continue their wonderful work for a grateful community.

Now it is my pleasure to ask Dr. Robben Fleming, president of the University of Michigan, to please come to the podium and do the honors for us.

Paul and Helen Zuckerman

50th birthday party for Paul Zuckerman, born in Turkey, with his son
Norbert

As a long-time friend of the man
we are honoring tonight, I'm happy to introduce Paul Zuckerman.

Paul certainly does not need a lengthy introduction, but
I'm going to give him one anyhow. At your plate is a souvenir
program, and in it is a brief biographical sketch which lists
most of his interests. I will not attempt to elaborate on his
activities. But, if you will bear with me, I'd like to relate some
anecdotes about Paul as well as to give you some of my

Introduction, Jewish National Fund dinner, Congregation Shaarey Zedek, June
1968.

impressions of this unusual personality. Tonight we will give him a little taffy instead of epitaphy.

Paul has the reputation of being a hard guy who is the softest touch in town when it comes to charity. His generosity is so great that it has helped our community set new high standards of giving to many important fund-raising projects. Because of the example he sets with his personal sense of *tzedakah*, he can solicit others more successfully than the average volunteer worker. I have never heard anyone criticize the size of his contributions. And you know that the one thing two Jews can always agree upon is how much a third Jew should give to charity.

My dear friend, Rabbi Nelson Glueck, president of the Hebrew Union College-Jewish Institute of Religion, told me a humorous experience he had with Paul. They both happened to be in Israel at the same time. Paul had taken his son Norbert on the young man's first trip to Israel. Dr. Glueck was there trying to complete plans for the building of a school of archeology and a Jerusalem branch of the seminary (incidentally, on land leased to him by the Jewish National Fund at $1.00 a year). The three men were in swimming at the Accadia Hotel in Herzlia-by-the-Sea. Dr. Glueck's project needed money, so he gave Paul a pitch for a contribution, and of course Paul said OK.

Because they were in swimming trunks, Paul asked Norbert to see if he could get a pen and a sheet of paper from the lunch stand near the pool. Norby came back with only a pen and said the waiters could not give him a sales slip to write on because they were all numbered. Without a change of expression, Paul asked Norby to go into the men's room and bring a square of tissue upon which Paul proceeded to write a check payable on the National Bank of Detroit for $2,000. He handed it to Glueck. Norby's jaw dropped, Nelson Glueck grinned (he still talks about it to this day), and, believe it or not, the bank cashed the check.

I remember the story about how Paul and Teddy Kollek, the mayor of Jerusalem, first became acquainted in 1957. This could only be a Paul Zuckerman story. Paul, who is our local leading iconoclast, is known to have no more awe for people in positions of importance than he does for the little man on the street. Paul was at the King David Hotel in New Jerusalem and received a phone call from Teddy Kollek's secretary. Teddy was then Ben Gurion's director general. The secretary conveyed the message to Paul that Mr. Kollek would like to meet him and that Paul should be at his apartment at six o'clock for a five-minute meeting so that Kollek "could get to know" Paul. Paul and his famous low boiling point exploded on the phone. "Five minutes! I've been married for twenty years and even my wife hasn't gotten to know me." Without waiting for an answer he hung up.

A few minutes later, Kollek called and suggested a meeting the following evening for at least an hour. Evidently, this satisfied Paul because at 6:00 P.M. sharp Paul arrived at Kollek's apartment. He rang the bell, the door was opened by Teddy, who sized up Paul without even saying hello, and poked friendly fingers into Paul's stomach to test his muscles. Paul returned the strange greeting by prodding Teddy's chest, strong and massive from his fisherman's days on the Sea of Galilee. Then these two characters started to wrestle on the floor; and they still had not exchanged a word of greeting.

Good friends ever since, Kollek has helped Paul create one of the most remarkable personal collections of Persian antiquities in this country today. Can you imagine this happening to anyone but Paul Zuckerman?

In a way, Paul is running his own private Jewish National Fund in Israel. A few years ago on one of his frequent trips to Israel, Paul complained to Teddy Kollek that Ben Gurion's cottage in the Negev kibbutz didn't have a blade of grass, a shrub or a tree around it. Teddy pointed out that none of the houses in that part of the desert were any better off, and because grass and shrubs were so expensive they just hadn't done anything about it. Paul left a check behind to landscape Ben Gurion's house and returned to Detroit. The next year, driving through the desert, he decided to look at Ben Gurion's home to see what had been done. He was stopped cold by armed sentries at least a hundred yards away from Ben Gurion's home. "How do you like that? They wouldn't even let me have the thrill of stepping on the grass I bought for him," Paul wailed. That will give you some idea of how sentimental Paul is.

Just a few weeks ago, Paul and wife Helen had lunch with Kollek in Israel. Paul mentioned that he marveled at the splendid beautifying job Teddy is doing in Old Jerusalem, especially with such limited funds. Sure enough, Teddy picked up the opening and convinced Paul that he should create a park in the Holy City to be called Zuckerman Gardens. Kollek said Paul should give this present to himself from "the man who has everything." And Paul did it, except that he called it the Detroit Gardens.

Those of you who have traveled in Israel have seen his name on walls and plaques all over the country, in the schools and hospitals. He has done the same here in our state. Not too long ago he gave Bloomfield Township the land for a library site. Among his current benefactions is the grant of a couple of hundred thousand dollars to Sinai Hospital. Next Sunday morning, at eleven o'clock, the hospital is dedicating the Paul and Helen Zuckerman Auditorium and Conference Center. You are all invited to come to the ceremony and to tour this magnificent, much needed, new facility at our hospital.

The Talmud, the body of old rabbinical civil and ceremonial law, relates a commentary on wealth. It tells that Rabbi Hanassi honored rich men. At first glance such conduct seemed surprising. Why should the possession of wealth make a person more worthy of honor? The rabbi explained that riches are in truth "deposits entrusted by God to individuals for the short span of their lifetime." It is obvious that the larger the sum involved the more trustworthy or dependable must be the persons to whom God entrusted the deposits.

Hence, reasoned Rabbi Hanassi, the fact that the Almighty has entrusted these men with such great fortunes or such powerful positions indicates their good credit and reliability in the eyes of God to utilize their wealth, power and position for good and worthy purposes. These people are therefore deserving of honor.

Paul Zuckerman has kept faith with his stewardship of wealth. So Paul gives money away without pain.

But giving money away is only one part of the character of this many-faceted man. His role as a mover and doer is even more extensive behind the scenes than in the public eye. We use his counsel on many aspects of our community life because he has the right, if you'll excuse the expression, *timber* in him.

Paul knows that all of us feel significant, primarily in terms of concern for others and what we mean to others. Cynics may consider this a sign of human vanity, but realists recognize this instinct as the fountain-head of honorable human endeavor.

I know dozens of people who have been helped by Paul in one way or another with their personal problems, and not just with money. He knows that there is a big difference between sticking your nose in other people's business and putting your heart in other people's problems.

Yes, people themselves are the source of his spirit, his Judaism. The most distant become intimate, very dear to him. His kinship with the people of Israel has given him ineffable delight.

Paul is on the board of Franklin Hills Country Club and loves to play golf. When I asked him about his questionable record of consistent low scores, he told me, "Let's put it this way—I play golf for my health, and a low score makes me feel better."

He has been honored by the Catholics, the Jews, and the Protestants. With the Arabs, he is not too close at the moment.

They tell the story about the time a little girl asked Paul if he'd buy some Girl Scout cookies from her. Paul thought he'd have some fun and asked, "Why should I buy cookies from you, why me?" She replied, "Because you are so handsome." He bought twenty-five boxes.

You should know also that he is distinguished by his independence of spirit and thought. And that is a euphemism. Some people just call him a maverick. I like that expression, because to me it means that nobody has his brand on him. He has the courage and audacity to speak his mind when he believes he has something to say.

Paul has amazing stamina and enthusiasm. His services to his fellow man are nonsectarian and interracial. He is the eternal optimist, declaring that there are no hopeless situations, only people who have grown hopeless about them.

We all pray, Paul, that you will be granted many more years of good health and happiness to continue your fine work for a grateful community.

Eleanor Roosevelt

Eleanor Roosevelt honored at the celebration for the establishment of
the Detroit Dormitory at Hebrew University

It was thrilling to hear the inspiring
message of Eleanor Roosevelt, the "great lady with the great
heart." It's a tremendous honor for us to live in the same generation with the best-loved woman of our times. Thank you
so much for being with us tonight, Mrs. Roosevelt.

In Mrs. Roosevelt's recent book, titled *On My Own*, I
read about her visit to Israel back in 1952. I was particularly
impressed with the statement she made, which I will quote
verbatim. She said, "Going from the Arab countries through
the Mandelbaum Gate into Israel was, to me, like breathing
the air of the United States again."

She also mentioned that when she visited the Arab

Presented at the Hebrew University of Jerusalem dinner, Statler Hotel, September 1959.

249

countries, before she arrived in Israel, she met some of the Arab leaders who wanted to know why she was so interested in Israel. One Arab leader said to her: "Madam, you have been friendly to Israel." And Mrs. Roosevelt replied: "Yes, I am friendly to all. I am equally friendly to your people." The Arab leader persisted with the statement: "But you have worked for Israel." And Mrs. Roosevelt answered: "That is true. When I think a thing is good, I also think it should be given help."

And that, in Mrs. Roosevelt's few words, is why we are all here tonight. The Hebrew University of Jerusalem *is* a good thing, and plays so large a part in Israel's present as well as in its future, that we all want to give it some help.

Most of us have been aware of the existence of the Hebrew University of Jerusalem, of its unique purpose, of many of its accomplishments and needs. And, Detroit has tried to be helpful in so many ways. One of these is through our yearly allocation to the University from the funds we raise in the annual Detroit Allied Jewish Campaign. However, the allocation that Detroit Jewry gives to the Hebrew University of Jerusalem is strictly for maintenance, or, as we understand it, for annual operating expenses of the University.

And now we are being asked to help Israel expand its national university by contributing a building on the campus to be called the Detroit Dormitory. This will play an important part in helping to educate their youngsters so that Israel may have the benefit of intelligent, trained minds urgently needed for the security of its future.

For all this generosity the Hebrew University and its five thousand students are deeply grateful. Perhaps we should properly say the entire state of Israel is grateful for this generosity.

And so tonight we have come together to launch the Detroit Dormitory project at the Hebrew University of Jerusalem.

Harvey and Jean Willens

Harvey and Jean Willens

I feel especially good tonight participating in this Israel bond testimonial honoring two very dear friends of mine, Harvey and Jean Willens. They have earned the respect and admiration of our entire community because of the splendid examples they set. They've shown how to make togetherness work. For about thirty-five years they've proven

Introduction, Israel Bond dinner, Raleigh House, October 1975.

that two people can be happy though married—to each other, of course.

I'm happy that we have this opportunity to show Harvey and Jean how grateful we are for all they mean to us. They are the kind of people who fully understand and appreciate the statement by the great rabbi of ancient days, Rashi, that "all Jews are responsible for one another." The Willens have an intense commitment to the welfare of their fellow Jews, no matter where they live in this world.

Because tonight is an evening for happiness, a *simcha*, I want to tell you some pleasant anecdotes about our friends, the Willens. I learned that they and their two daughters are native-born Detroiters. Harvey started his education at the Thirkel Elementary School. After his first day in classes, he came home and was asked by his dad what he had learned in school. He answered, "I learned for the first time that my name was not Harvaleh Boobaleh."

This kid was really smart. If you check the records you'll find that in 1929, at the annual Willens and Company banquet, Harvey, who was only eight years old, was elected vice-president of the company. Jean insists that the fact that Harv's father owned all the stock in the corporation had absolutely nothing to do with this fantastic promotion.

Harvey and Jean met while they were high school students. Their great romance flourished for about four years before our hero won the hand of the beautiful Jean. They loved to dance together, and today they are two of the greatest. They used to be called "Mr. and Mrs. Arthur Murray, Jr." But, in those early days, Harvey wasn't as good as he thought he was. At one of the school dances, Jean said to him, "Harv, please waltz a little faster; this is a fox-trot."

After Northern High School, Harvey went to the University of Michigan and graduated with a B.A. degree. While still at U. of M., he continued with his flying lessons. In 1940 he made his first solo cross-country flight. He was doing great until his motor conked out just beyond Sandusky, Ohio. Did he panic? I should say not. He found a clear spot and landed his plane. Guess where it was? Right in the middle of the Wimbleton Cup Rifle matches being held at Camp Perry's target site. Harv was greeted with a twenty-one-gun salute. The only trouble was that the guns were pointed at him! He made the front pages of the newspapers and was on all the radio stations, coast-to-coast. They called him "plucky Harvey Willens." Plucky isn't exactly what I would have called him.

In 1941, Harvey and Jean were married. They went to Havana on their honeymoon. They went on a cruise advertised as a trip they would never forget, and Jean says she sure won't. She said it was on that ship that she found out how the nautical term "heave-ho!" originated.

Soon World War II came and Harvey enlisted in the Navy Air Corps and went to war. He was a lieutenant junior grade stationed in China. Their daughter, Joanie, was born in 1946 while he was seven thousand miles away. He didn't see her until he returned to Detroit when she was four months old.

That was a long time ago. After he got back, his youngest daughter, Amy, was born in 1949. Now Harvey and Jean are grandparents of a darling four-year old boy named Jeffrey. They still live in Detroit on Hamilton Road across from Palmer Park. Harv calls it a very quiet neighborhood. Where else can you hear people whispering for help?

They travel a lot and have been to Israel twice, once on a Detroit service group study mission in 1966. Harvey was the group leader. They went again in 1973 with a group from Temple Beth El, of which he was a recent president. They loved the land of the Bible. Jean says she especially likes to eat in Israeli restaurants. "Where else can you get hot 'star-of-David' buns?" In Israel, you read from right to left. Harv told me that the last time he ate in a Tel-Aviv restaurant, he had the greatest "$4.95" he ever tasted. He saw a sign in Israel: "Please drive carefully—we need every taxpayer we can get."

One of Harvey's favorite hobbies is golf. And, incidentally, they tell me that in Israel you start playing golf beginning with the 18th hole, and then you work your way backward to the first hole. Harvey is really an excellent golfer. Back in 1968 he made a hole-in-one. I'll bet he's the only one in this room tonight who ever had that thrill. Jean is also an excellent golfer. Harv joined the country club just to be able to find a doctor on Wednesday afternoons.

Harvey is president of Franklin Hills Country Club this year. You see him often, entertaining some of his customers. He's quite a salesman. One time, when I played golf with him, I was in a sand trap about two hundred feet from the green, and he conceded my putt. And, I was not that good a customer!

Jean Willens is one of the loveliest ladies in town—in looks, in fashion, and in disposition. She is a wonderful wife, mother, and friend. Harvey says he has only one trouble with her: she goes out and passes good checks.

There is an old proverb—"Observe the face of the wife to know the husband's character." Need I say anything more? Harvey has the old-fashioned virtues of integrity and responsibility. I once heard him say that if God had believed in permissiveness, he would have given us "The Ten Suggestions."

Seriously, as we grow older, we begin to see that events of our life seem to arrange themselves in the image of our character, so that in a sense, we receive what we deserve. Maybe that will help you understand why Harvey and Jean are being honored tonight. On your table is the printed program for this affair. Please note the list of some of the many service and cultural organizations to which the Willens give so freely of their time, their funds, and their talents. So it seems to be true that we are what we do.

There is a story about the time Harvey and Jean were on one of their trips and struck up an acquaintance with a couple from New England. In the course of their exchanges of information about each other, the New Englander boasted, "Our family fought with George Washington, fought with General Grant, fought with Pershing, and fought with MacArthur. Whom did your family fight with?" Harvey replied, "Nobody. We get along with everybody."

And that pretty much describes the Willens family. So, there you have some seriousness mixed with some good-natured nonsense. All of it an expression of our great affection for Jean and Harvey.

And now the honorable Abba Eban will make the official presentation of the Israeli prime minister's medal to Mr. and Mrs. Harvey Willens.

Sam and Miriam Hamburger

L. to R.: Miriam Hamburger, Gertrude Wineman, Sam Hamburger

Thank you for your flattering introduction: I feel that I should lie down and let someone put some flowers on my chest.

Tonight we are honoring two of our friends, a husband and wife team that has earned the respect of the entire city, Mr. and Mrs. Samuel Hamburger—Miriam and Sam. For the first time, we are honoring a couple instead of an individual. You might say, we are "getting two for the price of one." I am happy that we can show them how grateful we are for

Introduction, Israel Bond dinner, Sheraton-Cadillac Hotel, December 1971.

their lifetime of assistance to those less fortunate. By their dedicated efforts they have proven that money is only as good as the good it can do. They have shown a deep consciousness of our responsibility to one another based on a nonsectarian, interracial level. In characteristically Jewish fashion, Miriam and Sam Hamburger have patterned their lives on the theory that God has given them stewardship of wealth to be utilized for good purposes.

But, I'd like to talk also about Miriam and Sam in a less serious way. I'll tell you some personal things about them which you may not know. For instance, they are native Detroiters. It is very unusual to find native Detroiters among our local Jewish "medicare kids."

Did you know that Sam has been a treasurer of our Allied Jewish Campaign for many years? I've always thought this was done with the idea, in the back of Federation's mind, that if any of the annual Allied Jewish Campaigns fell short of its goal, Sam would make up the difference.

I always enjoy being with Miriam and Sam as often as I can. Would you call that "*gelt* by association?" Did you know that Sam came from a poor family? His is a living Horatio Alger story. He has been working since he sold newspapers at the age of eight. He started the Production Steel Company during the depression years with borrowed capital. Together with other members of his family he built the business into one of the largest independent steel companies in America.

Miriam and Sam are supporters of practically every worthwhile local charity. No hand that is stretched out to them is left empty, because they are firm believers that *tzedakah* (giving) is a part of our way of life. I know of no charity to which they haven't given, and some of these organizations have not as yet found a disease to conquer.

I heard that Sam has been talking about retiring, and letting the United States government be self-supporting. Oh well, money isn't everything; and I wish I had a dollar for every time I've said that.

Miriam is quite a gal. Among her many extracurricular activities she has served for years on the board of our Welfare Federation's Capital Needs Committee and also on the board of the Fresh Air Society. Just the other day, Miriam was seen walking up to a little old man with a long white beard, wearing a red suit trimmed with white, and saying, "Santa, what do you need?"

She has shared with Sam their vital interest in Israel. They give all-out support to the United Jewish Appeal. Their combined Hamburger family gift is the largest of all the contributions we Detroit Jews give each year to our Allied Jewish Campaign. I don't know for sure, but they tell me Sam is so wealthy he sends Care packages to Howard Hughes.

Miriam and Sam are also leaders in our annual Bond campaigns. She is an Israel Bond Woman of Valor. Both of them are Double Golden Trustees of Israel. Their interests and benefactions are community-wide. They include cultural, humanitarian, scientific, and spiritual causes. Sinai Hospital and Children's Hospital are among their major beneficiaries. Art, education, and music are also among their main interests. Miriam and Sam are on the list of leading patrons of the Detroit Institute of Arts.

I almost forgot to tell you that Sam loves to play golf. He and his golfing buddy, attorney Harold Shapero, play at what I call *mashoogey* (crazy) hours. They sneak up on Franklin Hills Country Club in the dark, just before daylight, so they can be the first to tee off. They don't play for money. But, the rivalry that exists between these two rich competitors, for the prize of one golf ball each game, is really hard to believe. Sam has a saying: "Nothing counts in golf . . . like your opponent."

Miriam and Sam are truly unique. They are warm, soft-spoken, modest people who never put on airs. They don't flaunt their wealth. They are what I like to call *Haimashe menchen* (homey people). They are the salt of the earth, with a courageous, intense commitment to the welfare of others. And they do all these wonderful things, about which I've been telling you, *Le shame' show my yim*—without thought of personal gain or reward.

Maybe they are such wonderful people because they carry two of the most exalted names in our Bible. Miriam was the name of the sister of Moses, and Samuel was the last of our great prophets. Samuel, translated from the Hebrew, means "name of God."

To recap the life of a person in a few words is not easy, but if there is one word to characterize Miriam, it is "fairness."

She has a deep sense of fairness. She has empathy for people and understands their problems. Miriam is committed to the cause of justice for all people regardless of religion, race or national origin.

And, if there is one word to characterize Sam, that word is "integrity." He built a tremendously successful business because people found him completely trustworthy. Not long ago, I was with a man who is a purchasing agent for General Motors Corporation. We talked about the steel business. He told me about an incident at General Motors that required a great deal of confidential handling to keep GM from possibly becoming involved in an unpleasant situation. He said the powers that be at GM talked it over and decided there was one man in town they would trust with this special assignment. That man was Sam Hamburger.

You should know Miriam and Sam were reluctant to accept tonight's tribute. They felt that Jews should help Israel all they can for its own sake, and not because the Hamburgers were being honored. I told them "You are right, and we are right, too. We are both right." The Detroit Federation of Reform Synagogues needs your help to put over another successful Israel Bond event, for the benefit of Israel. Furthermore, it is especially important at this critical time, when the Arabs are again becoming bold and threatening Israel with another war, to test whether Israel can or cannot survive." They both spoke up: they would not refuse us anything. This was another example of their togetherness.

Before I close, I call to your attention that this is the fourth night of Hannukah, the holiday when we give gifts, usually Hannukah *gelt*. So, I'm asking you to use your *gelt* to help our brethren in Israel become self-supporting. Let's loan them some money as our Hannukah gift to them.

This kind of assistance is the highest degree of *tzedakah*. If there's any doubt about the accuracy of what I've just said to you, ask your rabbi.

We now come to the climax of our tribute to Mr. and Mrs. Sam Hamburger. We all pray that they will be granted many more years of good health and happiness together.

His excellency, Shimon Peres, will make the official presentation of the Israeli Prime Minister's Medal to Mr. and Mrs. Sam Hamburger.

Gus Newman Turns Ninety

Gus Newman

This is a big thrill for me. Today, the Jewish Home for the Aged is joining in the city-wide celebration of our beloved Gustav David Newman's 90th birthday, and I am given the honor of saluting Gus. I want to tell you some anecdotes about our dear friend which, I am sure, most of you have never heard.

But Gus, before I start bragging about you, I want you to know that I expect you to do the same for me when I reach ninety. Don't laugh; I'm getting there pretty soon, I hope.

Most of us know Gus quite well. He has been a member of the Home's board for forty-seven years. This gives him the unique distinction of being our oldest board member in years of service. He was elected back in 1934, before many of you were born.

For nearly all those years, the name of Gus Newman

Presented at Gus Newman's birthday celebration at the Detroit Jewish Home for the Aged, September 1981.

259

has been synonymous with the Jewish Home for Aged. No one has been more consistent in his devotion to the Home than Gus. He has held every important position in our organization. At times, Gus spent so much time at the Home that our residents thought he was a full-time paid staff member.

When Gus was president from 1954 to 1960, they say he considered installing oxygen masks with pay meters. I'm just kidding, of course.

He was chairman of our Admissions Committee for many years. With our then perennial president Jacob Levin, Gus went to most of our applicants' homes and talked to them with warmth and sympathy. They loved him because he spoke Yiddish fluently with them.

The cute stories Gus used to tell about some of these interviews would make a great book. His delightful sense of humor and charming manner have endeared him to all of us. Oh yes: did you know that Gus has led the *kiddush* on the second night of Passover at the Home for over thirty years?

Let me tell you some personal things about Gus that you won't find in the rounds. I dug these out by talking to some of his old friends, relatives, former girl friends, and some bartenders. I wish time permitted me to tell all of them to you, but unfortunately it doesn't.

Gus was born in Detroit. He has three sisters and three brothers. He is the eldest. He has been the head of the family since his father died when Gus was fifteen and one-half years old. He quit school and went to work. He is self-educated, and as a self-made man you have to agree he was a darn good mechanic.

The earliest story I heard about Gus goes back to 1896. When he was five years old, his grandfather, Abraham Jacobs, a custom tailor, made Gus a blue wool suit, with matching coat, cape, and cap and emblazoned with brass buttons. Gus strutted down the street resplendent in his new finery, got carried away with himself, and kept right on walking. He became lost. The police picked him up, brought him to the station. Thinking they would comfort him until his family would fetch him, they treated him to ice cream and cake. Shortly after, his two aunts came to the station to get him but Gus was enjoying himself so much he told the officers "I don't know who these ladies are."

In his youth, after his bar mitzvah at Shaarey Zedek, he became a leader in the activities at the old Hannah Schloss Center which preceded the Jewish Community Center. Gus played basketball and baseball. They tell me he was a great little athlete. Later he coached at the Young Men's Hebrew Association. In 1906, Gus became the first Jewish scoutmaster in Detroit.

Gus started to work at Henry the Hatter's when he was thirteen, delivering repair jobs to department stores. Mr. J. L. Hudson saw him and said, I'll pay you $3.50 a week to work for me." Gus said proudly, "I'm earning that much now, Mr. Hudson, so I think I'll stay with the hat store."

The owner of the hat store played the snare drums and sometimes played in the pit at the Temple Theatre. Through that connection Gus was allowed to stand in the wings. Gus Edward's' *School Days* was playing at the Temple with Eddie Cantor, George Jessel, Lila Lee, and Herman Timberg. Gus stood in the wings imitating the actors; Edwards saw him and was impressed. He said to Gus, "Kid, how would you like to join us and go on the road?" Gus said, "Fine, I'll tell my mother." When he told his mother he was going on the stage and become an actor, she said, "I'll teach you all the acting you need to know at home." So he retired from the stage before he started.

Even though Gus didn't join the Gus Edwards' review, he later became friends with many great entertainers, and he also befriended many struggling actors. Henry the Hatter became a popular rendezvous for many celebrities, and the Lafayette Building hat store was a picture gallery of famous people who were Gus's friends. Fight champions Jack Dempsey, Max Baer, and Benny Leonard were his friends. If you couldn't get tickets for any theater or sporting event, you called Gus, and you got the best in the house. Gus was a man of great civic influence.

Athletes, writers, and politicians were all friends of Gus. Community leaders Fred Butzel, Ike Shetzer, Judge Harry Keidan, Morris Zackheim, and Rabbis Abraham Hershman, Morris Adler, and Leo Franklin were among his treasured friends. Dr. Leon Fram is another long-time friend. Michigan Governors Fred Green, Frank Murphy, and Wilbur Brucker, and Senator James Couzens were also numbered among his intimate friends. So were most of the mayors and councilmen. During the depression he obtained jobs for many people at Ford Motor Company through his friends Harry Bennett and Charles Sorenson.

In his youth, Gus used to kill time and money by frequenting Detroit gambling houses. Just as Vegas does now, they gave you all the free drinks you wanted because it makes for better odds for the house. One evening he was feeling no pain and began to give away hats to the band, to the waiters, to everyone. Every cab driver in Detroit knew him, and they got him home okay that night. The next morning he got into the Michigan Avenue store, and they were really busy. He felt pretty good until he opened the cash register and found many little bits of paper with "OK one hat . . . Gus" instead of money.

I asked Gus to what he attributed his long and healthy life. And he told me: "I never smoked, drank hard liquor, or ran around with girls—until I was twelve years old."

Of course, you know that Gus is a walker and that he still walks five miles a day and still works out in a gym three days a week. His weight is the same today as it was sixty years ago. What you may not know is that he has convinced himself that his daily constitutional was dependent upon the long walk. No walk, no constitutional. The very first time Gus and Seymour Wasserman, who now owns Henry the Hatter, went to New York together they shared a bedroom on the train and neither slept very well. However, Gus insisted they get up at about six (the train did not get to New York until eight when it was on time). Gus also insisted that the porter make up the room at once. Then he proceeded to circle and recircle the room until Seymour got dizzy watching as Gus attempted to get in his five miles of walking. When Seymour suggested he use the train aisleway, he said, "Do you want folks to think I'm crazy?"

One of his idiosyncrasies is that he has never eaten a piece of watermelon in his life. Another is that he was probably the only automobile dealer in the world who owned an auto agency (Ford agency on Dexter) and did not know how to drive a car. He learned to drive at age sixty-five when his sister and brother-in-law moved to Oak Park, and he had no choice. He started driving late but is making up for it because he is still driving at age ninety.

Gus has been very active in our local Jewish charities,

not just the Home. He was president of the Hebrew Free Loan Association, the Detroit Service Group, the fund-raising arm of the Jewish Welfare Federation, and he has been honored every year for the past ten years at the Detroit Service Group's Annual Stag Day, including this year. He was a founder of the Hannah Schloss Old-Timers. He is active in the Jewish National Fund, Zionists, and the Allied Jewish Campaign.

During the early Federation campaigns, Gus, along with George Stutz, and sometimes Esther Prussian, would call on what they termed "Specials"—those people who did not fit into any regular category because they were gamblers in what we, in Prohibition days, called the Saloons, "Blind Pigs,"—to get the operators' pledges. They not only collected money but often would come home the happiest solicitors in town. They were plastered. Many of the gamblers, instead of mailing in the money, would walk into the hat store and say, "Gus, what's my marker?" And they would hand him their contributions. Some of the money came from non-Jews. Gus would turn in their money using cute names: Danny Sullivan, for example, became Danny Solomon.

For some unknown reason (maybe it was because he was the head of the family) as a young lad, Gus was nicknamed Zaidy (Grandpa), and all the kids he played with, black and white, called him Zaidy. Years later, at a Federation luncheon meeting at the Statler, Gus was sitting with Henry Wineman and other committee members when a black waiter said, "How do you do, Mr. Wineman." Then he spied Gus, and he greeted him with, "How you doing, *Zaidy*?" Of course, everyone got a kick out of that.

Gus never married, as you probably know. But he had plenty of chances. I know. I used to see the young gals and the widows chase after him.

I liked some of the very astute reflections he used to make about being a bachelor. He said, a bachelor is a man who comes to his office every morning from a different direction. A bachelor is a guy who can pull on his sox from either end.

Now that Gus is a nonagenarian, a guy who has been blessed by God and reached the Biblical three score and ten— plus twenty for good measure—and still going strong, I asked Gus to tell me all about it. After all, I'm seventy-seven and one of these days I hope to catch up with Gus. I asked him how it felt to reach ninety, and in his customary clever manner, he said, "Well, the best thing about growing older is that it takes such a long time."

He said he has reached the age when he has to put on his glasses to think, and every time he sees a girl he used to know—it is her granddaughter.

Gus then went on to say, "You know you have reached ninety when you light the candles on your birthday cake and the air conditioning automatically switches on."

He told me, "Now when I have a choice of two hobbies, I pick the one that lets me sit down."

He made many other very wise comments that I'm sure you will enjoy hearing, such as, "About the only thing that comes to you in life without effort is old age," and "The only thing about old age that I don't like is when you feel like the morning after, and you ain't been any place."

Gus prefers to stay home and watch TV rather than go out to the movies, because TV is closer to the bathroom.

He told me that last night he woke up about three o'clock, and his ear was ringing. He was so tired he let it ring four times.

He had a physical the other day and the doctor told him, "I'm happy to report that you are OK and should live to be ninety" Gus said, "But I am ninety." And the M.D. replied, "See, what did I tell you?"

Gus concluded our little conversation with, "Yes, God has been very good to me. But, I think He has let me live so long because He is testing the patience of my sister Doraella, with whom I live."

He said he hopes and prays that the day will come soon to the world when the lion and the lamb will lie down together in peace. But he's still betting on the lion.

And his advice to all of us is that we should live our lives so that if the mail brings a letter from the IRS, we can take our time and open it last.

Gus, you have made a fine beginning. Remember that the first Jew, Abraham, who started his mission to spread the idea of monotheism, did so at the age of ninety.

And don't forget, Gus, when you talk about Moses who lived to be one hundred and twenty and his brother Aaron who lived to one hundred and thirty, that you are just a kid.

Irving Berlin is past ninety. Rabbi Mordecai Kaplan was one hundred last June and is going strong. I could go on and list dozens of famous people who did great things after they reached the age of ninety, but my allotted time this morning has run out.

Gus, will you please come up here because it is now my extreme pleasure and privilege to present you with this plaque from the board of the Home. I will first read it to you and all those present.

A SALUTE TO GUS NEWMAN ON HIS 90TH BIRTHDAY

For close to five decades, Gus Newman's dedication and commitment to the Jewish Home for Aged has been exemplary. He has served the home in countless capacities, culminating in his presidency from 1954 to 1959. Gus has not only contributed significantly in his board leadership but also in his direct contact work with residents. Gus Newman's contribution to the Home helped create the foundation which has permitted the tremendous growth and development which we have seen throughout the years.

It is, therefore, a great privilege on behalf of the board of the Jewish Home for Aged to extend our heartiest congratulations to Gus Newman on his 90th birthday.

Gus, may you be blessed with many more years, filled with vigor, health, and happiness!

Presented: September 20, 1981

By: Leonard N. Simons

Red Buttons and Sammy Cahn

Sammy Cahn

Red Buttons

And now it is my pleasure to present for your pleasure two of the great names in the entertainment world.

Red Buttons is a composer, author, actor, and comedian.

He won an Oscar for his role in the movie *Sayonara*. He's equally famous for his performances on the stage, in the movies, and on TV. Just last Monday you probably saw him on Channel 4, the NBC network. He gave another great performance as the star of the Danny Thomas Show, "The Zero Man."

I've checked everywhere—at least six directories—and I can't find any other first name for him except "Red." Maybe tonight he'll tell us his real first name.

Among the songs he wrote is one entitled "The HO-HO

Introduction, Detroit Round Table of Catholics, Jews, and Protestants dinner, Cobo Hall, December 1967.

Song." Red, is that the theme song for the Jolly Green Giant?

Red told me that he came *All The Way* from Hollywood with his pal, Sammy Cahn, to *Make Someone Happy*. He said no one can *Call Me Irresponsible*. *I Should Care*, and I really do. I believe that *Day by Day* this is getting to be a better world. At least I have *High Hopes*. Sammy says *It's Been a Long, Long Time* since he was last here, and despite the weather Detroit is *My Kind of Town*. *Let It Snow, Let It Snow, Let It Snow*.

Red let me in on a secret. He said *Time after Time* I use *The Tender Trap* whenever I want Sammy to *Come Fly with Me*. I merely flatter Sammy by telling him *By Mere Bis Du Shane*, and it works every time. *It's Magic*. I also tell him he can play some of his favorite songs like *Three Coins in the Fountain, Love and Marriage, Be My Love, The Second Time Around*, and *The Best of Everything* that have helped keep Frank Sinatra at the top of the Hit Parade.

By now you must have realized that in my sneaky way I've just mentioned twenty of the tunes that made Sammy Cahn internationally famous and won five Oscars and Emmy Awards for him.

So Red and Sammy, *Come Blow Your Horn*; the stage is yours!

Harvey S. Firestone, Jr.

Harvey S. Firestone, Jr.

Twenty-four years ago, my partner Larry Michelson and I decided to hang out our advertising agency shingle. A wonderful little guy named Dick Hoy, of blessed memory, was working for the *Detroit News.* He took a liking to us, and no man could have done more for our embryonic business, even if he had been our own brother.

Then, there was another man, named McDermidt. I never found out his first name—they always called him "Mac"—who was the Michigan manager for the Firestone Tire and Rubber Company. Mac had his own ideas regarding local advertising. He asked Dick Hoy to recommend an advertising agency to him. Dick suggested us, with the following comment, so the story goes, "They're a couple of Jewish boys who are real go-getters." Dick told me that Mac replied, "Firestone doesn't care what church they go to. What we want to know is, can they write an ad that gets results, and are they nice people?"

Introduction, National Conference of Christians and Jews, Adcraft Club Brotherhood luncheon, Statler Hotel, February 1953.

I tell you this story so that you'll understand why the name Firestone brings a warm glow to my heart. Firestone was Simons-Michelson's biggest account for quite some time.

Today I have been honored with the privilege of introducing Harvey S. Firestone, Jr., to you.

What a famous name Firestone is, especially in Detroit. It is known by everyone, man, woman, and child.

Firestone ranks alongside Ford, Chrysler, Sloan, Kettering, and others, all names of men of automotive genius, men with deep faith in their fellowman.

Harvey S. Firestone, Jr., a famous son of a famous father, and I'm not just using adjectives loosely, for what I say is true. He has many of his dad's attributes, not the least of which is the same kind of deep faith in his fellowman. That is why he is here today; why he is spending a lot of time and effort, working to make this a better world, not just a world that runs better on rubber but a world that will run better on mutual understanding and respect.

In introducing Harvey Samuel Firestone, Jr., to you I will first tell you a few things about his personal life and also about just a limited number of his activities in an amazing long list of important organizations.

Mr. Firestone is fifty-four years old. After graduating from Princeton at the age of twenty-two, he became associated with Firestone. He is now their chief executive. Firestone Tire and Rubber Company has forty-eight plants in the United States, one for each star in the flag, and ten in foreign countries. During World War I, he enlisted in the United States Navy Aviation Corps.

He is the father of four children, one of whom is now a citizen of our town. Her name is Mrs. William Clay Ford, Martha to her friends. Mrs. Ford, like all the women in the Ford family, is a charming and lovely lady.

Harvey Firestone, during World War II, was the national chairman of the U.S.O. He was awarded medals from the governments of France, Spain, Finland, and Liberia.

Nineteen fifty-one saw him receive several more important honors:

Forbes magazine adjudged him one of America's twelve most outstanding business leaders. Northwestern University gave him an award in recognition of the impact which he has made upon his generation during a lifetime of distinguished service. Kenyon College awarded him a medal for devoted service to the Protestant Episcopal Church.

Truman appointed him to membership on the President's Commission on Internal Security and Individual Rights. He has also served on many other governmental committees.

He is a trustee of the Thomas A. Edison Foundation. He is on the National Commission of Community Chests and Councils, Inc. He is a member of the Board of Trustees of the National Society for Crippled Children and Adults. He is on the National Board of the American Bible Society and is a member of the International Committee of the YMCA.

He is a trustee of Princeton University, as well as of five other schools for higher education, and he is on the National Council of the United Negro College Fund. He is a member of the Vestry of his church, as well as a member of over a half dozen organizations affiliated with the Episcopal Church.

During 1951 and 1952, he was national cochairman of American Brotherhood Week, sponsored by the National Conference of Christians and Jews.

Quite a long list, isn't it? Yet, it is only a partial list. Time alone restricts me from mentioning the many other organizations served by Mr. Firestone. Obviously, here is the kind of man that we all like; the kind of man who is making America as famous for her humanitarianism as for her many other thrilling accomplishments.

So, now listen to the *Voice of Firestone*, the voice of Harvey S. Firestone, Jr., who will talk about something he considers as important as anything there is in the world, "The Brotherhood of Man under the Fatherhood of God."

Mr. Firestone.

Abram Sachar

Abram Sachar

When I came to the hotel for the Brandeis dinner, I ran into a friend who knew I was to speak on tonight's program. "Leonard," she asked, "are you nervous before you have to make your speeches?" I replied, "Not at all." "Indeed," she said, "then what are you doing in the Ladies' Room?"

If the truth be known, every speaker gets a few butterflies, especially when he has the honor and privilege to introduce as famous a man as Dr. Sachar. Most of us here have met him personally during his many visits to our city, and some of us have the good fortune to be numbered among his intimate friends. So, it is with much pleasure that I say a few words about our distinguished speaker, the president of Brandeis University.

The *Sachar* in Hebrew means "businessman," and since most names spring from some attribute or following of some ancestor, this name explains a lot. Now you know why so em-

Introduction, Brandeis University dinner, Book-Cadillac Hotel, November 1961.

271

inent a scholar has such a practical approach to Brandeis University. His cap and gown may be in the clouds, but his feet are firmly planted on the ground.

Dr. Sachar's fame is international. People throughout the world know about his fabulous work at Brandeis. He has made this first Jewish sponsored nonsectarian university in America one of the outstanding institutions of higher education in the world. All this he has accomplished in less than fourteen years, almost starting from scratch.

I will not go into detail about the school. Dr. Sachar will bring us up to date on that. But, I can tell you that Dr. Sachar's leadership, intelligence, and imagination at Brandeis add prestige to all Jews everywhere, a prestige that could not possibly be secured by us in any other way.

On my visits to Brandeis, I have particularly noticed a lot of activity, everybody keeps moving. One has to because Dr. Sachar has such an energetic building program that if you happen to stand still for five minutes, you will probably find a new dormitory being built right around you.

I have heard that applicants to Brandeis are scrutinized without their names or pictures; only their scholastic records are examined. This procedure assures equal treatment to all. I was told, "In this way we get the brightest young men and women. Those not so smart we send to Harvard and Yale."

Please permit me to tell you a bit about Dr. Sachar's background. He has studied or received degrees from Harvard University, Cambridge University, Wesleyan University, Washington University, Tufts University, University of Rhode Island, and the Rhode Island College of Education, as well as the Hebrew Union College. There is no question but that Dr. Sachar has dedicated his life to education. He has been elected to membership in Phi Beta Kappa, which is an honor given only to people of outstanding scholarship. He was the first national director of the B'nai B'rith Hillel Foundation. He has been a news analyst for NBC. He is an author of note and a great Jewish historian. You will find his books in every leading library in America. They are important contributions to the recording of our Jewish historical background. I could go on telling you about Dr. Sachar's many accomplishments, but time does not permit.

My feeling is that Dr. Sachar's greatest accomplishment

in his lifetime is what he has done, and what he is continuing to do, as president of Brandeis University. Abe Sachar is a genius, one of our great Americans. He is a man of amazing vision, a man of courage and intense devotion to an ideal. May God grant him good health and the strength to continue to make Brandeis more and more successful each year.

Next Thursday is Thanksgiving. Historians say that the pilgrim fathers established this holiday in the year 1621, based on Succoth, the Jewish holiday when God is especially thanked for the many blessings He has given us. Brandeis University is another way of saying thank you to God for the blessings of our good life in America, where we have always had freedom of worship and equal rights as citizens, and where we American Jews have lived for three centuries in dignity. Through the instrumentality of Brandeis University, the Jews, known as the people of the book, have found one way to make still another important contribution to American progress.

And now, because we are all anxious to hear more about our great university directly from its guiding genius, one of our great American citizens, it gives me extreme pleasure to introduce to you the only man who can tell tales out of school and make it pay, my good friend, *Mr.* Brandeis himself—Dr. Abram Sachar.

Pierre Mendes-France

L. to R., *front row:* the author, Pierre Mendes-France, Alfred Taubman;
back row: Alan Schwartz, Rabbi Hertz, Abram Sachar, Morton Scholnick,
Arthur Howard

Ladies and gentlemen. It is an honor
to have the privilege of presenting our distinguished speaker
at tonight's Brandeis University dinner. I was going to say
"introduce," but the Honorable Pierre Mendes-France needs
no introduction anywhere in the world, and in particular not
to the audience we have here tonight.

While we are all familiar with his international reputation as one of the leading personalities on the modern world
scene, I think you will be interested in some facts about his

Introduction, Brandeis University dinner, Book-Cadillac Hotel, November 1960.

personal life which my own research efforts brought to light.

I found out that Pierre Mendes-France is the scion of one of our oldest Sephardic families, with its roots in pre-Inquisition Spain. The *Jewish Encyclopedia* records a great many of his illustrious forbears with the family name of Mendes—rabbis, diplomats, and scholars who have written many a chapter in the cultural history of the past four and a half centuries in Holland, France, England, Italy, Turkey, and yes, in the United States too.

He himself attributes the hyphen in his name to a family alliance with the Francos; not, by any means, to the Franco of today's Spain, but the historically famous Jewish Francos of Portugal, where some of his ancestors took refuge after 1492.

The cause of higher education which Mister Mendes-France speaks for tonight is one traditionally identified with his family. And, Pierre Mendes-France himself, still young at fifty-three, has added lustre to a great name in the annals of our people.

Born in Paris on January 11, 1907, he studied at the Sorbonne and was graduated at the age of eighteen. He received the degree of Doctor of Laws and was admitted to the bar as the youngest lawyer in France. Later, he became one of the most eminent French jurists. The author of a number of books on financial subjects, he served for a time as professor in the School of Social Studies at the University of Paris.

In 1932, at the age of twenty-five, he was elected to the Chamber of Deputies. And here, too, he was the youngest member of the august body. A few years later he became mayor of the city of Louviers in Normandy. At the age of thirty he was appointed under secretary of state for finance in the cabinet of Premier Leon Blum.

Then, with war clouds on the horizon, Pierre Mendes-France became one of the most outspoken men in his country against Nazism. Mobilized in September 1939, he served as a lieutenant in the French Air Force in Syria. Back in France at the time of the German invasion, he attempted to stop the conclusion of an armistice with Germany. He helped organize the Opposition to General Petain's policy of collaboration with Germany.

Persecuted, arrested, and imprisoned in Lyon, he escaped in June 1941 and lived in hiding for a while as one of

275

the leaders in the French Underground anti-Nazi movement. Pierre Mendes-France then succeeded in reaching London in February 1942 and joined the French Free Forces under General de Gaulle. He flew many missions in the French bomber group "Lorraine."

In November 1943, our honored guest was appointed by General de Gaulle as finance commissioner of the French Committee for National Liberation. In this capacity, he headed the French delegation to the Bretton Woods Conference in the United States.

After the Liberation, he was given so many important government positions and responsibilities that to try to enumerate all off them would be absolutely impossible in the few minutes allotted me.

Unquestionably, the highlight of his career was his confirmation as premier of France on June 18, 1954. Pierre Mendes-France electrified the French people and the western world by promising to achieve peace in the strife between France and Indochina within one month or he would resign. This promise was made on June 18, 1954. He missed that self-imposed deadline by so few hours that his countrymen forgave the slight lapse in his timetable and he returned to Paris on July 21, a hero, from the Geneva Conference, where the armistice was signed as he had promised. In similar fashion he ended the exhausting warfare in Tunisia which was sapping the vitality of France.

And here's something of which we all can be proud: our speaker has been decorated four times by his government. He has the right to wear the ribbon of the Legion of Honor, the Croix de Guerre, also the medal awarded to French escaped prisoners of war and the medal which identifies him as a member of the Resistance.

One of the special programs of Pierre Mendes-France was his effort to get the people of his country to switch from alcoholic drinks to milk. This apparently has not been achieved. When I was in Paris a couple of years ago, my own inspection of the glasses on the tables along the Champs-Elyseés did *not* count as many glasses of milk as glasses of Pernod.

You will also be interested to know that Mr. Mendes-France is a family man with a lovely wife and two sons.

Our community takes special pride in a bond between

our honoured guest and our city. He has relatives in Detroit, and I am happy to say that they are with us in the audience.

Of special interest to the Brandeis family is the fact that a year ago last summer Mr. Mendes-France came to our campus as the special guest of the University, delivering a series of lectures at Brandeis and receiving an honorary degree at commencement. He returned to the United States a couple weeks ago especially to appear on behalf of Brandeis in a limited number of cities, of which Detroit is one. The subject of his talk is, "A forecast of the rivalry of the East and West during the next fifteen years."

Ladies and Gentlemen, the Honourable Pierre Mendes-France!

Nelson Glueck

Nelson Glueck and the author

G*ood evening, ladies* and gentle-men. I am honored tonight to introduce the man whom we all came to hear. Dr. Nelson Glueck is well known to an audience like this one. His fame is international and not only among scholars. The man on the street, too, has read of some of his achievements because they are romantic as well as scholarly. His achievements are spectacular and smack as much of derring-do as of research. He has implemented what so many of us dream of and, in adding to the world's store of knowledge and his own reputation, has tasted more than once the heady wine of adventure. He has lived history, walked with kings of past millennia, and helped quicken to life the printed pages of the Bible.

Yet, in spite of the stature of the man, I, who know him well, can tell you that he is a very humble and simple man, unpretentious and with a delightful sense of humor.

Introduction, Wayne State University, Department of Near Eastern Languages and Literatures lecture series, 1960.

Wayne State University is to be congratulated on his acceptance of our invitation to be here tonight. This is Dr. Glueck's third appearance in the notable events sponsored by Wayne State University's College of Liberal Arts, Department of Near Eastern Languages and Literatures, headed by Dr. Abram Spiro. This relatively new department of the University created on the recommendation of Dean Victor Rapport has achieved nationwide acclaim because of its programs. Tonight's lecture is another in the Near Eastern Lecture Series established by the generosity of Walter and Leah Field.

You must turn to *Who's Who* for a complete recapitulation of Dr. Glueck's career. It is a long and lustrous one, which I can only describe briefly.

Nelson Glueck holds a great many scholastic degrees from universities both in America and abroad, including the honorary degree of Doctor of Laws from the University of Cincinnati. He also received the Cincinnati Fine Arts Award. One cannot say of him that he is without honor in his own hometown.

For the past twenty years (1947–66) Dr. Glueck has been president of Hebrew Union College, the oldest Jewish theological seminary in America, or for that matter in the world today. A member of its faculty since 1929, which he joined as instructor, his rise through the ranks to the presidency was a rapid one; 1929 to 1947 in the world of an educator is a short time indeed to win and enjoy the recognition which is his.

Dr. Glueck is a man of many parts. He is one of the world's greatest archaeologists. The *Detroit News* not too long ago ran a feature story about Dr. Glueck on its magazine page and described him in the caption as "The Rabbi Who Digs for the Truth."

On one of his previous visits he recounted something a prominent newspaper friend had told him: "that next to rape and murder, archaeology is third in public interest."

Archaeological research is continually revealing that much of what we once accepted in the Bible as apocryphal is factual. A great deal of this new evidence has been unearthed by our guest this evening. He has uncovered more than one thousand sites in the Holy Land. His explorations in Transjordan mark the first time that an entire country has been archaeologically studied, square mile by square mile. The novelist

279

Rider Haggard may have written of King Solomon's mines, but Dr. Glueck found them. It was he who first located the copper mines of King Solomon and excavated the great king's port city of Ezion-Geber on the Red Sea.

I spoke a while ago of the heady wine of adventure in Dr. Glueck's career. He has lived it; often with the Bible tucked under one arm and an armed guard to protect him, he has sought for the evidence that is helping to turn parable, legend and hearsay into history. It is said by men who accompany him on these expeditions that our scholarly guest sets a stiff pace for his companions, takes the sun and the sand in his stride.

I could go on telling you about Dr. Glueck's many great scientific discoveries, but time does not permit. It is interesting to note, however, that this very busy man, in addition to his many other activities, has made the time to publish a number of important books.

Dr. Glueck is a member of the Archaeological Institute of America, the Central Conference of American Rabbis, the American Oriental Society, Sigma XI, and Phi Beta Kappa. He belongs to the Explorers Club and has many times risked his life among the Arabs in Palestine, Transjordan, and northern Arabian Peninsula.

I am so proud to say that Dr. Glueck is a personal friend of mine and that I have the pleasure and honor of being associated with him in a small part of the good work that he is accomplishing as president of the Hebrew Union College-Jewish Institute of Religion. Not too long ago I participated in a memorable event which celebrated Dr. Glueck's tenth anniversary as president of the Hebrew Union College. Everyone in the huge dining room stood up and cheered when Dr. Glueck came to the podium because we, who were there, realized and appreciated the significant contribution that this great, dedicated man is making in the fields of religion, as well as in biblical archaeology. So it gives me extreme pleasure to introduce to you our speaker of the evening and my good friend, Dr. Nelson Glueck.

Samuel Sandmel

Samuel Sandmel

W_{ayne} *State University* is fortunate, and we here tonight are to be congratulated, on the first speaker in the new lecture series of the College of Liberal Arts' Department of Near Eastern Languages and Literatures.

I have been honored with the privilege of introducing Dr. Samuel Sandmel, one of America's distinguished scholar and the world's leading Jewish authority on the New Testament. Dr. Sandmel, a native of Dayton, Ohio, moved to and attended public schools in St. Louis. He graduated from the University of Missouri with the B.A. in 1932 and the Ph.D. from Yale; he was ordained rabbi in 1937 at the Hebrew Union College in Cincinnati. He served as director of the Hillel Foundation at Yale from 1946 to 1949, and was Hillel Professor of

Introduction, Wayne State University, Department of Near Eastern Languages and Literatures lecture series, 1959.

Jewish Literature and Thought at Vanderbilt from 1949 until 1952, when he was appointed to the faculty of Hebrew Union College (he was named provost of his Alma Mater in 1957 and still holds that office): these are the milestones in his academic career.

Awarded the President's Fellowship of Brown University, Dr. Sandmel wrote *A Jewish Understanding of the New Testament* published in 1956 and reprinted in 1957. It is recognized as a significant treatise in the field of religion. His book, *Philo's Place in Judaism* appeared, too, in 1956. *The Genius of Paul* was published in 1958. Prolific as well as profound, our guest even now is putting the final touches on *An Introduction to Bible*, scheduled for early publication. Dr. Sandmel has devoted a lifetime to research on interpretation of the New Testament in its relation to Judaism: these are the milestones in an erudite and articulate literary career.

During World War II, Dr. Sandmel served for four years as a Navy and Marine Corps chaplain.

What I have given you thus far is serious, factual chronology. But our speaker tonight is a man of many parts. The publisher of *Who's Who* might omit an account of these other interests. So, as one who is a friend of Dr. Sandmel, I am assuming the privilege of shedding a little light on the nonacademic and nonliterary facets of Dr. Sandmel's activities. .

I can tell you that he is as fast on a baseball diamond as he is adept in fielding a Greek participle. He has written musical notes, as well as footnotes to the history of the Bible, that have inspired admiration. He is recognized to be as fluent in Hebrew as he is with the gag that rocks 'em back on their heels. Back at Hebrew Union College they still talk of the finest play ever given there. Our guest not only wrote the libretto but the music; he had to be restrained from playing the snare drum, and only desisted from shifting the scenery because the representative of the Scene Shifters' Union who objected was bigger than he is. And Sandmel, as you can see, is no little fellow. The world of the scholar may be the gainer, but Broadway is the loser, because Dr. Sandmel chose education instead of entertainment.

Dr. Sandmel's subject tonight is "Judaism and Christianity in the First Century." He is an authority on this particular period of world history. I am sure his lecture will make a real contribution to our understanding of the life and times of the biblical era.

Ladies and gentlemen, anything more I could say would be, as the classical Greek phrase goes, "piling Ossa on Pelion." Permit me, then, to present Dr. Sandmel.

Norman Bentwich

Shalom. Over the years I have introduced many men and women whom I proudly call great Jews. Tonight is another such occasion. I have the honor and privilege of presenting to you my friend Professor Norman de Mattos Bentwich of London and Israel. He is equally famous as an author, a historian, and as an outstanding lawyer specializing in international law.

Professor Bentwich's career has been long and illustrious. He was born in London and is four times twenty-one years old. You know, eighty-four does sound better that way.

He is a famous son of a famous son. His grandfather as a boy came from German Poland to become a jeweler in the city of London. In his later years he devoted all of his time to the synagogue. His grandmother belonged to a family that settled in England in the 1700s.

Norman Bentwich is one of eleven children. His parents had nine girls and two boys. When I read that statistic I wasn't sure whether Bentwich was Jewish or Catholic.

All eleven children were musicians. Professor Bentwich's mother saw to it that each child was taught an instrument—piano, violin, cello—and by school standards they all excelled in music. Norman played the violin.

Particularly interesting to us all is the fact that his father, who was a lawyer, founded and then became the first president of the first English lodge of the International B'nai B'rith. Some of the earliest planning for the establishment of the Jewish state of Israel took place in Professor Bentwich's father's home. Back in 1895 his father, together with Israel Zangwill, sent invitations to leading Jews in London to come and meet Dr. Theodore Herzl of Vienna. Herzl was to be an occasional visitor in the Bentwich home.

Although Professor Bentwich was educated at Cam-

Introduction, Midrasha College of Jewish Studies, January 1967.

bridge University, he states that the teacher who had the deepest influence on his early education was Solomon Schechter, the great rabbinic scholar, who taught him Hebrew. Rabbi Schechter, who became president of the Jewish Theological Seminary of America, was responsible for Bentwich writing three books on post-biblical history for the Jewish Publication Society of America. They were studies of Philo, the mystic philosopher of Alexandria, Josephus Flavius, the renegade Jewish historian; and the third was on the larger movement of Hellenism in its relation to Jewish tradition.

Talking about books, Norman Bentwich has authored forty-five! Think of that, forty-five books on Israel, international affairs, biographies, etc. He wrote his first book on Palestine back in 1919. It was called *Palestine of the Jews*. He wrote his latest book on Palestine together with his wife, Helen, in 1965, called *Mandate Memories*. During those forty-six years he has written many other books about Palestine and Israel, so that today the world is richer because of what Norman Bentwich from personal observation and experience has recorded for posterity about the Holy Land.

During his early years, Zionism came to play a large part in his life. His father had taken him, while he was still a school boy, to the Zionist Congress at Basle in 1899, and Norman Bentwich himself was a delegate to the Congress at the Hague in 1907. He continued to be an annual delegate to the Zionist Congress until 1912.

Professor Bentwich was called to the Bar in 1908 and practiced as a barrister until 1912. He then accepted a post in the office of the Egyptian Ministry of Justice in preparation for his career in Palestine. He was a lecturer at the Royal Law School at the University of Cairo, 1913–15.

When World War I broke out, he was assigned to the British forces in Egypt, and he was a major in the Camel Transport Corps during the Palestine campaign of 1916–18. Norman Bentwich has been decorated with the order of the British Empire and the Military Cross.

In 1918, he was appointed senior judicial officer of the British military administration in Palestine, and when Sir Herbert Samuel was appointed high commissioner, Bentwich became legal secretary and then attorney general of Palestine during the Mandate from 1919 to 1931.

He was professor of international relations at the University of Jerusalem from 1932 to 1951. And he is now the Chaim Weizmann Professor of International Relations emeritus of the Hebrew University of Jerusalem. He also has been deputy chairman of the Board of Governors of the Hebrew University of Jerusalem since 1953. He has served as chairman of the Board of the English and Irish Friends of the Hebrew University of Jerusalem since 1946.

When the Hitler persecutions started in 1935, he was engaged in rescue and emigration work, first as deputy of the League of Nations Commission for German Refugees in London, 1933–36, and he was vice-president of the Jewish Commission for Relief Abroad, 1944–48. He also served as chairman of the National Peace Council, 1944–47 and has been chairman of the United Restitution Office since 1948.

He has played an important role in numerous other relief, rescue, and rehabilitation movements and in organizing legal aid for refugees from Nazism.

In 1915 he married Helen Franklin. I only wish that time permitted me the opportunity to tell you about her, as well as about her famous husband. In her own right she is a fabulous woman. She has spent a lifetime as a civic leader and worker. She rates twenty lines of listings in *Who's Who in World Jewry*. And I know there must be quite a romance between these two wonderful people because so many of Professor Bentwich's books are dedicated to his wife, Helen. You might say that that "speaks volumes." Incidentally, they split their time between Israel and London every year.

Professor Bentwich is a former president of the Jewish Historical Society of England, and he holds honorary degrees from Dropsie College in Philadelphia, Melbourne University of Australia, Aberdeen University of Scotland, and the Hebrew University of Jerusalem.

And all that I've just told you represents just a brief resume of this great man's career. So I can't help but say what a great opportunity this is for all of us tonight. I only wish that Professor Bentwich had the time to speak to us at length about the tremendous changes he has seen in world Jewish history. To have lived and actually participated to the great extent that he has in the rebirth of Israel, in the renaissance of the Jewish people during the past fifty years or so, is a thrilling experience that God has given to but very few.

Life has never been boring for Norman Bentwich or his wife. In just the last few months, he traveled to Leningrad to attend a conference of international lawyers and recently spent time in Ethiopia helping the Falasha Jews of that country. Now, on this visit to the United States, he has speaking engagements at the Jewish Theological Seminary in New York as well as its branch, the University of Judaism in Los Angeles. He is also speaking at the Hebrew Union College-Jewish Institute of Religion in Cincinnati, New York, and Los Angeles.

If you want to read about this great man's fascinating three-quarters of a century of life, up to 1961, I recommend that you get his autobiography, the book *My 77 years*.

In closing I'd like to thank Professor Bentwich for coming to Detroit so that we could have the great pleasure to meet him and his dear wife in person.

Esther Prussian

Esther Prussian

It is my privilege tonight to be the spokesman for the Detroit Service Group in honoring a very lovely lady, whom we all know as the First Lady of our Jewish Welfare Federation, Esther Prussian. And when I say "First," I really mean first. She was the first person to become a staff member when Federation was founded, and she has been with us for the entire fifty years that the Detroit Service Group has been in existence. That entitles her to a big round of applause.

Esther was interviewed recently. It was part of the new plan to keep an oral history of Federation, as remembered by some of us who have been around for a long time. In the Detroit Service Group/50th Anniversary Booklet in front of you, which I like to call "The Book of Esther"—our "Megillah"— you will find excerpts from her interview. When you read it you will learn about Esther's great record of the service which

Introduction, Detroit Service Group 50th Anniversary dinner, Tam O'Shanter Country Club, September 1976.

she has rendered to organized Detroit Jewish charity for over half a century.

She played a very important part in our history. She has found her satisfaction in life by serving us. Although once I did hear her say, "52 years with Federation, and *whom* has it got me?"

The taped interview discussed her career with Federation. But, all people in the business world also have a personal side to their life. I would like to talk a little about Esther's. To know her is to love her, respect her, admire her . . . a reflection of her own extraordinary capacity for understanding and love, those qualities of the spirit by which we of Federation and the Detroit Service Group have gained much. She is what our Jewish Bible describes as a true woman of valor.

She says her secret of happiness is not in doing what you like, but in liking what you do.

Although she was born in Boston, she has lived here so long that we think of Esther as a native Detroiter. When I once asked her how old she was, she said, "I will be perfectly honest with you: I won't answer."

When she was a youngster she was known as Ruth Prussian, even though her full name was Esther Ruth Prussian. She liked Ruth, but Detroiters liked Esther better so she went back to her original biblical name.

Her hobbies used to be singing and piano playing. She quit singing when she was heard singing "The Star Spangled Banner" and was then investigated by the U.S. House Un-American Activities Committee.

Now she plays piano, or would play the piano, except she has no piano in her apartment.

So, she watches TV and she loves to read mystery books. Esther is a great sports fan—baseball, football, hockey—you name it. She never used to miss the opening Tiger games, rain or snow. It made no difference if it conflicted with the openings of Allied Jewish Campaigns or not. Once, because of her hero, Hank Greenberg, on Rosh Hashona, New Year's Day, she went to see Detroit win the American League championship. But she salved her religious conscience by refusing to ride to the game. She walked to and from the ballpark!

Esther collects elephants, all shapes, sizes, and colors. She has over three hundred of them, and maybe that is why

Max Fisher loves her. But don't tell him she is a Democrat.

Esther has gone on three Study Missions to Israel, the first one back in 1955. She loves to travel but gets sick most of the time. She thinks they should change the name from Study Missions to Kaopectate Festivals.

Seriously, despite Esther's years, she is still vigorous and vital. Her mind is still sharp, and she knows and remembers almost everything of any consequence about every contributor to the Allied Jewish Campaign. In fact, I called her "Detroit's Dun & Bradstreet."

To have anyone work for you for fifty-two years is, in itself, a great accomplishment. It certainly speaks highly of the leaders of our Federation and how nicely we treat our staff people. I am proud of that. And, Esther is our shining example.

But then how could anybody treat Esther any differently than we have? All of us whose lives have come in contact with her feel the enrichment.

It has always been and still is a pleasure to work with her. She always helps you get things done, done well and on time. As King Lear said, "Her voice was ever soft, gentle and low . . . an excellent thing in a woman."

She dedicated her life to two things: Federation and her relatives. Few people know that even though she never married, she is still thought of as mother by some of her nieces and nephews whom she helped raise when her brother and his wife died years ago. These lovely people are with us tonight because we wanted them to see how much we love Esther, too.

Yes, Esther, you are quite a gal. We have come a long way together. You won the confidence and friendship of every local Jewish community leader over these past fifty years. You encouraged and inspired all these men and women to share your vision of a better tomorrow, for Jews everywhere, no matter where in the world they lived. You have given so much of yourself, such dedication to our Jewish values and loyalties, that today Detroit ranks unique among American cities as one of the best, if not the best, of all Federation Jewish communities.

We thank you from the bottom of our hearts, and we are grateful for everything you mean to us. Thank goodness you are still around to hear us tell you how we feel about you. You are a very unusual and exceptional person. We treasure you as a source of strength to our community. We thank you for being you. We hope you continue to stick around, even on a part-time basis, to help us for many more years.

And now, Esther dear, if you will please come up to the podium, on behalf of the Detroit Service Group on its 50th Anniversary, we wish to present you with a token of our affection and hope you wear it for many years, in good health and happiness.

Max M. Fisher

Max Fisher and the author

I want to say a few words about the man who is the 1957 chairman of this greatest of all Detroit Allied Jewish Campaigns; Max Fisher.

As a fund-raiser, he is tops because of his own magnificent personal example as a giver. Long ago he realized that the joy of living is the pleasure of giving. He is so good at getting money from his prospects that his associates tell this story about him.

Presented at the 1957 Allied Jewish Campaign meeting, Jewish Welfare Federation of Detroit, May 1957.

A youngster once swallowed some pennies that his father had given to him. His mother screamed to her husband, "Call the doctor!" The father said, "You don't want a doctor; let's call Max Fisher." His excited wife asked, "Why Max Fisher?" The husband calmly replied, "Because Max Fisher can get money out of anybody."

Max has not yet reached the age of fifty, but he has already reached an enviable position as one of, if not the, outstanding Jewish citizens in our community. His fine reputation is acknowledged by people of all faiths in Detroit and the nation.

Max has everything anybody could hope for. I remember the time when he wasn't feeling well and went to see a friend who was a psychiatrist. "Doctor," said Max, "I'm in perfect health, and I am the head of a very successful business that makes a lot of money. I'm married to a beautiful girl who loves me, and I love her. We have four wonderful children. I just built a beautiful mansion on an estate next to Franklin Hills Country Club. I've been given many honors, and I have a million friends. Tell me, Doctor, what is my problem?"

While we all know that the great Jewish emergency this year made all of us open our hearts and pocketbooks a little wider, few of us know that this man has given almost 100 percent of his time during our entire campaign in order to make it the big success it is. No one has ever worked harder or with greater sincerity. Max alone handled about one hundred prospects. And his record for increases is fabulous. Detroit can be proud that Max Fisher has arrived to fill the shoes of our late, beloved leader, Fred Butzel.

Max Fisher has earned our appreciation and a great round of applause to acknowledge what he is doing for us and our fellow Jews around the world.

Leo M. Franklin

Rabbi Franklin

*T*hank you President Bonner, Provost
Stevens, and Mary Shapero. I am proud and pleased to accept
the Leo M. Franklin Award in Human Relations. I like to think
that if Dr. Franklin were still with us, he would be pleased
also. He was my friend.

You know, the human brain is a remarkable instrument.
It starts clicking the moment you are born. And it never stops
working—until you are expected to make a speech in public.

So, it's smart to get your thoughts down on paper. When
I was one of the bosses at the old Simons-Michelson Co. advertising agency, I would put some of our clever copywriters
to work preparing my speeches, until one day I got up to talk.
I couldn't wait to hear what I was going to say. I pulled the
envelope with my speech out of my pocket, and I started off
great. When I finished page one and turned to the second, all

On receiving the Rabbi Leo M. Franklin Memorial Award in Human Relations,
Rackham Memorial Building, April 1982.

I found was a totally blank page, except for these words—
"OK, wise guy—you're on your own now."

Since then, I write all my own talks. This is a day of
nostalgia for me. Almost thirty-four years ago, my rabbi of my
youth, Leo M. Franklin, died after having served Temple Beth
El and all Detroit for about a half century. He was short in
stature but a giant of a man, vitally concerned with human
relations, a humanitarian in the finest sense of the word. I can
say that with authority because I knew him well. I'm proud
to help honor his memory today.

I remember back in 1948, when Rabbi Franklin died, my
friend, Nate Shapero, came to me—we were both on Temple
Beth El's board—and asked if I would help him raise money
to establish a Dr. Leo M. Franklin Memorial Fund for some
worthy purpose. Of course, I said yes, and then I added that
my partner, Larry Michelson, and I would like to be the first
ones to make a contribution to the fund.

Little did I think that some day I'd be getting the money
back with interest. Paraphrasing the Bible, "Cast your bread
on the waters, and it will come back—cake." The Annual
Franklin Award in Human Relations is a check for $1,000, as
you have heard. That's a lot of money. Just think, now I get
$1,000 cash for being good. Up to now, I could be good for
nothing.

I am donating the award money to the Wayne State
University Press to be used to help take care of its building on
Woodward Avenue. After all, it carries my name and that's
the least I can do. Or, Dr. Bernard Goldman, the Press director, can use the money for whatever University Press purpose
he decides. In a world full of commas, semicolons, and pe-
riods, "Bern" Goldman is an exclamation point.

Again, to give credit where credit is due, the next year,
when Nate Shapero became president of Beth El, he came up
with the idea that the money we raised be offered to Wayne
State University to establish a Rabbi Franklin Award in Human Relations. Wayne was enthusiastic about the suggestion
because it had great respect for Dr. Franklin. Ten years earlier,
Wayne State University had given him an honorary doctorate.
In 1923, the University of Detroit had given Rabbi Franklin an
honorary degree, also.

I once heard that a minister, whose last name was Fiddle, turned down an honorary Doctor of Divinity, a D.D. degree, because he did not want to be known as "Fiddle D.D."

In Temple Beth El's archives, I found a copy of a letter written by Rabbi Franklin; he wrote, "If I were asked what I regard as the chief function of the Rabbi, I would say that it is to touch life at every point. *I am interested more in human beings and their problems* than in some of the activities others might deem to be of greater importance.

A *Detroit Free Press* lead editorial called "Leo Franklin the Detroit citizen who *stood in the forefront* among men in the advancement of every worthy thing we think of when the word humanitarianism is spoken."

Rabbi Franklin was actually the founder of Detroit's interfaith movement between Christians and Jews. Back in 1902, he brought together six ministers of different religions and many people of various religious persuasions for a citizens' interdenominational Thanksgiving Day Service, the first religious service of its kind held anywhere in America. He was also one of the organizers of the Detroit Round Table of Catholics, Jews, and Protestants. I guess today he would be called an ecumaniac.

Rabbi Franklin participated with Bishop Gallagher in the fight against the anti-parochial school amendment which our state legislature was considering, making it compulsory for all students to attend public schools. The bill was defeated. On the other hand, he was Fr. Couglin's adversary in a celebrated dispute regarding bigotry. He fought slum housing conditions in Detroit and brought about new housing laws and regulations. It was a fact that there were no social, civic, or philanthropic movements begun in Detroit during his lifetime with which Dr. Franklin was not identified.

Rabbi Franklin taught that minorities have rights and majorities have responsibilities. His was the cry of the Psalmist: "Ye who love God hate evil."

Over the years, Rabbi Franklin asked me to help him in some of his many projects which involved human relations and which were close to his heart. Soon they were close to mine also.

When I think of the words "human relations," I think of a great many things: being concerned about people, their problems, their achievements, and their interests. I think of improved public welfare, alleviation of human suffering, social reforms, goodness, kindness, compassion, and empathy; and we cannot forget philanthropy—the name of the game: money.

Rabbi Franklin gave generously of his limited income, and I do mean limited. Have you ever heard of a rich rabbi? Would you believe that during the Great Depression of the 30s, Dr. Franklin served as Beth El's rabbi without pay because the synagogue could not afford to pay him. He told me this himself.

Rabbi Jacob Marcus, the eminent Jewish historian and head of the American Jewish Archives, wrote me that in his opinion, Leo Franklin was a great rabbi. Dr. Marcus knew Rabbi Franklin as well as any other rabbi in America. Dr. Marcus just celebrated his 70th year at the Hebrew Union College—the seminary from which Rabbi Franklin was ordained ninety years ago, at age twenty-two, as the youngest rabbi ever to graduate from Hebrew Union College.

I've never forgotten the message about the importance of human relations and human rights that Dr. Jacob Marcus gave us when he preached at Beth El a few years ago. I've quoted him many times because what he said makes its point in an unique way. He reminded us that during this atomic age we must all work together because the atomic bomb is not anti-Jewish, anti-Catholic, anti-Protestant, anti-Muslim, Anti-Negro, or anti-anything. If the atomic bomb falls, it will fall on everyone alike. In an atomic war all men are cremated equal.

I started going to Beth El with some friends when I was about sixteen years old. I was impressed with the way Rabbi Franklin preached. I learned a lot from him about my religion and human relations that I've carried with me to this day. I learned that no person can say, "I am viable; I can go it alone." "Viable," the dictionary tells us, means "Likelihood or capability to live, develop, and survive on its own as a separate entity."

None of us is viable. You may think you are, but you are not. In this life, you are dependent on other people from the moment of your birth until you die.

I may sound naive talking about human relations when all about us when all we see and hear in the media are wars between nations on all continents, terrorism, murders, fraud and dishonesty, racial and religious prejudice, selfishness and betrayals. But, for the future of our children and posterity, we still must try to make this world a better place in which to live.

My religion teaches in the "Sayings of the Fathers" that *It is not thy duty to complete the work but neither art thou free to desist from it.* In other words, do not be disheartened by the difficulty of what is before you. Do as much good in this world as is in your power. And that certainly makes sense.

Well, this is Leonard Simons of the disappearing generation talking. I'm happy to say that I have reached my ripe old age, and I do have a rich storehouse of wonderful memories. I know I still have a lot of good deeds left in me, even though it seems that the only thing that is holding me together is static cling.

Time keeps marching on. Last July, on my birthday, one of my young granddaughters baked me a cake. Instead of the "77" I expected on the frosting, there was a "9$^{1}/_{2}$." I asked her the reason. She said she thought that this year I'd rather remember my shoe size.

I wish to thank the rabbis for the previews of my eulogies. I'd like to thank Temple Beth El for the jackpot. And, my sincere thanks also to all you nice people for sharing this day of happiness with me.

I'll close with my favorite aphorism: There is a big difference between sticking your nose in other people's business and putting your heart in other people's problems.

Richard Hertz

Rabbi Hertz

Dear friends, Mahnish tah nu? ("Why is this night different?") Our answer to this ancient and famous question of the Jewish Passover is that "this night, also, is definitely different," because Rabbi Hertz's retirement marks the end of another historic era in the life of Michigan's oldest Jewish congregation. It is a bit sad. Yet, tonight we are happy we can show Dr. Hertz how grateful we are for his almost thirty years of dedicated ministering to the spiritual needs of our members.

I have been asked to reminisce about Dr. Hertz. But to try to encapsulate Dr. Hertz's long career at Beth El in a few words is obviously impossible. I will recall just some things that occurred in his early years here. As Mark Twain once said, "When I was young, I could remember anything—whether it happened to me or not."

Talk given on the retirement of Rabbi Hertz as the spiritual leader of Temple Beth El, June 1982.

In a sense, I helped start Dr. Hertz' career in Detroit. I was his first president at Beth El, and he was my first senior rabbi when I served as president. We spent our first two years together getting acquainted and discussing plans for Beth El's future. Often we agreed, and often we argued. There was never a dull moment.

First, however, let me remind you of the state of emotional and mental distraction in which we at Beth El found ourselves thirty years ago when our beloved Rabbi B. Benedict Glazer died at the early age of fifty. We were dazed and bewildered at the shock . . . completely unprepared, but we had to carry on.

I was vice-president, our president was leaving on a round-the-world cruise. We had no associate or assistant rabbi. Suddenly, we were a congregation of over sixteen hundred families without a rabbi; and I became president *pro tem*, pseudo-senior rabbi, and imitation assistant rabbi.

Thank goodness Dr. Glazer, with characteristic foresight, had selected Minard Klein, the president of the Hebrew Union College-Jewish Institute of Religion graduating class, to be our assistant rabbi. Young Rabbi Klein arrived in June after being ordained, and we were back in business. No longer did members come to me for counsel on family troubles and help on religious questions. I admit, I was a horrible substitute rabbi. On a scale of one to ten—I was about a $2^1/_4$.

I served on the quickly appointed rabbinical selection committee. Meyer Prentis and Nate Shapero were cochairmen. We had to work through the Rabbinical Placement Committee of the Central Conference of American Rabbis. We asked about Rabbi Hertz, but they thought he was unavailable because he was in line to succeed his senior rabbi at a larger temple in Chicago. However, we insisted he be asked if he would be interested. Well, he was. We invited him for an interview and were very impressed. He had ten years experience with large congregations. Dr. Hertz agreed to join Beth El and was elected in January, 1953. He succeeded Dr. Glazer as our thirteenth rabbi.

Thirteen, as many of you know, is a proud and lucky number in Judaism. Proud, because that is the age of bar and bas mitzvah—when Jewish boys, and nowadays girls also, reach the status of an adult in the observance of our Holy Commandments; lucky, because all the relatives and friends give gifts.

We had made our choice, and we were anxious to have Dr. Hertz with us quickly. But, he had to perform his Chicago duties through the High Holy Days. My wife Harriette and I flew down to Chicago to attend Sinai Temple's farewell service for Dr. Hertz.

It was a very cold winter Sunday morning. The sanctuary was packed with about fifteen hundred people. There were speakers from the congregation and from the outside, both Jews and non-Jews, all praising Dr. Hertz and saying how much he would be missed. Finally, Dr. Hertz spoke, beautifully and eloquently. I forget what he said, but I remember the people loved every word. I saw men and women wiping tears with their hankies. There wasn't a dry eye around me except for the stony-faced man sitting next to me. So I asked him facetiously, "Aren't you sorry to see Dr. Hertz leave?" "No," he answered, "I'm a stranger here. I just came inside to get warm."

Dr. Hertz was installed on April 3rd, 1953, at our Woodward and Gladstone temple. I remember that date well. As president *pro-tem*, I stood in the receiving line with Dr. Hertz's family, which included his lovely mother and his father. Dr. Maurice Eisendrath, president of the Union of American Hebrew Congregations, spoke; so did that great president of the Hebrew Union College-Jewish Institute of Religion and Middle East archaeologist, Dr. Nelson Glueck, followed by Dr. Louis Mann, Rabbi Hertz's senior rabbi for the previous six years and who, incidentally, was also his father-in-law.

I insisted upon standing in line next to Dr. Glueck because my grandmother had always said to me, *Zol zein mit glueck*. For the benefit of those who don't understand Yiddish, that means, "You should always stay well."

The following month, May 1953, I was elected Temple's 33rd president. At the same time, I was president of Franklin Hills Country Club. If you think it was easy to please and satisfy two rabbis and over two thousand Jewish families in both organizations, all at one time, I'm here to tell you that was an experience no one in his right mind should deliberately have. I think when I took on both jobs, I had a full head of hair.

Things started to happen when Dr. Hertz arrived. Reform Judaism is called Reform because we are not afraid to change if the change is meaningful to us in our minds and in our hearts.

In December, 1953, the year Dr. Hertz came; we reintroduced bar mitzvah to Beth El after a lapse of about fifty years. As our thirteenth rabbi, Dr. Hertz was the logical one to do it. I recall dear old Clarence Enggass, the jeweler, telling me that he was the last member of Beth El to be bar mitzvah before the ceremony was replaced by confirmation, the ritual which we Jews borrowed from the Protestants. Incidentally, all religions copy from each other. Catholic priests wear their little skullcaps which Bishop Fulton Sheen called beanies. These are copied from our *yarmalkies*. Christians copied kneeling from the Jews. It was originally a Jewish custom. I think we dropped it because it was too tough for many of our well-fed, overweight ancestors to get up from their knees.

Dr. Hertz's first couple of years with us are still vivid in my mind. I remember Dr. Hertz inviting his mentor and dear friend, Dr. Jacob Marcus, the great historian of American Jewry, to come to Beth El in 1954. Dr. Marcus spoke gloriously about the Jewish Tercenternary, the 300th anniversary of the first Jews coming to America in 1654. His entire talk was reprinted in *The Beth El Story*.

The Beth El Story was the title of our one-hundred-year history book. I remember the help Dr. Hertz gave us to get it finished. With his advice, Irving Katz's research and rhetoric, and with support from the Leonard Simons Fund at Beth El, we finally, after five years of work, completed our book. The Wayne State University Press published it, and it then went on to win a national prize as one of the best-designed books of the year.

I remember the wonderful evening when one of the great women in American history, Eleanor Roosevelt, widow of President Franklin D. Roosevelt, accepted Dr. Hertz's invitation to come to Beth El. She spoke to a packed house. We had the privilege of hearing a warm, charming, inspiring talk. She thrilled all of us.

I also remember Dr. Hertz bringing us some financial *mazel*, good luck. One month after he became our rabbi, Temple received a gift from an unknown admirer who had died in Florida. Her will brought us $150,000 in cash, and no one even asked for or wanted a plaque.

Beth El had about sixteen hundred families when Dr. Hertz came. But, we were losing ground because our members were moving farther northwest. We were beginning to suffer from what I call "seventh day absenteeism." Dr. Glazer was the first to see the exodus. He had given a couple of sabbath sermons and several serious talks to his board of directors about our need to move where all our members would increasingly have their new homes. We listened and followed his advice.

We bought land, twice. While the consensus was to move eventually, the question was when? We had a gigantic task ahead of us. We had to make sure we did not do anything prematurely. Dr. Hertz, like most of us, was not anxious to move from our beautiful old temple. But, when he became convinced we were correct in our thinking, he joined us wholeheartedly in planning our new house of worship.

Dr. Hertz' advice led us in making our historic move. I remember how often, and how strongly, he gave us verbal shots in the arm. He urged us from the pulpit, at special meetings, and in personal contacts with our leaders to build our new temple. He urged we do it for our own sake and for the sake of our children. I remember his words. Dr. Hertz reminded us *we* had not built the Woodward and Gladstone Temple: our fathers and grandfathers did it for us. They planned it, designed it and gave the money for it. We just inherited it. Now, he said, the time has come for us to see that the next generation of Beth El membership is cared for as well as ours was, or even better.

His constant and continuous appeals were successful. Our members made fantastic efforts and gave personal contributions that were unbelievably generous. Dr. Hertz never let the pace of fund raising slow down, up to and including these last few weeks.

We are now over eighteen hundred families. We remain strong from every standpoint after 132 years of existence. Look about you. What you see is what we all dreamed of having: another magnificent temple to God. With Dr. Hertz' help, we built this new temple, and now, coincident with his retirement, we hope to have it debt-free.

We have put a plaque on nearly everything in our temple, in commemoration of the donors who provided funds to finance our edifice complex. Honestly, there is nothing left of sufficient importance to be named in honor of Dr. Hertz. That's why I'd like to say, in all sincerity, our glorious Temple Beth El stands as the properly important monument to you, Dr. Hertz, and your twenty-nine years of service to us.

It would demean Dr. Hertz' contribution to seem to allege he did it all alone. But, it enhances his image to acknowledge the many others who followed and responded to Dr. Hertz's leadership. All the members made our new temple a reality.

Dr. Hertz' career as an American and a Jew has been motivated by the ideals of our Jewish faith. During his years at Beth El, he has participated actively in many eminently worthy causes—Jewish, interfaith, civic, human relations, health, etc.—locally, nationally, and internationally. He has been a strong supporter of Israel.

He has transmitted the imperishable values our generation of Jews has inherited from our forefathers. Dr. Hertz inspired and elevated our congregation with eloquent messages from the pulpit. He is a fine teacher of Judaism, fulfilling his obligation as a rabbi. He has well merited the affection of his congregants.

I often wonder how many of us would have the courage and stamina and disposition to be a rabbi. Long ago I came to conclusion that being a rabbi of a large congregation is one of life's most difficult jobs. There are many good aspects and satisfactions, of course, but to try to satisfy the presidents a rabbi must contend with—and I deliberately use that word "contend"—is a Herculean task. Dr. Hertz had nineteen presidents with nineteen different sets of ideas and plans and suggestions in his twenty-nine years at Beth El. That averages out to a new president about every year and a half. And could *you* remember the names and faces of about six thousand people, members and their families? No wonder rabbis have a saying in their fraternity: "Laugh at your troubles, and you'll never run out of things to laugh at."

Dr. Hertz, you can take pride in knowing that you made a great many contributions to Beth El's enviable history. You did your job exceedingly well and now join the illustrious Dr. Leo M. Franklin as one of only two rabbis emeriti in Temple Beth El history. May you, as he did after his retirement, continue to be a powerful factor for good at Beth El and in our community for many more years. We are counting on that.

While you have reached the retirement age as our senior rabbi, please remember, Dr. Hertz, that reaching the age of sixty-five is not a sin. It's the time of life when you still feel young—but only once in a while.

You know, being retired or partially retired isn't all that bad either, Richard. I'm getting to be an expert on that subject. Retirement is that marvelous time of life when the sun rises and you don't. Alarm clocks become past history.

In closing, Dr. Hertz, on behalf of our entire congregation, may I thank you for all you have meant to us, for all you have done for us over the three decades you have served. *Yasher koach*—May you go from strength to strength. And we pray, Richard, you may enjoy the balance of a long life of happiness and good health with you dear Renda.

And so may it be.

Henry Longhurst

Henry Longhurst

T*hose of us* who love golf were shocked last weekend when we heard the report on network television that Henry Longhurst had passed away at the age of sixty-nine. Henry was the popular British golf columnist and TV commentator whose voice, in recent years, became so well known to all Americans. I, especially, was sad because he was a friend of mine for over thirty years. It is true that Henry had been ailing for quite a while, but we never anticipated that his voice would be stilled so soon. What a shame.

Henry became one of America's great favorites through his part in televised major golf tournaments. The Associated Press called him "a master of dry wit and understatement. Mr. Longhurst brought a civilized, literary style to television golf commentary. . .." His unique style of delivery, his sophisticated command of the English language combined with his British accent, his amazing knowledge of the game of golf, his

Portions of this eulogy were included in Jack Saylor's golf column in the *Detroit Free Press*, January 1979.

great sense of humor, and his ability as a raconteur of golf anecdotes pertaining to the most famous golf stars of today and the past forty years or more made him a great favorite of golfers everywhere.

Even though the ABC and CBS networks only brought Henry over a few times a year to handle the results at the 16th hole of the Masters, US Open, PGA, The British Open, and the Women's PGA Championships—when *Golf Digest* magazine (to which he usually contributed a clever monthly article on golf) recently ran a poll to see who was their readers' favorite TV golf announcer—Longhurst was the fourth most popular out of the fifty names mentioned. This was quite a tribute to his popularity.

How did a golf "hasher" in Detroit like me become a friend of Henry Longhurst, who lived thousands of miles away in the tiny village of Hassocks, Sussex, about four miles outside of Brighton, England?

I must go back to 1945, when the US Women's Amateur Golf Championship was held at the golf club to which I belong, Franklin Hills Country Club in Franklin, Michigan. I was appointed chairman of the committee to publish the usual tournament program book. Because I did not want it to be just dull pages of advertisements, I looked for some interesting golf articles. I saw one comparing British and American golf in the *New York Times Sunday Magazine* section, written by Henry Longhurst.

I wrote the editor and asked permission to use the unique story, explaining that we couldn't pay anything for the privilege because the project was a labor of love on my part. The paper said OK so far as they were concerned, but suggested I get final approval from the author, Henry Longhurst, and gave me his address. I wrote and gave him the same story. He replied that he was flattered to have his article included, and, of course, we could use it without charge.

When the program book was completed, I sent Henry Longhurst a copy and thanked him again. Because the war had recently ended, I asked if he would let me send him a little gift of appreciation, something he hadn't been able to secure for a long time because of the war. I also asked him what his wife and children might like. He answered saying it wasn't really necessary, but if he could have some American golf balls he'd be very pleased; his wife would appreciate some rice, and his children would love some chocolate.

That's how we started our "pen pals" relationship. He told this story in his book on his travels, *You Never Know Till You Get There.* A couple of years later he had occasion to fly over to the States, and he phoned me. I invited him to come to Detroit as my guest and arranged for him to stay at Franklin Hills Country Club. We met and had a most enjoyable weekend together. The first time he played our course he shot a 79, and, as many of you know, Franklin Hills is considered a tough course. From then on my wife and I exchanged visits with Henry and his Claudine (whom he called "The Queen Mother"). We would meet in London or Hassocks or New York or Detroit, etc.

I learned many things about this unusual man: for instance that back in the 1930s, when Bobby Jones made his famous grand slam of golf, winning the Amateur and the Open of both the United States and England in the same year, Henry Longhurst, at the age of twenty-one, was the captain of the Cambridge University golf team. By invitation, he came with a team of ten fellow students to play five weeks of matches in Philadelphia, Boston, New York, and at various country clubs against other school and club teams, including the University of Pennsylvania and Harvard. When he returned, he wrote of his experiences in the States during our Prohibition days. He said he'd never forget "Knock 3 times and ask for Charlie . . . Buddy can you spare a dime . . . Al Capone and Stutz Bearcats . . . Raccoon coats and hip flask liquor poured from teapots . . . Rah, Rah, Rah." He brought back the report that those five weeks in America were *worth two years at the university.*

In his youth, he was quite good as a golfer. He was the Amateur Golf Champion of Germany in 1939 and the loser by the last putt on the final green in the French Amateur finals the following year. He also played in the 1936 US Amateur, and he got past the first round before losing. He related that after winning in Germany the group retired to the "19th hole" for a drink. When the waiter asked him what he'd like, he answered, "a dry Martini." A few moments later the waiter returned with three Martinis! "Dry," or "drei," in German means "three."

He knew them all, all the English golf stars and American golf greats. But, as he put it, "My own affection for Walter Hagen bordered almost on hero worship. Walter's staggering self-assurance, wit, and good humor, wide-open smile, inexhaustible zest for life, his ability to combine wine, women, and song with the serious business of winning golf championships—that was Hagen. A fellow whose like you meet once in a lifetime." And so Hagen was, as we knew him also.

Henry lived and traveled well. He met and knew some of the most celebrated people, including royalty, millionaires, clergy, scholars, politicians, champion golfers, hunters, fishermen, military people . . . you name it. He was wined and dined all over the world. Men and their families vied for the privilege of sharing his company. He was a connoisseur of good food and good liquor. In fact, he used to say he preferred to drink his calories.

As another of his good friends once wrote, "Henry Longhurst was one of those rare and exceptional men who possessed a combination of a great many blessed attributes. He was observant, objective, and above all, had a keen sense of humor. Combine these things in a man and there you have a companion for any occasion."

Henry first started playing golf at the age of eleven "with a small sawn-off club on a three-hole course before the grown-ups surfaced for breakfast. Within a matter of an hour I was hooked for life." At the age of thirteen he won his first tournament, for juveniles age six–fourteen, and he had a caddy!—a seven-year-old boy.

Longhurst's first article in print appeared in *Golf Illustrated* magazine in 1930. Henry Longhurst's name was well known by nearly everyone you met in England. When I'd ask English people if they knew my friend Henry Longhurst, they'd all say, "Of course I've heard of him; he's the golf writer for the *London Sunday Times!*" And that he was, for twenty-one years. His column appeared every Sunday, and he never missed an issue. His article was placed in the middle of the back page so that it had great visibility to all readers regardless of whether they were interested in golf. If I remember correctly, the paper had a circulation of several million, with distribution all over the British Isles.

Yes, Henry was called the man with the priceless talent;

he could write and talk brilliantly and briefly about golf and anything else. He played golf for over fifty years. At times he had a handicap of "Plus One." He enjoyed an enviable reputation as a globetrotting, golfing journalist and broadcaster who entertained a tremendous public all over the world.

I have all the books Henry Longhurst wrote—about a dozen—going back to 1941. I thumbed through them to refresh my memory about some of his thoughts. His first book was titled *It Was Good While It Lasted.* Alongside those words he inscribed to me, "Such a pity it didn't last! Henry."

It is such a pity that it didn't last longer, so that we could have continued to enjoy Longhurst's articles on golf, his reminiscences, and his great fund of knowledge about golf, golfers, and golf history.

Yes, Henry Longhurst lived life to the hilt. Not many journalists or sportsmen ever had it so good.

His career was interrupted by the madman, Hitler. Beginning as a "learner gunner" in the Royal Air Force, he advanced to captain and ended as a member of the British House of Commons for two years, the "Honorable and Gallant Member for Acton (Middlesex)." The theme of the campaign for election to Parliament was "Churchill asks you to vote for Longhurst," and this time they did. How proud he was to be an MP. All of this is recorded in his book *I Wouldn't Have Missed It.* Incidentally, Churchill liked him and wrote a foreword to one of his books.

For countless years he always wore his favorite tie. It was the one given to members of the St. Andrews Golf Club of Scotland. He wore it proudly, with all its food spots and wrinkles, as if it were a medal from Her Majesty. Recently he was honored by the Royal and Ancient St. Andrews Club (where Jack Nicklaus just won the 1975 British Open). They made him a life member.

As I think back to some of the things I learned about this unforgettable man of character, I remember that he was a lifelong Sherlock Holmes addict and a member of the Sherlock Holmes Society of London. He had a tremendous collection of Sherlock Holmes books. I helped him locate some that were published in America.

Henry Longhurst was an exceptional student of the game of golf. In one of his books, titled simply *Golf*, he expressed beautifully and successfully his philosophy of what the game of golf should mean to all of us. *"Your first concern is to learn the art of hitting the ball well enough to derive pleasure from the game ... the only excuse for playing it."* To which most of us will say amen. He wrote this book after exchanging views with leading American and British golfers. He came up with the opinion that there is no correct way of hitting a golf ball. He showed, with photos of various golf champions and by quoting them verbatim, that golf is not an exact science. He loved the game because "it is, after all, the only adult outdoor game that lasts a lifetime and in its small way helps to turn us into a nation of players instead of a nation of spectators."

The last book he wrote was his autobiography, published in 1971. The title was *Henry Longhurst: My Life and Soft Times.* His earlier decision to call it "Golf Has Been Good to Me" evidently didn't tell it all. Henry often said "Golf has been *incredibly* good to me and if I could go back and make a fresh start, I should be sorely tempted to do it all over again."

Henry wrote in his autobiography that he "can claim to have done the first 'live' outdoor radio broadcast on golf when the BBC set up a glass box on stilts at some vantage point on the Little Aston golf course outside Birmingham, overlooking two greens and three tees." Whether he could claim to have done the first "live" television of golf, he wasn't sure. But, he said he was "in at the birth," way back in the days when "practically none of the public had TV sets anyway."

He loved American cars. As he put it, "Every thirty-three years I go down and collect a light blue American motor with a huge V-8 engine—1932, a Hudson Terraplane and in 1965 a Ford Mustang," ordered through Jerry Bielfield's Ford agency when Henry was in Detroit. The cars were roadsters and the pride of his life. He didn't believe in the American philosophy of car obsolescence. He treated his cars with T.L.C. (Tender loving care).

Henry wrote, "If I have a regret, it is finding myself living in the permissive society at the age of sixty-plus. Rather like opening the stable door when the horse is no longer fit to bolt . . . with which elevating thought I wish you, for a while, farewell."

Longhurst described his life as a golf correspondent for over forty years as "giving pleasure to other people, and until you've had such a job, you don't know what a deep satisfaction there is in that. The knowledge that one's writings may entertain, amuse, and divert from their trivial daily routine some hundreds of thousands of people lends inspiration to one's efforts. I liked to fancy myself as a kind of intermediary between the sunny, carefree world outside and the prisoners in their offices in the city."

It was Mr. Winston Churchill who wrote: "Rational, industrious, useful beings are divided into two classes—those whose work is work and whose pleasures are pleasure . . . and . . . those whose work and pleasure are one. Fortune has favored the children who belong to the second class." Henry always said, "My work and pleasure were one."

His newspaper sent him to the four corners of the earth to find new and interesting stories primarily about golf. From what he wrote, I doubt if there are many countries and places that Henry did not visit. If they had a golf course, Henry played it. In his book *Round in 68* he relates his odyssey of sixty-eight days around the world playing golf in many countries on many courses, with local friends and new acquaintances. This book tells about one of his visits to Detroit.

Henry Longhurst visited Detroit often. He had a great many friends in out town. He was a part of the teams that handled the television broadcasts of at least two national golf championships that I remember at Oakland Hills Country Club: the PGA in 1972 and the Carling World Open in 1964.

From what I knew about this man after thirty years of friendship prompts me to say that there are few men in this world who had more friends, and knew more people in more parts of the world, than Henry Carpenter Longhurst. He will be sorely missed.

The Associated Press in its news release of July 23 stated, "Henry Longhurst, the British golf commentator and writer, has died at his Sussex home after a long battle against cancer, his family announced today. He was sixty-nine years old." The Bible tells us that the average man's life is three score and ten . . . seventy years. Henry beat par.

Gates Brown

Gates Brown and the author

     Under the direction of Leonard Si-
mons, Gates Brown, pinch-hitter extraordinary for the Tigers,
was presented a new car last week by a group of Jewish sports
fans of this city.

This presentation was made at Tiger Stadium; the text of the talk appeared in
the sports sections of the *Detroit News* and the *Detroit Free Press*, fall 1968.

In making the presentation Simons said: "Gates Brown, on behalf of a group of us from the Standard-City Club of Detroit, it is my privilege tonight to present you with a gift of appreciation.

"We selected you, Gates, among all the heroes of the 1968 Tiger baseball team because you represent the constant dream of American young men, that of being able to come through and deliver results when needed, and especially during crucial moments under extreme pressure.

"This you did, magnificently, time and time again, throughout this entire season. No player in the history of baseball ever did such a fantastic job of pinch-hitting.

"While we are not attempting to depreciate the thrilling efforts of all your Tiger teammates as well as the great direction of manager Mayo Smith, we felt that it would be unique if we honored you as the outstanding ballplayer who was *not* a regular on the team.

"And we know we are justified in choosing you because seldom, in any sport, has any athlete who has not played regularly on a team contributed so much to the realization of a championship.

"Your enviable record deserves more than just a pat on the back. We notice that Jimmy Campbell and the Tiger management have already paid you a high tribute by putting your name all over the outside of the stadium and on the tickets . . . Gates 1—Gates 2—Gates 3—and so on.

"We wanted to do something special for you, too, for all the honor and the thrills you have given to the citizens of Detroit, for the great job you did to improve our city's image when you helped bring us the American League championship. So we all thank you from the bottom of our hearts. Our wives thank you. Our children thank you. And I thank you.

"Here are the keys to a brand new 1969 Chevrolet. If, next year, you do another great job for the Tigers, we'll give you the car.

"I'm just kidding, of course. It gives us great pleasure to present you with this gift from a grateful group of Tiger fans. Use your new car in the best of health, and may it bring you a lot of additional happiness.

"Keep on swinging."

Donors included Harold Allen, Maurice Aronsson, Sidney Bertin, Louis Blumberg, Sol Eisenberg, Max Fisher, Nate Freedland, Adolph Goldberg, Irving Goldberg, Phil Gross, Emanuel Harris, Sidney Heinrich, Jason Honigman.

Arthur Howard, Milton Howard, Harold Kaplan, Harry Korman, Elwood Kukes, Dr. Irvin Kurtz, Dr. Mort Lazar, Syd Levison, Edward Levy, Irving Mahler, Larry Michelson, Jack Miller.

David Schimmel, Jules Schubot, Nate Shapero, Abe Shiffman, Bernard Siegel, Leonard Simons, Joe Slatkin, Richard Sloan, Ed Slotkin, Cy Wagner, Jack Wainger, Max Zivian, and Paul Zuckerman.

Harry C. Saltzstein

Behold, I have taken the cup of trembling from thy lips.
Thou shalt drink of it no more.

—Adapted from Isaiah 51:22

Harry C. Saltzstein

A Festschrift is a "volume of learned articles, essays and the like—'festival writings'—contributed by colleagues and admirers as a tribute, especially to a scholar." In this instance, the scholar is that very fine gentleman and physician, my longtime friend, Dr. Harry C. Saltzstein.

To be asked to contribute was an honor I could not refuse, though I am not certain I belong in this pleasant project. I am not a medical man and, thus, cannot qualify as a colleague; most certainly, however, I am one of his admirers, and this is one of the specifics.

What can I do to a journal like this? Would it be appropriate for me to express publicly my personal affection for this compassionate human being? Should I hail Dr. Saltzstein with

From the Sinai Hospital *Bulletin*, April 1976.

paeans of praise—no pun intended? And would it also be appropriate to add a bit of levity about doctors in general and this doctor in particular, in a volume otherwise so formal and dignified? The editors assured me that this, too, was a contribution.

Over the years, Dr. Harry and I have worked together on mutually interesting projects, especially Sinai Hospital. We served on the boards of the Southeastern Michigan Chapter of the American Cancer Society and the Michigan Cancer Foundation. They gave us many opportunities to work together and to discuss the changes we have seen in medicine, in the life of a doctor, in the care of patients, and in the problems of hospital administration.

We would talk about these matters seriously, but often we would exchange humorous quips. He has a good sense of humor, even if it is not apparent on the surface. Many a true thing has been said in jest; sometimes we laugh through our tears. But, if we can still enjoy a good laugh at ourselves or at our problems, there is still some hope for the future. Humor is so important to the world. The question we ought to be asking people is, "What have you done for me lightly?"

I could relate many anecdotes from our conversations. But because I wanted to go beyond my own experiences with Dr. Saltzstein, I spoke to some of his relatives, colleagues, former students, and patients. Some of the humorous stories told to me are true, but some, I am sure, are apocryphal. So, here goes. "Once a pun a time. . . ."

Some funny stories came out of the old days of the North End Clinic. For instance, there was one doctor whose sense of humor was expressed in this fashion. He would fit out a patient with a combination neck brace, back brace, and hernia support and then say, "Wear it in good health!" One elderly patient complained, "I have had my gallbladder out, my appendix out, my tonsils out. I get the feeling that God is taking me back on the installment plan."

When Dr. Saltzstein's practice became so large that he could use some help, he started training some assistant surgeons. Today the list of men who served under him would name many who went on to become famous surgeons in their own right.

Some of Dr. Harry's better quips are:

What this world needs is a placebo that works.

The best malpractice insurance of them all is a cure.

A recent survey proves that people who live longest are rich relatives.

A specialist is a doctor whose patients can be ill only during office hours.

Does "M.D." stand for "Malpractice Defendant"?

I asked Dr. Saltzstein if he thought medicine is as much fun today as it used to be. Harry replied, "Well, I am eighty-five years old and nothing is as much fun as it used to be."

Not too long ago I saw the United States Census annual report which showed that the medical profession is the highest paid of all professions.

If the medical profession is the highest paid, income-producing, profession, how come Dr. Saltzstein is not rich? He never married, had no children to support, and has always had spartan spending habits. I guess the answer is that his timing was poor. He should have been born about fifty years later. But, even if he had been, I will bet he would still have been the same type of person, caring more about patients than money. He has always said, "The secret in caring for the patients is you have to *care for* the patients."

I was going to say, "They do not make many like him any more." But then I thought, "What am I saying? I am almost seventy-two years old, and at my age I cannot afford to alienate any doctor. I never know when I will need one." Of course, I look through the *Journal of the American Medical Association* every week, even though I do not understand most of it. My wife insists that one of these days I am going to die of a misprint.

Seriously, I would like to pay my compliments to Dr. Saltzstein and his lifetime of service to his fellow man. I will not attempt to capture, in a few sentences, the richness of this man's life. A person is so much more than what can be said about him or her.

I remember the summer of 1941. Dr. Saltzstein invited a group of us to a meeting at a friend's house. He solicited our help in getting a hospital established in Detroit under Jewish auspices. He was anxious to do this because Dr. Golub's (of New York City) survey, made public in 1938, showed that of the 344 Jewish physicians in Detroit, only 30 percent had inpatient appointments at our local hospitals, *many of which were in name only, without provision for active hospital service.* The opportunities for advancement in graduate medical education, in clinical research, and in clinical teaching were limited.

The large proportion of Jewish doctors who could not get staff appointments at hospitals felt that their chance for maximum professional development was hampered without a Jewish-sponsored hospital in Detroit. But Dr. Saltzstein believed that Detroit Jewry could make its own contribution to better medical care for *all* people living in our community. He was right! Then came World War II, and, of course, all activity stopped on the new project. His plans were delayed, but he was not to be denied. On January 15, 1953, his dream came true.

To prove again that Dr. Saltzstein is a medical man of great determination and dedication, let me quote Dr. Michael J. Brennan, President of the Michigan Cancer Foundation

A central interest of Dr. Harry C. Saltzstein, all the while he has been in Detroit, is the registration of cancer cases.

When Dr. Saltzstein first came here from New York, he was the leader in the advocacy and operation of the Harper Hospital Cancer Register. Later, when Sinai Hospital was opened, Harry saw to it that it had a Register from day one. Hospital cancer registers are important but they deal with only the one segment of a regional population that happens to go to a particular hospital.

Twenty-five years ago, Doctor Saltzstein, Dr. Harry Nelson, Mr. Edward Tuescher, and Dr. Osborn Brines of the Wayne State University Medical School, Dr. Frank Hartman of Henry Ford Hospital, and Dr. William Simpson at the then Detroit Institute of Cancer Research were the moving forces behind the establishment of the Michigan Cancer Register under the direction of Mr. Isadore Seltzer. By 1959, it included twenty-five of the larger hospitals in Detroit. Our government then decided to establish in Detroit its largest permanent unit of SEER Cancer program (Surveillance, Epidemiology, and End Results).

Now the total cancer experience of 4,500,000 people, being treated in 85 hospitals, by over 7,500 physicians is recorded in this registry.

Harry Saltzstein can look back with justifiable pride in this product of his vision, industry, and persistence. In a very real way, the largest cancer registry and follow-up unit *in the world today* stands as a living monument to Doctor Harry and that small circle of farsighted doctors who laid its foundation here in Detroit.

His family told me that from the time Harry Saltzstein was a youngster, he loved two things above all else, medicine and people. He believed that the role of a physician was a responsibility given to only a few of the almost four billion people in the world.

He has lived his life quietly and confidently. He developed a special hypersensitivity to the sufferings of others, which was responsible for his tenacity of purpose. Dr. Saltzstein's aims were always restoration of health and joy for the patient. He was known always for his sympathy for the poor and underprivileged. Harry built an enviable reputation for integrity, for refusing to be tempted to compromise. Under his hand, many lay down in sleep, entrusting the thread of their life to his careful skill.

Dr. Harry C. Saltzstein was certainly one of the foremost surgeons in Michigan. I have been told by medical men that he had a national reputation as a surgeon. He was known as the physician's surgeon. Dr. Saltzstein was a very important factor in the improvement and development of surgery in our town. He contributed his own excellent surgical skills, and he was ever interested in teaching and training many young doctors specializing in surgery. He demanded high standards not only from others, but from himself as well. His is a record of achievement of which any doctor would be proud.

A passage in George Eliot's famous book *Middlemarch* could very well have been describing our friend, Dr. Saltzstein. "Early in his career he became imbued with the conviction that the medical profession, as it might be, was the finest in the world; presenting the most perfect interchange between science and art; offering the most direct alliance between intellectual conquest and social good."

So now Dr. Harry C. Saltzstein has reached the venerable age of eighty-five. Although he has been an unexcelled surgeon all his life, with an impeccable reputation and extensive practice, he has not been a great financial success. But let him define that word "success." He has lived his life doing well what he always meant to do: being a compassionate, excellent physician and surgeon. Certainly no one can dispute that as a goal, or question his full achievement of it.

Raymond C. Miller

L. to R.: Alfred M. Pelham, Msgr. Edward J. Hickey, the author, Raymond Miller, Harvey Merker, Reuben Ryding

*W*ednesday, *April 30*, was a sad day for us. We paid our last respects to one of the best friends and staunchest supporters the Detroit Historical Society has ever had.

To encapsule the life of a wonderful person like Ray is really not fair to his memory. I recall a great many things about him, but space limitation permits me to mention but a few.

Ray was not a native Detroiter, but he loved his adopted city, Detroit. He was born on May 20, 1899, in the little town of Belle Plains, Kansas, a town that even today has less than one thousand in population, proving again that "tall oaks from little acorns grow."

From The Detroit Historical Society *Town Crier*, Annual Report, 1980.

Prior to coming to Wayne State University in 1924, he taught at several colleges and universities, including the University of Chicago and Eastern Michigan. He spent forty-four years at Wayne and was chairman of the History Department when he retired in 1968.

His colleagues at Wayne State acclaimed him for the important part he played in the university's growth and success. He was the chairman of the committee in charge of their centennial celebration.

Dr. Miller was a gentleman in every sense of the word, and a gentle man. He was a humble person in spite of his erudition, and one of the most unpretentious people I have ever known. His friendly manner endeared him to all. He smiled easily and often.

Ray and his dear wife Julia were married fifty-five years; they were childhood sweethearts. Both were loved by all who knew them. They were an ideal married couple; so close, they lived for each other's happiness. In her recent illness, Ray took care of Julia's needs every moment of the day. No registered nurse could have been more proficient, more devoted, more tender.

I will mention just a few things about the consistent record of over thirty years of service Dr. Miller rendered as a labor of love to the Detroit Historical Society, the Detroit Historical Commission, and the Detroit Historical Museum.

My memory takes me back to the early 1940s, when Ray and I stood at the side of the president of the Detroit Historical Society, George Stark. We promised George we would stick with him until the campaign for funds to build our museum was a success; we did, and it was!

Ray secured a special Wayne State University assignment which permitted him to be loaned as the first director of our Historical Museum. And he served in that capacity for two years without pay. He was to spend half of his time as head of the university's History Department and half as director of the Museum. As it turned out, Ray ended up with two full-time jobs, running concurrently, for two years!

He hand-picked Henry Brown as his assistant director and trained him until he felt Henry was ready to take over as director. Ray continued to watch over Henry, and the rest of us, like a mother hen. He served as a Detroit Historical Society board member until he died; in fact he introduced the main speaker on April 18, 1980, at the Local History Conference.

These many years of service, of time and energy, were given freely because Ray loved history and loved Detroit. The Detroit Historical Society elected him a life member of the board and cited him for his three decades of service to the board, his many contributions to local history, for his services as editor of the Society's *Bulletin*, for the history books that he authored and for his lifelong efforts to inspire students in the field of history and local research, as well as for his contributions to the development of our local heritage based on sound scholarship.

The Raymond C. Miller Memorial Fund has been established in his memory at the Detroit Historical Society.

Raymond Miller was given many other honors—the Detroit Historical Society Guild's Patriotic Award, the WSU Faculty Service Award, the WSU Alumni Service Award, and the Award of the American Association for State and Local History for his book on the history of the Detroit Edison Company. He was also given the Mayor's Medal of the City of Detroit in 1971.

As I reflect, I think about how Ray Miller took the initial Detroit Historical Commission, which included four history novices, a newspaper reporter, an advertising man, a society matron, and a manager of real estate property, and held our hands and educated us as to how an historical museum should function. He gave us direction. He taught us the purpose of a museum and what our philosophy about museum operation should be.

We could not have operated so effectively if it were not for Dr. Ray Miller's efforts and his advice to us during all these years. I ought to know, for he was my mentor, too.

So, dear Ray, for all you meant to us, for sharing part of your life with us, we thank you again from our hearts. We loved you, dear friend, and we greatly miss you.

The Real McCoy

Elijah McCoy

I was at an affair recently where the master of ceremonies said, "The next speaker needs no introduction. He needs none because he did not show up."

We have the same thing here today: the next speaker was supposed to be Commissioner Charles Hagler, but he evidently couldn't make it. So, I bring you greetings from the Detroit Historical Commission. I am pleased to participate in the dedication today of this official state historical marker.

I am pleased because it honors the memory of an outstanding Detroit man—Elijah McCoy—whose genius as an inventor brought Detroit and McCoy national and world fame.

You have all heard the expression "the real McCoy." It has been used by people to indicate that the item referred to is genuine, authentic—not false or an imitation. The expression originated in Detroit and referred originally to Elijah McCoy's reputation for quality merchandise. Well, it is the real

Given at the dedication of the State of Michigan historical marker at St. Dominic's Church, Detroit, May 1975.

325

McCoy when I tell you that the Detroit Historical Commission is proud of the good efforts of the Black Historic Sites Committee. We are proud because, at long last, proper recognition is being given to many deserving black men and women who did so much for Detroit.

We of the Detroit Historical Commission are primarily concerned with preserving and telling the story of our town's history and heritage. This story cannot be told completely unless full credit is given to all segments of our population.

Like the Roman god Janus, who had two faces on one head—one facing the front and the other the rear—we Historical Commissioners live our lives facing both toward the past and the future. We try to learn from the lessons of the past, while at the same time, we try to plan for the future.

Appreciation of history is important because it shows the advancement of human life from one generation to another. We especially want our younger generation to know something about the progress that is being made slowly but surely.

I want you to know how very proud I am to be a part of today's marker dedication honoring a black Detroiter, Elijah McCoy, who truly deserved to be honored. It is another step in the right direction. It is another step forward by decent-thinking Detroiters trying to create the kind of world in which we want to live, the kind that God intended when this world was created.

And to that I say "Amen."

Frederick Stearns' Telephone

Frederick Stearns

Batting *in the* 9th position, so to speak, there doesn't seem to be much I can add to what has already been said about the first telephone in Detroit, and the Detroiter, Frederick Stearns, who had it. So, I will make my few remarks in the same vein as did our director of the Historical Museum.

I showed my daughter today's program and the picture of the Stearns telephone historical marker. Would you believe that until today she had always thought that the telephone was invented by Don Ameche? I, of course, knew better. I remember noticing when I got my first job that my boss had three telephones on his desk. When I asked his secretary why, she said that was so he could hang up on more people.

Seriously, Frederick Stearns was an outstanding citizen, a dynamic business man who helped make history for our city by making Detroit world famous for its pharmaceutical prod-

Dedication of the State of Michigan historical marker in downtown Detroit, July 1972.

327

ucts—just as others at the same time were making Detroit famous by putting the world on wheels.

When I was a kid Frederick Stearns was in the drug manufacturing business. I liked his Zymol-Troches cough drops. I figured that any product with a name like that had to be good. He also created Astringesol and several other products that are still sold today by his successor company.

You know how we all take for granted certain things that we use every day, like the telephone. I consider the telephone one of the three great inventions for the benefit of mankind: the wheel, electricity, and the telephone.

And, talking about the date of the first telephone in Detroit, I will never forget a couple of other famous dates in American history. They were Blue Monday, October 28, and Black Tuesday, October 29, back in 1929. Those colors, black and blue, were very appropriate. Many of you undoubtedly remember these dates quite well, also.

That's when the stock market crashed to an all-time low. Fortunes were washed out. People who were investors in the market—and who wasn't?—went from riches to rags overnight. Nearly all of us were broke. Nobody had any money left. To show you how important cash was, I remember putting a nickel in a coin telephone box and a voice said, "God bless you."

And with that apocryphal story, I also say, "God bless all of you."

George Washington Stark

George Stark

At a moment like this you can appreciate my feeling of ambivalence, the mixed emotions that I have. I am happy and proud to help dedicate this living memorial to George Washington Stark, the man I knew as my friend. But I regret that he is not with us to see the tribute we have created to show, in some small fashion, how grateful we are for his many years of service to Detroit, the city he loved so much.

George was the president of the Detroit Historical Society at the time when the Detroit Historical Commission was established by city charter. This was accomplished because George was determined that our town would have a handsome municipal-owned historical museum to help perpetuate our local heritage. George Stark made it possible. I know whereof I speak because I was privileged to work at his side

Talk given at the dedication of Stark Hall, Detroit Historical Museum, December 1973.

during the many months it took to design the plans and to raise the money needed to build this museum.

The history of Detroit was the love of George Stark's life, second only to his love for his wife, Anne, and his children. The museum was his dream, and he lived to see it become a reality, serving thousands of families every year. If any building ever was a monument to one man's efforts, this is it.

George's charm and wit, his unrivaled memories of early Detroit, and his erudite articulation combined to help him disseminate knowledge of Detroit history in a masterful manner. He wrote a great daily column in the *Detroit News*. He was in constant demand as a public speaker. His avocation was being the perennial president of the Detroit Historical Commission and the official City of Detroit historiographer. He was also the author of nine books on Detroit history.

There is a great temptation for me to continue on about George Stark. But, I remind myself that he was a very modest man. To those who never had the good fortune to have known him personally, I hope I have given you some idea of the warm, friendly person he was. George was a real sweet person—a man's man but still a gentle man and a gentleman. During my lifetime, I have known but a very few men of his quality.

Yes, Detroit can and does remember George Stark with thanks for everything he did for our town, for what he meant to us, and also for "his" museum in which we are dedicating the George Stark Detroit Hall this afternoon.

I now invite you to join Ann Marie and George Washington Stark II, two of George's grandchildren, who will unveil the plaque dedicating this exhibit hall in his memory.

On Ed Tuescher's Second Retirement

L. to R.: Dr. Dorin Hinerman, Chairman, MCF Board of Trustees, the author, Walter Greene, Chairman MCF Board of Directors, and Edward W. Tuescher

It seems that I go through life making farewell speeches to Ed Tuescher. The last one was September 11, 1967, almost eight years ago. I guess it didn't take. Are you sure you really mean it this time, Ed?

But, Ed, we are glad you came back to finish out your business career with the Michigan Cancer Foundation because you have been so closely identified with us from our earliest days. When I was asked to speak today, my first impulse was to pull out a copy from my files of my last farewell speech to

Talk presented at Board of Trustees meeting, Michigan Cancer Foundation, May 1975.

you and repeat it because you probably don't remember what I said anyway. Even I don't remember it.

I do remember, however, telling everybody about that great idea you originated to fight cancer by quitting smoking. It was called the "Tuescher Nicotine Anonymous Plan." When you feel a craving desire for a cigarette, you simply phone another Michigan Cancer Foundation volunteer. He comes over and you get drunk together.

I probably should start thinking about retiring soon also, Ed, even though I have my own business. But I wonder if that would be wise. I talked to one of my friends who has not been busy since his retirement; in fact, he admits that these days, the only time there is something he has to do is when he gets up in the middle of the night. I am sure things will be more interesting for you.

My working relationships with you go back over thirty years, when we first became acquainted through our mutual interest in fighting cancer. I can call to mind many exciting moments, including trips together to the International Cancer Congress in Russia, the one in Japan, and last year, when we went to Italy. I am so proud that the board has seen fit to name the community meeting room in your honor. That makes us roommates because I've got one, too.

Except for Dean Arthur Neef, I think I am the oldest member on the Board, in years of service. I have worked with you very closely during all those years, and I know I am not exaggerating when I say that all the fine success of the Michigan Cancer Foundation is due in large measure to the work and ideas that you contributed to this project. Your groundwork gave Dr. Brennan a splendid start in bringing international fame to our cancer-fighting organization. I am very happy to add my personal thanks to you for everything you have meant to us.

I am pleased to be able once again to participate in a tribute to my good friend, Ed Tuescher, this time on his second and positively final retirement party.

Postscript
The Michigan Cancer Foundation called Ed Tuescher back to work again twice because they needed his expertise and help on so many projects!

Epilogue

I hope you enjoyed *SIMONS SAYS*. It was published to mark my 80th birthday in July of 1984. Books like this have been called tombstone editions, but I hope to stick around for a while longer to help those I love and to irritate those I don't. I have tried, at appropriate occasions, to combine my serious message with a bit of nonsense. This is my format for a speech or a talk. Not that I originated this style of presentation, but experience has taught me what my audiences like and how to keep them interested and from going to sleep during my talk. And it works. So, this is my advice to other amateur speakers.

I start with a little humorous story, and usually the laugh is "on me" or something that is appropriate for the evening's subject. For instance, I used this one to open my talk at a Rotary Club luncheon meeting. After I was introduced, I told the audience that the chairman had said to me "Mr. Simons, you talk just as long as you want. We leave at 1:30."

Then I gave my message with a few more bits of humor. To leave them smiling, I ended with, "and in conclusion, I want to thank you for inviting me and for giving me your undivided attention. We will now give out the prizes for the best doodles drawn on the tablecloth."

Start and finish with a smile. Spread a little happiness. This world needs a lot more smiles, fun, and jokes combined with the thought-provoking messages.

If you are called on to give many talks, don't be afraid to repeat a joke or story that earned a big laugh. That idea gave me a big problem in this book. I have used many of the same jokes over and over again for different audiences because they never failed to get big laughs. Hence, when this book was suggested, I had to go over every talk and eliminate the repeaters. I hope I did a good job of surgery.

Remember, if a joke is new to you, and makes you laugh, chances are it will be accepted in the same way by the people sitting in front of you. When you hear or read a good joke, write it down and save it for the right audience. Build a file of jokes for your own amusement.

And finally, remember the Chinese orator whose name was "On Tu Long."

There is a big difference between sticking your nose in other people's business—

and *putting your heart in other people's problems...*

Leonard N. Simons

LEONARD N. SIMONS